The Quest
for the Dark Tower

ALSO BY ALISSA BURGER

The Wizard of Oz *as American Myth:
A Critical Study of Six Versions
of the Story, 1900–2007* (McFarland, 2012)

*The Television World
of* Pushing Daisies: *Critical Essays
on the Bryan Fuller Series*
(edited by Alissa Burger, McFarland, 2011)

The Quest for the Dark Tower

*Genre and Interconnection
in the Stephen King Series*

ALISSA BURGER

McFarland & Company, Inc., Publishers
Jefferson, North Carolina

This book has undergone peer review.

LIBRARY OF CONGRESS CATALOGUING-IN-PUBLICATION DATA

Names: Burger, Alissa, author.
Title: The quest for The dark tower : genre and interconnection in the Stephen King series / Alissa Burger.
Description: Jefferson, North Carolina : McFarland & Company, Inc., Publishers, 2021 | Includes bibliographical references and index.
Identifiers: LCCN 2021007018 | ISBN 9781476676982 (paperback : acid free paper) ∞
ISBN 9781476642802 (ebook)
Subjects: LCSH: King, Stephen, 1947- Dark tower. | King, Stephen, 1947- — Criticism and interpretation.
Classification: LCC PS3561.I483 Z62245 2021 | DDC 813/.54—dc23
LC record available at https://lccn.loc.gov/2021007018

BRITISH LIBRARY CATALOGUING DATA ARE AVAILABLE

ISBN (print) 978-1-4766-7698-2
ISBN (ebook) 978-1-4766-4280-2

© 2021 Alissa Burger. All rights reserved

No part of this book may be reproduced or transmitted in any form or by any means, electronic or mechanical, including photocopying or recording, or by any information storage and retrieval system, without permission in writing from the publisher.

Front cover image © 2021 Shutterstock

Printed in the United States of America

McFarland & Company, Inc., Publishers
 Box 611, Jefferson, North Carolina 28640
 www.mcfarlandpub.com

Acknowledgments

Like all books, writing this one has been a challenging process and I have been well-supported along the way.

My fellow scholars at the 2017 International Conference for the Fantastic in the Arts provided invaluable feedback on my foundational infographic approach to this project, as did those at the 2019 International Gothic Association Conference. I similarly shared this work with my colleagues at a Culver-Stockton College faculty colloquium. I am grateful for the productive discussions, important questions, and new considerations that came from each of these conversations and count myself lucky to be part of such dynamic and supportive scholarly communities.

Library staff have—as always—been lifesavers in helping me track down elusive sources and tackle the inherent mysteries of research. I am particularly indebted to the Culver-Stockton College library team, including Amber Strub-Lay, Julie Wright, Katie Marney, and our excellent group of student workers.

I couldn't have written this book without the support, encouragement, and patience of my friends and family, particularly my dad, Rick Stickler, who is a fellow *Dark Tower* fan and was the first to read my chapter on the Western genre. Jenny Collins and Scott Giltner were great idea bouncers and "What about...?" questioners. Finally, Jason Burger, my partner in this wild and exciting life, deserves thanks for putting up with my writing stress and my piles of books and stacks of research materials, and for always saying "You've got this" instead of "Really? *Another* project?"

Thank you all—this book would not be what it is without you.

Table of Contents

Acknowledgments   v
Preface   1
Introduction   4

1. Epic and Legend   11
2. Fairy Tale   29
3. Fantasy and Science Fiction   44
4. Western   63
5. Horror   79
6. *'Salem's Lot*   97
7. *The Stand* and *The Eyes of the Dragon*   110
8. *Insomnia*   123
9. *Desperation* and *The Regulators*   136
10. *Hearts in Atlantis* and Other "Low Men"   149
11. *The Talisman* and *Black House*   162

Conclusion   174
Chapter Notes   183
Works Cited   191
Index   201

Preface

Stephen King is an immensely popular and prolific author, and in recent years, academic and scholarly interest in King has boomed, with authors critically considering King's fiction, adaptations of his work, and his impact on the larger popular culture landscape. Many of King's best-known works have become cultural touchstones, instantly recognizable to a wide audience, even those who have never read one of King's books. For example, t-shirts offer the advice to "Keep Calm and Take Carrie to the Prom," while the narrative and key elements of *The Stand* (1978; revised and expanded 1990) were invoked in discussions of the COVID-19 pandemic that began in 2020. King's work is making its way more frequently into the college and university classroom, his contributions to literature have been acknowledged by both the National Book Awards and National Endowment for the Arts, and his contributions to contemporary American literature are incalculable.

While scholars have analyzed a wide range of King's work, addressing nearly every novel within his expansive career, one area that has been often overlooked is King's *Dark Tower* series. There are eight *Dark Tower* books: *The Gunslinger* (limited edition 1982; expanded and revised 2003), *The Drawing of the Three* (1987), *The Waste Lands* (1991), *Wizard and Glass* (1997), *Wolves of the Calla* (2003), *Song of Susannah* (2004), and *The Dark Tower* (2004) comprise the original series, followed by an additional *Dark Tower* novel, *The Wind Through the Keyhole* (2012), the action of which chronologically takes place between *Wizard and Glass* and *The Wolves of the Calla*. While critically considering King's *Dark Tower* series is no easy feat, spanning more than three decades and thousands of pages, it is essential in understanding King's work as a whole and his position within the larger literary landscape. This is because in the creation of his *Dark Tower* series, King draws upon and engages with a wide range of genre influences and specific texts, from Sir Thomas Malory's *Le Morte Darthur* (1485) and J.R.R. Tolkien's

Lord of the Rings (1954) to Shirley Jackson's *The Haunting of Hill House* (1959) and Sergio Leone's *The Good, the Bad, and the Ugly* (1967). In addition, the narrative action of the *Dark Tower* series doesn't simply impact the characters and world within its stories, but reverberates through much of King's other fiction, though interconnection, returning characters, and overlapping worlds. The universe of King's Dark Tower also expands far beyond the page, through Marvel Comics extensive adaptation of this narrative, Nikolaj Arcel's feature film *The Dark Tower* (2017), and the potential influence of the Dark Tower universe and its interconnections in the Hulu Original series *Castle Rock* (2018–2019).

My work here builds upon the encyclopedic considerations of King's Dark Tower universe chronicled by Bev Vincent in *The Road to the Dark Tower: Exploring Stephen King's Magnum Opus* (2004) and *The Dark Tower Companion: A Guide to Stephen King's Epic Fantasy* (2013) as well as Robin Furth's *The Dark Tower: A Complete Concordance* (2012, revised and updated edition). However, while Vincent and Furth chart these interconnections and provide brief overviews of distinct elements, my aim here is to dig deeper into those connections, to analyze the influence, impact, and negotiation of King's inspirations and the Dark Tower-connected King texts to consider their significance and to position the *Dark Tower* series at the intersection of King's literary influences and within the context of King's own fictional canon as a whole.

In developing this sustained analysis, the first half of the book is focused on genre influences, including specific genre characteristics, key texts in each of the genres considered, and their presence and negotiation in King's *Dark Tower* series. This first section includes chapters on epic and legend, fairy tale, fantasy and science fiction, the Western, and horror. In the second half of the book, I turn my attention to the *Dark Tower* series' interconnection with King's larger body of work, with chapters on Dark Tower connections in *'Salem's Lot* (1975) with the return of Donald Callahan; the figure of Flagg in *The Stand* and *The Eyes of the Dragon* (1986); the cosmological consideration of *Insomnia* (1994); the parallel narratives of *Desperation* (1996) and *The Regulators* (as Richard Bachman, 1996); the "low men" and voracious cars of *Hearts in Atlantis* (1999), *From a Buick 8* (2002), "Ur" (2015), and "Mile 81" (2015); and the Territories and passages between worlds central to *The Talisman* (1984) and *Black House* (2001), both of which King co-authored with Peter Straub.

Each of these chapters moves beyond noting and charting these connections—whether of genre or other King works—to consider how King negotiates and transforms these elements, why these connections matter, and what they mean, both for reading King's *Dark Tower* series and King's fiction more broadly. As one of King's characters, Jake Chambers, notes in *The Gunslinger*, "there are other worlds than these" (King, *The Gunslinger* 266) and in this consideration of genre influence and King interconnection, I work to map those worlds, the connections between them, and the impact they have on one another and on King's work as a whole. The *Dark Tower* series stands at the center of King's canon and the overlapping worlds of his creation, and any cohesive, comprehensive analysis of King's fiction and his position within the larger literary landscape must consider the *Dark Tower* series' inspirations, interconnection, and influence.

Introduction

Stephen King is one of the most popular and prolific writers of the late 20th and early 21st centuries. He has written more than fifty novels and ten short story collections, charted new territories in publication, and become an icon of popular culture as well as literature. King is beginning to be recognized and respected as a literary voice of a generation, evidenced by the growing body of scholarship surrounding his work, his 2003 National Book Awards Medal for Distinguished Contribution to American Letters, and his 2015 National Endowment for the Arts' National Medal of Arts, though these honors haven't silenced the old guard of literary critics who dismiss King as a "popular" or "genre" writer. As America's premiere boogeyman, King is best known for his tales of horror, whether it is the supernatural terror of vampires, monsters, and other things that go bump in the night or the all-too-human horrors of abuse, murder, and real-world violence. Building on the rich tradition of the horror genre, King draws inspiration from masters like Bram Stoker, Mary Shelley, Edgar Allan Poe, and H.P. Lovecraft, though he is also a writer firmly invested in the contemporary moment, with his fiction abounding with music and popular culture references, slang, brand names, and current events. Just as King's work draws on hybrid influences of the classic and contemporary, he also frequently challenges and transgresses the boundaries between genres and defies expectations, and his canon includes the fantasy tales of *The Talisman* (with Peter Straub, 1984) and *The Eyes of the Dragon* (1986), and the mysteries like *The Colorado Kid* (2005) and the *Bill Hodges* trilogy (2014–2016) in addition to the horror for which he is most well-known.

At the center of King's sprawling canon is his eight-book *Dark Tower* series, which has spanned almost the entirety of his career. Beginning with the first installment of King's serial publication of *The Gunslinger* in 1978, the *Dark Tower* series follows the adventures of Roland Deschain, the last survivor of a world that has "moved on," and his quest for the Dark Tower, which is the linchpin of all existence across multiple, interconnected worlds. Following *The Gunslinger* (which was collected in a limited edition in 1982, published as a trade paperback in 1988,[1] then revised and expanded in 2003), the *Dark Tower* series continues with *The Drawing of the Three* (1987), *The Waste Lands* (1991), *Wizard and Glass* (1997), *Wolves of the Calla* (2003), *Song of Susannah* (2004), and *The Dark Tower* (2004). King published an additional *Dark Tower* novel in 2012, *The Wind Through the Keyhole*, the action of which chronologically takes place between *Wizard and Glass* and *Wolves of the Calla*. As Roland pursues this quest throughout the series, he draws companions into his world to form a *ka-tet* (a group bound by purpose and destiny) in his search for the Tower. Along with Eddie Dean, Susannah Dean, Jake Chambers, and the billy-bumbler Oy, Roland crosses great swaths of Mid-World and beyond, always guided by the Beams that point the way toward the Tower. The *ka-tet* encounters both friends and foes along their journey, defending those who ask for their help and standing against the emissaries of the Crimson King, whose driving goal is to bring down the Dark Tower and, with it, all existence.

In addition to its enormous scope, the *Dark Tower* series has two distinctive characteristics: its genre hybridity and its interconnection with the larger canon of King's work, both of which provide unique opportunities for reading, interpreting, and responding to the series. As Cyrena N. Pondrom explains, "a (literary) text is, by definition, a dialogue with other texts" (qtd. in G. Miller 107), and with the *Dark Tower* series, this "dialogue" is complex and dynamically engaged. King is tremendously well-read and draws upon a wealth of literary traditions and influences as he constructs his *Dark Tower* universe. Taking direct inspiration from Robert Browning's poem "Childe Roland to the Dark Tower Came" (1855), the *Dark Tower* series engages a number of distinct and at times dissonant genre traditions, including those of Arthurian romance, fairy tales, the fantasy epic, science fiction, the Western, and horror, playing with established patterns and familiar narratives to create something new through negotiation, subversion, and combination. Similarly, the *Dark Tower* series is integral to King's larger body of work, with connections to many of his novels and stories that take place in worlds other than Roland's own. As King writes in the afterword of *Wizard and Glass*, the fourth *Dark Tower* novel, "I am coming to understand that Roland's world (or worlds) actually *contains* all the others of my making" (697, emphasis original). Some of these interconnections are overt and sustained—such as characters from King's other novels appearing in the world of the Dark Tower, like Father Donald Callahan of *'Salem's Lot* (1975) or Ted Brautigan of *Hearts in Atlantis* (1999)—while others are more subtle, evocations and echoes between worlds rather than a fully-developed narrative intersection. As a result of these two characteristics, the *Dark Tower* series is among King's most complex work and a core to his larger body of literature, in which many roads lead to the Dark Tower, whether by direct or more circuitous routes.

Despite the central position of the *Dark Tower* series within King's larger canon, these books remain some of the most under-represented of King's work within the scholarly discussion. There are excellent encyclopedic guides to King's *Dark Tower* universe, including Robin Furth's *The Dark Tower: A Complete Concordance* (2012, revised and updated edition) and Bev Vincent's *The Road to the Dark Tower: Exploring Stephen King's Magnum Opus* (2004) and *The Dark Tower Companion: A Guide to Stephen King's Epic Fantasy* (2013). These guides are invaluable resources, charting the interconnections of specific elements and references throughout the series with brief entries on key people, places, things, and influences. However, while these reference books do a remarkable job of cataloging these details and providing readers with the puzzle pieces of the series, they offer little critical engagement, analysis, or consideration of how these pieces fit together as a cohesive whole and what these interconnections might ultimately mean in a critical reading of King's work, whether the *Dark Tower* series specifically or his larger body of literature. In addition, given the complex combination of influences and interconnections in the *Dark Tower* series, scholars who have tackled it have often understandably done so by focusing on a single element of the series and isolating a particular genre influence, tradition, or connection to specific source material, such as Arthurian legend, Browning's poem, or T.S. Eliot's "The Waste Land" (1922). Finally, a more holistic approach in scholarship on the *Dark Tower* series has been to "emphasize the hybridity of genres and influences that appear in the series" (J. Miller 203), as addressed by James Egan, Patrick McAleer, and Heidi Strengell, among others. However, just as the encyclopedic treatments of the *Dark Tower* series may miss the forest for the trees, the hybridity-focused approach effectively identifies the larger trends and traditions of the series, but with little opportunity to dig deeply into some of its details. My aim with this book is to combine these different approaches to critical analysis, foregrounding genre hybridity and interconnection while also providing in-depth consideration of specific genre traditions and King connections.

This book is organized in two main sections: the first on genre and the second on interconnections with King's larger canon. Genre classifies works into particular "types" and Bernice Murphy explains that "popular fiction's reliance upon classification by genre is one of its most significant characteristics" (46). Genre can be broadly defined as the collection of specific elements or characteristics needed for a work to fit that categorization: for example, imaginative secondary world building is central to the fantasy genre, while a work cannot be properly called horror without elements of the terrifying, unsettling, or grotesque. This is essential in understanding not just the narratives themselves but perceptions of literature as well as contemporary marketing and consumption. While there are certainly deviations and a diverse range of subgenres, genre is a defining feature of contemporary literature. However, the *Dark Tower* series refutes this expectation, employing and combining a wide variety of genre traditions, which both individually and collectively provide the reader with a range of interpretive lenses to consider in terms of general literary analysis, narrative convention and expectations, and contextualizing the series within the scope of King's larger body of work. Each of these genre-focused chapters provides an overview and application of the specific genre traditions engaged by King's series as well as consideration of relevant texts with which King engages, from Sir Thomas Malory's *Le Morte Darthur* (1485) to Sergio Leone's *The Good, the Bad, and the Ugly* (1967).

King's *Dark Tower* series is frequently referred to as an epic, both in terms of its narrative approach and its formidable size, and Chapter 1 begins by analyzing the elements of epic and legend that serve as the foundation for King's *Dark Tower* universe and the characterization of Roland Deschain, with key texts including Malory's *Le Morte Darthur*, *The Song of Roland*, Browning's "Childe Roland," and Eliot's "The Waste Land," each of which engages with and builds upon the epic qualities and narrative elements of the works which have come before, highlighting a pattern of inspiration and negotiation over several centuries. Chapter 2 examines the fairy tale tradition and the allusions to classic and contemporary fairy tales that inform King's series, from Charles Perrault and the Brothers Grimm to the imaginative world of L. Frank Baum's Oz, as well as considering the significant role of storytelling within the *Dark Tower* series, particularly in *The Wind Through the Keyhole*. The central role of the Turtle in Mid-World fairy tales and that being's prodigious power also connects the *Dark Tower* universe to King's Derry, *IT* (1986), and the children who must stand against It's evil. Chapter 3 unpacks the conventions of fantasy and science fiction, first by exploring the fantasy quest tradition and the influence of J.R.R. Tolkien's *The Lord of the Rings* (1954) in King's *Dark Tower* narrative and secondary world building, then shifting to consider the influence of science fiction within the series, where robots, nuclear weapons, and degenerated technology exist side by side with magic and the supernatural. Roland's world and the gunslinger himself are distinctly Western genre archetypes and Chapter 4 applies a range of Western genre conventions to King's series, including the frontier, its challenges and conflicts, the code by which the Western hero operates, and the guns he wields to do so. Roland is a Clint Eastwood–style hero (or antihero), and just as King has noted Browning as a direct influence on the *Dark Tower* series, he has similarly discussed the inspiration of *The Good, the Bad, and the Ugly* as well as John Sturges' *The Magnificent Seven* (1960) and Sturges' own inspiration, Akira Kurosawa's *Seven Samurai* (1954). Finally, the section on genre concludes with horror in Chapter 5, with a consideration of King's definition of different types of horror laid out in his critical analysis of the genre *Danse Macabre* (1981) as well as the influence of horror greats including Edgar Allan Poe, Shirley Jackson, and H.P. Lovecraft in the *Dark Tower* series. These close readings demonstrate the ways in which King utilizes and subverts this wide range of genre traditions, with Maroš Buday arguing that "metafiction serves as the central pillar around which each and every postmodernist element in the series revolves ... an ever-resonating refrain for [King's] literary epic" (136). Taken both individually and together, these chapters are designed to provide both an in-depth consideration of specific genre influences on the *Dark Tower* series as well as highlight their overlappings, interconnections, and hybridity.

In addition to drawing on a wide range of genre traditions and diverse literary and popular culture texts, the *Dark Tower* series connects with several of King's other works, including recurring characters, intersecting narratives, and common themes. Considering the central position of this series to King's larger body of work, Tony Magistrale argues that "*The Dark Tower* can be appreciated as a means for unpacking the King canon, an umbrella text encompassing the whole of the writer's fictional oeuvre ... a kind of Unified Field Theory for King" (*America's Storyteller* 150–1). The second half of this book explores these intertextual connections and their significance in creating the world of the Dark Tower within the larger scope of King's work as a whole. One of the most significant ways King's *Dark Tower* universe connects with his larger body of work is through the appearance of familiar characters. Chapter 6 focuses on *'Salem's Lot*, the ways in which King utilizes the vampire trope in the *Dark Tower* series, and the role of Donald Callahan, the disgraced priest of Jerusalem's Lot who turns up again in the *Dark Tower*'s Calla Bryn Sturgis, as King fills in blanks between *'Salem's Lot* and Callahan's reintroduction, providing him with a new story among new friends. The connections between the *Dark Tower* series and *'Salem's Lot* are metatextual as well, with Callahan discovering a copy of the novel *'Salem's Lot* in the midst of the group's adventures in Calla Bryn Sturgis and opening it to find his own past described as a fiction, an experience that is intensely disorienting and existential, and serves to foreshadow the continuing metatextual approach of the *Dark Tower* series' later books, in which King becomes a character in his own fiction. Another recurring character throughout King's canon is Randall Flagg, who has been alternately known by a host of names including Walter o' Dim, The Man in Black, Richard Fannin, Marten Broadcloak, and The Walkin' Dude, among others. Flagg is the main focus of Chapter 7, which looks at *The Stand* (1978; revised and expanded 1990) and *The Eyes of the Dragon*. In addition to highlighting the genre hybridity of King's larger canon, including the post-apocalyptic narrative of *The Stand* and the fantasy tradition of *The Eyes of the Dragon*, this chapter provides a close reading of Flagg himself, both as an individual character that can be traced back to King's college poem "The Dark Man" and as a larger, symbolic cipher in the series' macro-thematic exploration of good and evil. While *'Salem's Lot*, *The Stand*, and *The Eyes of the Dragon* focus on the interconnections between worlds and the characters who cross these boundaries, with Chapter 8's consideration of *Insomnia* (1994), the macro-cosmic impact of actions rather than individuals between worlds becomes apparent, with mythological Fates in the guise of "little bald doctors" warning Ralph Roberts of the consequences of the Dark Tower's potential fall, a disaster which hangs in the balance in Derry, Maine, and which threatens to destroy all worlds. *Insomnia*'s young Patrick Danville is later drawn into King's *Dark Tower* universe in the final book of the series, but it is the saving of this boy's life in *Insomnia* that ensures the Tower's safety well before his path crosses with Roland's. In the series' exploration of multiple worlds and parallel realities, King presents these infinite possibilities as events that could well be happening on another level of the Tower, a nod to the chaos theory belief that the smallest actions (or inactions) can completely alter the course of all that may come after. Commonly referred to as "the butterfly effect," this positing of possible realities is central to King's simultaneous publication of *Desperation* (1996) and *The Regulators* (1996), the first published under his own name and the second under his by then well-known pseudonym of Richard Bachman, and these two books are discussed in Chapter 9. The pairing of these two novels—which include characters of the same names but in different settings, situations, and relationships with one another—offers a kind of parallel universe/alternate reality engagement that echoes the complexity of time and place engaged throughout the *Dark Tower* series. Similarly underscoring these interconnections between multiple worlds and possible realities, there are echoes between these works and the *Dark Tower* series, including the Destoya Mountains, shared terminology (such as *can-tak* and *can-toi*), and the appearance of enforcers referred to as "regulators" in the *Dark Tower* novels *Wizard and Glass* (King 344) and *Wolves of the Calla* (King 290). Chapter 10 looks at King's interconnected series of novellas *Hearts in Atlantis*, which is one of the most direct and sustained examples of interconnection between the *Dark Tower* series and King's larger body of work, particularly in its introduction of Ted Brautigan and the paranormally powerful agents known as "Breakers" who are kidnapped and pressed into service by the emissaries of the Crimson King, forced to use their power to chip away at the Beams that keep the Dark Tower standing. Brautigan and the Crimson King's "low men" are central to the collection's opening novella, "Low Men in Yellow Coats," and these enforcers and their uncannily living cars feature prominently elsewhere in King's work, including in *From a Buick 8* (2002), "Ur" (2015), and "Mile 81" (2015), highlighting the more subtle encroachments of the "low men" and the malevolent influence of the Crimson King beyond the bounds of Roland's own world. The final chapter of this section examines *The Talisman* and its sequel *Black House* (2001), both of which King co-wrote with Peter Straub. In *The Talisman*, Jack Sawyer crosses from his own real world into the fantastical land of The Territories, which overlaps with that of *The Eyes of the Dragon* and Roland's own. While the similarities in *The Talisman* are fairly subtle, *Black House* draws King and Straub firmly into *Dark Tower* territory, including overlapping narratives that share common characters, the monstrous Crimson King, the abduction and abuse of Breakers, and a portal between Jack Sawyer's world and the Mid-World of Roland Deschain and the Dark Tower.

In addition to the focused analysis of each individual chapter, taken together as a whole this book charts the influences and interconnections King draws upon and develops in his *Dark Tower* series, providing readers with a critically-informed overview that moves beyond charting these connections or spotting King "Easter eggs" to instead contextualize, consider, and reflect upon what these engagements signify, both individually and collectively. Though King's most recent *Dark Tower* book was published in 2012 (*The Wind Through the Keyhole*), as the central axis of his literary universe, the *Dark Tower* series has unsurprisingly continued to make its presence felt in the intervening years, in both King's own writing and in other popular culture incarnations of his work. This enduring influence makes understanding the *Dark Tower* series essential in critically considering King, his work, and his lasting impact on literature and popular culture.

1

Epic and Legend

Storytelling is as old as humanity itself, with oral traditions preceding and influencing modern literary and narrative conventions. The telling of stories communicates the values of individual groups and societies, from creation stories to tales of the exploits of legendary heroes, reaffirming the culture's commitment to these ideals with each retelling. The best and most resonant stories get told and retold, passed down through generations, echoed in the works they have inspired and taking on new forms and functions in their telling to meet the shifting needs of their audiences. As King writes in *Song of Susannah*, "some stories *do* live forever" (271, emphasis original) and these timeless narratives speak to the very foundation of what it means to be human. These stories are epitomized in the literary tradition of epics and legends, many of which King incorporates in his *Dark Tower* series, including legends of King Arthur, the 11th-century French epic *Song of Roland*, Robert Browning's "Childe Roland to the Dark Tower Came," and T.S. Eliot's modernist classic "The Waste Land."

The term "epic" has been regularly and loosely applied to King's *Dark Tower* series, both in reference to its scope and its size, with a prodigious length of more than 4,000 pages. However, in considering the connections between King's *Dark Tower* series and the traditional epic narratives which influence it, a more specific literary definition is required. Epics are tales of heroic adventures or battles and can be either passed down through oral storytelling traditions or crafted as narrative fictions (White 81). From classics like the Sumerian *Epic of Gilgamesh* (c. 2100 BC), Homer's *The Iliad* and *The Odyssey*, and the Anglo-Saxon *Beowulf* (c. 800) to more contemporary works like Tolkien's *Lord of the Rings*, epics are built around a central hero and play out on a grand scale. Drawing on *The Columbia Encyclopedia* definition of the epic, Ben P. Indick identifies key features as including "a hero who embodies national, cultural, or religious ideals and upon whose actions depends to some degree the fate of his people; a course of action in which the hero performs great and difficult deeds; a whole era in the history of civilization; the intervention and recognition of divine or supernatural powers; [and] the concern with eternal human problems" (qtd. in Indick, "Stephen King as an Epic Writer" 56). T. Gilchrist White adds to this list of characteristics "beginning *in medias res*, or 'in the middle of things'; a series of flashbacks to tell the hero's history; [and] vast settings that cover many nations, the world, or the universe" (81).

King's *Dark Tower* series bears many of the characteristics outlined by Indick and White. Roland epitomizes the culture and traditions that have disappeared around him, as the world of his childhood and young manhood has "moved on" (King, *The Gunslinger* 3), with this phrase frequently repeated throughout the series in considering the past, as well as the present state, of Mid-World. Roland is the last gunslinger, the last in the line of Arthur Eld, and the last survivor of the now-gone Gilead. The ideals for which his father and all the gunslingers before him fought and died live on through Roland, a legacy and a burden that commemorate that past and cultural identity as part of All-World. Roland stands against great odds and almost always triumphs, whether his opponents are human, monstrous, or somewhere in the middle, like the Crimson King's *taheen* (part-human, part-animal hybrids). The reader is ushered into Roland's story *in medias res* at the start of *The Gunslinger*, in Roland's pursuit of the Man in Black, with no context or background narrative provided, though those earlier occurrences and conflicts are sketched in through Roland's storytelling and flashbacks. The first book of the series, *The Gunslinger*, was originally published as five separate installments in *The Magazine of Fantasy and Science Fiction* (1978–81), and the individual narratives each focus on a flashback of Roland's past, providing the reader with a glimpse of who he once was, as well as who he now is, told through his recollections of the slaughter in Tull, his childhood witnessing of the palace cook Hax's execution for treason, his boyhood home of Gilead, and his test of manhood against his teacher Cort. Roland's past and the stories he shares with his *ka-tet* are also the central narratives of both *Wizard and Glass* and *The Wind Through the Keyhole*, offering insights into Roland's identity through these recollections. Intersections of the supernatural and the problems that preoccupy humanity abound throughout the series as well and align the gunslinger's narrative with the epic tradition, as Roland and his *ka-tet* face challenges both mortal and supernatural in nature, from Keystone World hitmen to speaking demons, the monstrous Crimson King, the were-spider Mordred, and the guiding power of the Turtle, with each encounter a step along the way in their hope of saving the

Tower, restoring the deteriorating world, and seeking redemption for the humans who live within it, as well as honoring the memory of individuals and civilizations past. Finally, as the definitions provided by both Indick and White emphasize, the events of the epic extend well beyond Roland himself and his quest for the Dark Tower, with the fate of untold and interconnected universes depending on his success or failure.

While many epics are fictional creations, some of them draw on historical people, places, and events, blurring the lines between epic and legend, the latter of which "lies somewhere between myth and historical fact and which, as a rule, is about a particular figure or person" (Cuddon 484). The intersection of legend and epic highlights the connection between actual events, the stories they inspire, and the legend-making impulse that elevates individual endeavors to a larger scope, representing a truth applicable to the larger society or even humanity as a whole. The works upon which King draws in his *Dark Tower* series engage with this tradition, as well as becoming part of the web of the interconnection and inspiration between individual works, each of which build upon, reference, and remake some of those which have come before.

King Arthur

The legend of King Arthur has influenced literature and popular culture for more than five hundred years, with countless stories, books, and films telling the tales of Arthur, Queen Guinevere, and the Knights of the Round Table. Arthurian narratives are an excellent example of Cuddon's definition of legend as blurring the lines between history and story, though Mike Ashley explains that the historical reality is ultimately inconsequential, as "the historicity of King Arthur is irrelevant to the legend other than in depicting a valiant hero protecting Britain from invasion, decline and ruin" (57). Sir Thomas Malory collected and synthesized a wide range of Arthurian narratives in his *Le Morte Darthur*, selectively choosing and emphasizing the themes he found most intriguing as "he reshaped his originals, omitted much that was not relevant to his purpose, and even created new sections to advance his themes" (Lupack 134). Closer consideration of specific stories and their historical context also highlights the shifting representations and meanings of Arthur achieved through this storytelling. As Ashley notes, "The legends, drawing from their variant sources, offer different perspectives of Arthur, and in the three centuries from Geoffrey [of Monmouth] to Malory, Arthur moves from the heroic centre stage to become a tragic figure and victim of fate ... [as] Arthur's enemies become those within his kingdom, not external" (57). Malory's *Le Morte Darthur*, widely considered to be the definitive recounting of the Arthurian legend, tells of the adventures of Arthur's knights, their duels and feuds with both enemies and one another, the quest for the Holy Grail, the forbidden love between Queen Guinevere and Sir Lancelot, and Arthur's death.

There are several major influences of the Arthurian tradition that resonate throughout King's *Dark Tower* series, including the legendary figure of Arthur Eld, the quest narrative, and the presence of an antagonistic Mordred. As Furth explains, within the universe of the Dark Tower, Arthur Eld was "Mid-World's greatest mythical hero and the ancient King of All-World" (90). Arthur Eld's exploits and battles are Mid-World legends and the quest to protect the Dark Tower can be traced directly back to Eld, who is the figurehead and ideal of the "gunslinger-knights" (Furth 90) who have risen to continue his mission. Chivalry and courtly practices are central to Roland's recollection of the Gilead of his childhood, as well as the tales and historical accounts he shares with his *ka-tet*. Just as with King Arthur's knights, Eld's gunslingers are bound by a moral code known as the Way of Eld, which prescribes the gunslingers' "rigorous physical and mental training as well as their sense of honor and duty" (*ibid.*). As Eddie sums up the Way of the Eld in *Wolves of the Calla*, "If you decide we *can* help them, then we *have* to help them. That's what Eld's Way really boils down to…. And if we can't get any of them to stand with us, we stand alone" (King 162, emphasis original). In drawing a band of new gunslingers around himself, Roland is continuing the line of Arthur Eld, philosophically rather than by blood lineage, though these lines at times seem to blur, as in Roland's claiming of Jake as his son, Eddie's noted similarities to Roland's old *ka*-mate Cuthbert, and Eddie's recurring sense of reincarnation (King, *Wolves of the Calla* 203). Like Britain's King Arthur, Arthur Eld carried a legendary sword called Excalibur, and the barrels of Roland's guns are made from that sword's metal (King, *The Dark Tower* 608), a detail which figures significantly in the prophecy of the Crimson King's defeat. Roland is recognized as being of the Line of Eld both by his guns and by his demeanor, as he upholds the Way of the Eld and speaks with "the voice of a king" (King, *Wizard and Glass* 598).

As with King Arthur, Arthur Eld has both mythical and historical qualities: while a King named Arthur Eld reputedly lived and reigned approximately seven hundred years before Roland's own quest, there is also the Arthur Eld of myth and legend, who "was the first king to arise after the Prim receded" (Furth 91), the driving back of the monstrous Great Old Ones to quiet chaos and make civilization possible. King's Roland is the last surviving descendant of Arthur Eld and the final gunslinger left to continue this legacy. However, the line of Arthur Eld is complicated and at times, contradictory. As Furth explains, just as Roland is a direct descendent of Arthur Eld, so is the Crimson King, which divides the line of Eld into two diverging paths of light and darkness: "Both bloodlines are obsessed with the Tower, which is their birthright, yet while the line of Deschain is sworn to preserve it, the Red King and his son—the *dan-tete*, or little king—have pledged to destroy it" (91). While King Arthur's Round Table was challenged and dismantled from within due to discord among his knights, in the *Dark Tower* series, the fate of the Tower depends upon the fault lines and conflicts of the two surviving branches of the Line of Eld.

Another similarity between legends of King Arthur and King's *Dark Tower* series is the central position of the quest narrative. Roland's central, all-encompassing quest is to find and gain the Dark Tower. In Malory's *Le Morte Darthur*, the principal quest is the knights' pursuit of the Holy Grail, though as with many Arthurian romances, Malory uses "the technique of interlacing, sometimes called *entrelacement* ... [which is] the interweaving or alternating of different plot lines that focus on the adventures of individual knights" (McMurray 73). While Roland and his *ka-tet* are set toward the Dark Tower, their quest takes them in a variety of different directions as they work to ensure the Tower's safety, with King building on the tradition of *entrelacement* as well, at times echoing the narrative structure of Malory's *Le Morte Darthur*. These divergent quests are particularly significant in *Song of Susannah* and *The Dark Tower*, the last two books of the series. In *Song of Susannah*, Susannah ventures to New York City, Castle Discordia, and beyond to give birth to Mordred, while Roland and Eddie go to Stephen King's Maine in 1977 to palaver with their author and creator. Similarly, in *The Dark Tower*, the *ka-tet* is divided on separate quests within the quest, with Jake, Callahan, and Oy facing the vampires, low men, and *taheen* of The Dixie Pig, while King's Maine once again demands Roland and Eddie's (and later Jake's) attention and intervention. Each of these individual quests are central to reaching the Dark Tower, drawing the *ka-tet* ever closer to Roland's goal even as they are separated from one another. Additionally, Rachel McMurray explains that "at their core ... the quest for the Dark Tower and the quest for the Grail are both quests for knowledge" (46), though this knowledge, once gained, can be potentially destructive. The human is not meant to behold the divine, as with the Grail, and in *The Dark Tower*'s final pages, Roland at last reaches the Tower and makes his ascent, only to find that the knowledge he has so long sought may destroy him, as he is turned back to the Mohaine Desert, forced to begin his quest anew. Horrified by this revelation, it is likely a blessing that

Roland soon forgets. As the Voice of the Tower itself tells Roland, "*each time you forget the last time. For you, each time is the first time*" (King, *The Dark Tower* 828, emphasis original). Roland is doomed to repeat the same quest, seek the same knowledge, and experience the same horror, presumably until he gets it right, though what constitutes that "rightness" remains unclear. As Roland begins again at the series' conclusion, there are some significant differences, such as his possession of the Horn of Eld, which had previously been lost at the Battle of Jericho Hill, and the reclamation of which symbolically serves as a "*promise that things may be different ... that there may yet be rest. Even salvation.... If you stand. If you are true*" (King, *The Dark Tower* 829, emphasis original). This theme of "standing," holding one's ground in being true to personal values and the greater good echoes throughout much of King's fiction, including in *The Stand*, "The Body" (in *Different Seasons*, 1982), and *IT*, which each feature variations on this theme in the language of standing together and refusing defeat against overwhelming odds, whether of the human or supernatural variety. The notion of standing is integral to the *Dark Tower* series as well and Roland tells Eddie, "Unless we stand true, we'll never get within a thousand miles of the Tower" (King, *Wolves of the Calla* 163). As Jenifer Paquette explains, in King's fiction, "heroes decide to stand, but they don't have to; they can choose to run and hide like everyone else. The decision to stand and deal with the aftermath is what makes them heroes" (158). With this consideration in mind, the emphasis on Roland's need to stand in order to end his cyclical repetition of gaining and once again losing the Tower underscores his development as not just a man and as a gunslinger, but as a hero as well. In this respect, the conclusion of *The Dark Tower* offers some hope. As McMurray argues, the presence of the horn "seems to indicate that Roland has become, or will become, a better knight" (62), less likely to make some of the same mistakes that have haunted him throughout his previous versions of his quest. In this conclusion, King also draws on the Arthurian quest tradition, which is inspired by the Wheel of Fortune and "the Arthurian convention of leaving and returning to the same place" (McMurray 63), in this case encompassing time as well as place.

Finally, both the legends of King Arthur and King's *Dark Tower* series feature a Mordred who complicates the direct royal lineage and subverts or challenges the protagonist's aims. In the Arthurian tradition, Mordred is a complex and shifting character across different versions of the narrative. As *The Arthurian Encyclopedia* recounts, Mordred is often central to stories of Arthur and his name "appears almost as early as does that of Arthur" (Thompson 394). In earlier versions of the Arthurian legend, Mordred is Arthur's nephew, though beginning with the Vulgate *Mort Artu*, Mordred becomes Arthur's son, the unwittingly incestuous child of Arthur with his half-sister Morguase (*ibid.*), a paternal relationship that is maintained in Malory's *Le Morte Darthur*. In Malory's account, Mordred is a traitor and kills King Arthur, dying himself in the process, as "right so he smote his father, King Arthur, with his sword holding in both his hands, upon the side of the head, that the sword pierced the helmet and the tay of the brain" (513). The Mordred of the *Dark Tower* series is a melding of the two divergent lines of Eld, fathered by Roland and the Crimson King through the sexual intercessions of disembodied Speaking Ring demons. Mordred is gestated in the shared body of Susannah Dean and an incorporeal being called Mia and as Furth explains, "Mordred unites the mortal and nonmortal worlds.... Two of his parents—Roland Deschain and ka-mate Susannah Dean—are human. However, his other two parents—the Crimson King and Mia, daughter of none—are not" (141). Mordred's form echoes this hybrid nature, sometimes taking on the appearance of a human child and at other times, a monstrous spider. In the legends of King Arthur, despite Mordred's treachery, in many tellings he is presented with consideration and complexity, such as in "the alliterative *Morte Arthure* [which] offers a sympathetic portrait of Mordred as a figure who suffers genuine remorse for his deeds" (Thompson 394). This complexity is another characteristic of Mordred that King draws from the Arthurian tradition into his *Dark Tower* series. While Mordred's motivations for his betrayal remain largely unexplored in Malory's *Le Morte Darthur*, Mordred Deschain's thoughts and emotions are detailed in *The Dark Tower*, and he looks upon Roland "with love and hate, loathing and longing" (King 169–70). Mordred is often hungry and cold; he is nearly always alone and he envies Roland and his *ka-tet*, hating them for the warmth of their fire and even more for the comfort of their camaraderie and togetherness, which Mordred is himself denied. Mordred is a key to both the destruction of the Dark Tower (through his planned murder of Roland) and the gaining of the Tower (through the hourglass pattern on his spider belly that can unlock the door). While Mordred finds himself conflicted and yearning for Roland's love and approval, his final act is murderous, as he attacks Roland and kills Oy. In his version of Mordred, King highlights the character's complexity and internal conflict, with McMurray arguing that "the use of Mordred in the *Dark Tower* series reveals King's skillful interpretation of Malory, while at the same time offering modern readers a new perspective from which to read Malory's version of Mordred" (54). King's characterization both heightens and mitigates Mordred's monstrosity, transforming him into a literal monster as a were-spider, while simultaneously affording readers a sympathetic glimpse into the thoughts and emotions that drive his vengeance. As with his tales of the legendary Arthur Eld and narrative traditions of Arthurian legends (the quest, the cyclical structure), this version of Mordred demonstrates the ways in which King draws upon, negotiates, and remakes the Arthurian tradition in the *Dark Tower* series, claiming and reshaping familiar legends for a contemporary audience.

The Song of Roland *and "Childe Roland to the Dark Tower Came"*

In addition to drawing on tales of King Arthur, King's *Dark Tower* series takes inspiration from two legendary Rolands: the protagonist of the French epic *Song of Roland* and Robert Browning's poem "Childe Roland to the Dark Tower Came," which themselves draw both on Arthurian traditions of knightly conduct and the quest narrative.

The Song of Roland is a *chanson de geste* (or "song of deeds") dating back to 1100, likely written by the Norman poet Turold, based on the author's self-identification in the poem's final lines. Translator D.D.R. Owen argues that "none of the eighty or more surviving Old French epics encapsulate better than the *Song of Roland* the crusading warrior spirit of the feudal nobility" (2). These *chansons de geste* were recited and performed, fluid texts that were always changing and adapting to their specific audience and surrounding culture, much like the ongoing creation reflected in Arthurian narratives and later, in King's use of these texts in his *Dark Tower* series. Following in the tradition of Arthurian narratives, in which the lines between history and legend are blurred, *The Song of Roland* is based on an actual battle that took place in 778, when "Charles, King of the Franks, suffered a military reverse in the Pyrenean pass of Roncevaus" (Owen 4). The story of Roland at its center is a created narrative, though it takes inspiration from the historical figure of Hruodlandus, who was governor and defender of one of the borderlands of Brittany (Vincent, *The Road to the Dark Tower* 283). As a result of this combination of historical truth and narrative creation, *The Song of Roland* "has long been used as a test case in the debate over epic origins and how history came in this way to be transformed into legend" (Owen 8). Three key characteristics of *The Song of Roland* that resonate throughout King's *Dark Tower* series are the figure of Roland, a battle in the face of impossible odds, and the central importance of the relationship between soldiers to the battle and the narrative.

The *Song's* Roland is arrogant and headstrong, preoccupied with his own reputation and eventual legend, "the paragon of the unyielding warrior victorious in defeat" ("Le Chanson de Roland"). When Charlemagne's rear-guard, including Roland, are vastly overmatched by the pursuing Saracens and his friend Oliver encourages Roland to sound his horn to call Charlemagne and the rest of the army back to fight beside them, Roland refuses, saying, "I'd rather die than thus be put to shame; / If the King loves us it's for our valour's sake" (Turold 94). Roland's pride is maintained, though the battle is lost and all the French soldiers are killed, including Roland himself. Like the *Song's* Roland, King's Roland can be stubborn and prideful. Echoing the refusal of the Song's Roland to call for help when he and his men face impossible odds, when King's young Roland and his first *ka-tet* gain an understanding of the dangers they face in Mejis, Cuthbert wants Roland to send word back to their fathers, arguing that "even if it's too late for *help* to come from Gilead, it's not too late for *advice* to come from Gilead" (King, *Wizard and Glass*, 372, emphasis original). However, Roland refuses, distracted by his love for Susan and believing that they have the situation in hand, with no need for their fathers' help or advice, and even scolding Cuthbert that "it's comfort you're looking for ... not advice" (*ibid*.), unaware of the disaster which lies ahead. Similarly, when he meets Jake, Eddie, and Susannah, Roland has a clear mission and is resistant to and dismissive of anything that gets in the way of his quest for the Dark Tower, which even results in him letting Jake fall to his death in *The Gunslinger*. Roland's single-mindedness frustrates his *ka-tet*, particularly as they are getting to know Roland and the new world in which they find themselves. Early in the series, Roland is steadfast in his belief that *ka* will guide him: the Dark Tower is the destination towards which he is unswervingly moving and everything else is of little consequence, a faith that his newfound companions struggle to reconcile themselves with in *The Drawing of the Three* and *The Waste Lands* particularly. Similarly, guided by the Way of the Eld, Roland will not flee from a fight, even when the odds are stacked against him. When he is attacked by the citizens of Tull, a battle he recounts in *The Gunslinger*, he refuses to run, even though the fight pits him against the town's entire population, all of whom he leaves dead. Roland and his *ka-tets* stand against overwhelming odds in *Wizard and Glass* and *Wolves of the Calla* as well, fighting because it is the right thing to do and to stand for those who need and deserve their protection.

However, the most overmatched fight in the *Dark Tower* series and one from which Roland does not emerge victorious is told only in brief mentions and through Roland's dreams: the Battle of Jericho Hill, where he lost his original *ka*-mates, Cuthbert Allgood and Alain Johns, the latter of whom is accidentally killed by his own friends. Echoing *The Song of Roland*, at the Battle of Jericho Hill, Roland and his *ka-tet* are betrayed and outnumbered. Though Roland and Cuthbert run side-by-side into this overmatched battle and fight valiantly and with honor to their final moments, Roland is the lone survivor (King, *Wolves of the Calla* 169–72), escaping only by concealing himself in a cart full of dead bodies (King, *The Dark Tower* 175). Roland remembers the Horn of Eld—an echo of the *Song*'s Oliphant—lost at Jericho Hill, and which is returned to him as he begins his quest anew at the conclusion of *The Dark Tower*. Even more significantly, however, he remembers his friends, Cuthbert and Alain, part of the original *ka-tet* of his boyhood and young manhood, after whose loss he traveled alone until the drawing of his new companions in Eddie, Susannah, and Jake. The relationship and devotion between Roland, Cuthbert, Alain, and some of the other fellow gunslingers of his youth epitomize the "relationship between fellow-knights that is known as *compagnonnage*" (Owen 11). In this chosen brotherhood, which connects the *Song*'s Roland and his friend Oliver as well, these young men, who are "not related by birth but who may have received their chivalric training in the same household, might freely pledge to each other loyal comradeship and brotherhood in arms. Their pact was not necessarily formal; but its effect was to link the knights' destinies as firmly as any feudal or even blood connection" (*ibid.*). Roland and his fellow gunslingers trained together with Cort and their first loyalty is to one another, their shared aim of protecting Gilead, and later, seeking the Dark Tower. While Gilead falls and Roland reaches the Tower alone, his companions are still with him in spirit, with Roland calling each of their names as he approaches the Dark Tower, honoring his fellow gunslingers and their sacrifices. This loss also influences the man Roland becomes, as Michele Braun argues that "the deaths of his initial companions weigh heavily on the quest, and part of Roland's progress toward the Tower lies in redeeming his humanity by developing an emotional attachment to his new companions" (75), becoming a different kind of gunslinger. The memory of Jericho Hill and Roland's love for and camaraderie with his *ka*-mates even result in Roland adapting and making different choices when a fight proves unwinnable, as when he and Eddie are pinned behind the East Stoneham, Maine, general store and Roland reflects that "all this was too close to what had happened in Jericho Hill.... It was time to beat a retreat" (King, *Song of Susannah* 134). In this change—and in the cyclical nature of the narrative that gives Roland the chance to try again, to do better next time around—King's *Dark Tower* series is more optimistic than *The Song of Roland*, whose protagonist dies in battle because he refused to call for help in the face of impossible odds.

While the influence of *The Song of Roland* on King's *Dark Tower* series is fairly subtle, achieved through King's riffs on some of the epic poem's key characterization and themes, the *Dark Tower* series' relationship with Browning's poem "Childe Roland to the Dark Tower Came" is more overt and sustained. In his "Argument" that prefaces *The Drawing of the Three*, King notes that his *Dark Tower* series is "inspired by and to some degree dependent upon" Browning's poem (9), which itself draws inspiration from the quest narrative structure of Arthurian legend and from William Shakespeare's *King Lear*, in which Edgar, feigning madness, declares that "Childe Roland to the Dark Tower came. / His word was still 'Fie, foh, and fuh, / I smell the blood of a British man'" (III.iv.195–197).[1] Browning's poem recounts the quest of a young knight named Roland and his "world-wide wandering ... drawn out thro' years" (Browning 59), as he travels through a blighted land to reach the Dark Tower, which ultimately reveals itself as a "round, squat turret, blind as the fool's heart, / Built of brown stone, without a counterpart / In the whole world" (Browning 64), ugly and potentially meaningless. Todd K. Bender describes Roland's quest as a "magnificent failure" (414). The description of the wasteland through which he passes suggests that this failure is larger than just Roland's own, that there is something fundamentally wrong with the world through which he moves. Browning describes the land as bearing "a starved ignoble nature" (Browning 60) and of the grass, that "it grew as scant as hair / In leprosy; thin dry blades pricked the mud / Which underneath looked kneaded up with blood" (Browning 61). This could be the desiccated land following a brutal battle or a post-apocalyptic vista: there are signs of devastation and violence, but no hope, a despair that carries over in Roland's arrival at the Dark Tower. This description is ominous, reflecting not just the land through which he passes, but Roland himself, as the poem can also be read as "a journey into the mind, a psychological rather than a physical quest" (Bender 414). When Browning's Roland arrives at the Tower, he recalls the friends he has lost along the way as "one moment knelled the woe of years" (Browning 65) and he blows his horn, though whether he does so in triumph, resignation, or a simple declaration of his presence is undetermined. In "Childe Roland to the Dark Tower Came," Roland's quest for the Dark Tower is also a quest into himself and his own past, plumbing the depths of his despair and the loss of those he has loved. Indick argues that the poem's conclusion "is one neither of victory or defeat. If anything, it deepens the mystery" ("Stephen King as an Epic Writer" 65). Harold Bloom offers the interpretation that in these final lines "either the entire poem beings begins again, in a closed cycle ... or else Roland proclaims his story's inevitable lack of closure" (qtd. in Indick, "Stephen King as an Epic Writer" 65). There is no resolution for Childe Roland, who has gained his Tower but is still not victorious.

King's *Dark Tower* series follows a similar trajectory: while the Tower itself is clearly Roland's end-goal and the linchpin of all existence, the choices he makes and those he loves (and loses) along the way are integral to his quest as well, with those relationships and his own memories informing his final approach to the Dark Tower, as he cries out the names of his fallen and departed friends (King, *The Dark Tower* 801–2), echoing Browning's description of "Names in my ears / Of all the lost adventures of my peers" (Browning 65). In addition, just as Browning's poem reveals Roland's psychological state, when King's Roland nears and finally enters the Tower, he finds himself drawn further into his own mind and memories, as "each level represents some element of his life: an event, a memory, or a token of a developmental milestone" (Braun 72), immersing him in sensory recollection and surrounding him with faces and memories ranging from his birth to his final approach to the Tower. Finally, this preoccupation with identity, memory, and the past is dramatically and literally realized, when Roland opens the door bearing his name only to find himself turned back once more, returned to the Mohaine Desert and his pursuit of the Man in Black, stripped of his memories as he must begin his quest—and his (re)making of himself—anew (King, *The Dark Tower* 827–30). Browning's Roland sees the Tower and finds it ugly, while King's Roland gains his Tower only to be set to more striving and suffering, a purgatorial cycle that forces him to begin his quest all over again. In both cases, while the Dark Tower seemed to promise knowledge and solace, it leaves these two Rolands in uncertainty, with even more questions and no promise that they will ever be answered or that their quests will be fulfilled.

Some of the connections between Browning's poem and King's *Dark Tower* series rely on the similarity of names: Roland himself, his friend Cuthbert (Browning 62), and the iconic Tower. But in the final book of King's series, *The Dark Tower*, King draws Browning's poem itself into Roland's world, an intertextual engagement that offers a clue to the gunslinger's destiny. As a character within his own fiction, King leaves Roland and Susannah a copy of Browning's poem, with certain stanzas circled for emphasis. As they read, Roland and Susannah see overt parallels to their own recent experiences and narrow escape from the monstrous Dandelo, a kind of emotional vampire that nearly destroyed Roland and whom the gunslinger identifies as Browning's "hoary cripple" who "lied in every word" (Browning 59), though this description applies just as neatly to *Wizard and Glass*'s Rhea of the Cöos and to Roland's long-time foe Flagg, in all his many guises (King, "Afterword" 590). Roland also sees connections between Browning's poem and his own long quest, with the mention of Cuthbert and echoes of the events in Mejis as recounted in *Wizard and Glass* (King, *The Dark Tower* 695), including the young gunslingers' fight over Susan Delgado and whether or not Roland had forgotten his duty (King, *Wizard and Glass* 425–32). These connections are slippery and disorienting, doubling back upon themselves as Roland speculates that Browning is telling their story and Susannah argues that King was inspired by Browning in his own writing of the gunslinger. As Susannah thinks, "It was too confusing. Like trying to figure out which came first, the chicken or the egg. Or being lost in a hall of mirrors" (King, *The Dark Tower* 693). Browning and King's Rolands both seek the Tower and the knowledge it promises, but after trying to reconcile Browning's poem with their own experiences, Susannah decides there are some things better left unknown and refuses to read further (King, *The Dark Tower* 695). The revision of these Rolands—and the larger narrative traditions upon which they draw—is also indicative of their specific audiences, contexts, and readers. As Braun argues in her consideration of genre and the influence of Browning and *The Song of Roland* on the *Dark Tower* series, "In the *Dark Tower*, Roland's deeds are translated into a dark 20th-century fantasy. Roland's metamorphosis reflects changes in genre, changing conventions of the hero, and changes in the attitudes, values and anxieties of the culture in which the book is written and received" (67). These echoes, overlaps, and reversals are indicative of the ways in which King incorporates genre influences, specific texts, and connections to his own larger body of work throughout the *Dark Tower* series: they allow the reader to dig deeper into the world and characters before them, negotiate and at times even trespass the boundaries between reality and fiction, and immerse King's characters and readers in an web of texts and conventions that span literary history, from the classic to the contemporary.

T.S. Eliot's "The Waste Land"

Browning's "Childe Roland to the Dark Tower Came" prefigures another poem with which King's *Dark Tower* series engages, as "Browning's use of a wasteland as a symbol for man's alienation and his evocation of a failed courtly quest foreshadows T.S. Eliot's *The Waste Land*" (Bender 415). "The Waste Land" also draws on the legend of the Holy Grail in its "relation to the Fisher King, whose lands will die if he is not healed" (Auger 189), once again emphasizing the connection between the individual and the state of the world which surrounds him. Norris J. Lacy explains that the Fisher King is a guardian of the Holy Grail in many Arthurian narratives, most notably in Chrétien de Troyes's *Perceval*,[2] though he appears in many forms and by different names in a wide range of narratives, including as Pelles in Malory's *Le Morte Darthur*, "a ruler whose injury has caused his lands to become barren and desolate wastelands" (McMurray 25). In claiming and remaking the Fisher King legend for a modern audience, Eliot "adapted the perfect symbol for modern society and its ills" (Lupack 20), in a post–World War I world that was all too familiar with devastation and destruction. The Fisher King's illness is echoed in the deterioration of his lands, meaning that the success of the Grail quest will restore both the Fisher King and his world. Eliot writes of a land comprised of "A heap of broken images, where the sun beats, / And the dead tree gives no shelter.... And the dry stone no sound of water" (lines 22–24), a desiccated and arid land that offers no relief.[3]

In King's *Dark Tower* series, the land is similarly blighted, first by conflict and later by the devastation of some cataclysmic rupture, and rather than the Fisher King being the key to its restoration, the answer lies in the Dark Tower itself. While signs of this ruin are apparent in many of the places though which Roland and his *ka-tet* pass—and in multiple worlds—the most direct engagement with Eliot's poem is found in the third book of King's *Dark Tower* series, aptly named *The Waste Lands*. The notion of the waste lands defines the worlds through which they pass, particularly once they reach the dystopic and disintegrating city of Lud, where Eddie reflects that "all of Mid-World had become a waste land, haunting and haunted" (King, *The Waste Lands* 489), with this observation encompassing both the physical and spiritual state of the world in which they find themselves, which has moved on and in its wake, left only destruction. One of King's epigraphs to the novel is an excerpt from Eliot's poem, including the description of the land itself, ending with Eliot's admonition "I will show you fear in a handful of dust" (line 30), a line that Jake Chambers uses to preface his own disjointed school essay, "My Understanding of Truth" (King, *The Waste Lands* 141). Both King's epigraph and Jake's school essay also draw on Browning's "Childe Roland to the Dark Tower Came," bringing these two poems into direct conversation with one another: King's epigraph highlights the blighted nature of the land through which Roland passes, in which the growing things are "bruised as to balk / All hope of greenness" (Browning 61), while Jake's choice reflects his doubt and terror with his inclusion of Browning's opening line: "My first thought was, he lied in every word" (Browning 59). Both Roland and Jake take on some characteristics of the Fisher King's deterioration throughout the first part of *The Waste Lands* as well, as they struggle to reconcile their two disparate memories of one another—alive or dead, real or imaginary—with each going mad in his own respective world as a result of this doubling. Bringing Jake into Mid-World will not save the world itself, but it will save Roland and Jake's sanity and enable the quest to continue toward the Dark Tower, which may be the key to setting the world right.

This isolation is similarly echoed in King's references to Thomas Wolfe throughout the *Dark Tower* series, most notably in his evocation of Wolfe's litany of *"a stone, a leaf, and unfound door.... And all of the forgotten faces"* (1, emphasis original) from *Look Homeward, Angel* (1929). In the *Dark Tower* series, the leaf becomes a rose, but the symbolism remains the same, encompassing a world and the possibility that all can be lost or saved. Wolfe's litany is the key to Jake's return to Mid-World as well, as he reflects in his final essay, *"I can't go home again unless I find a stone a rose a door"* (King, *The Waste Lands* 142, emphasis original). Wolfe continues his rumination of this isolation, which bears similarities to Roland's own, in the search for *"the lost lane-end into heaven, a stone, a leaf, and unfound door. Where? When?"* (1, emphasis original). The rose and the doors—both those Roland finds and those he creates—are his means of building a *ka-tet*, forging new relationships, becoming a better gunslinger, and perhaps one day succeeding in his quest and earning his redemption. But as Eliot and Wolfe's work suggest, there is the isolation of the waste land, memory, and the self with which the gunslinger must first contend.[4]

Finally, in *The Waste Lands*, Roland and his *ka-tet* get a close look at how bad the land itself has gotten, as they pass over the devastated terrain outside of Lud (King 570). As they travel above these lands on Blaine the mad monorail, they get a close look at the devastation below, with its scorched, smoking earth and monstrous, impossible beings (King, *The Waste Lands* 570–1). This vista makes it clear that something has gone fundamentally, structurally wrong, perhaps even allowing the monsters to return from the legendary Prim, the chaos that had preceded All-World's civilization untold generations before. Whatever the cause, the natural order has been subverted and broken, and the land itself reflects this breakdown, one that can hopefully be reversed if Roland gains the Dark Tower. Even after being reunited with Jake and having his sanity restored, Roland remains a conflicted protagonist. The waste land and its horrors also reflect Roland's own internal state, following the tradition engaged by Browning in "Childe Roland to the Dark Tower Came," as well as the Gothic tradition of externalizing the internal horror. As Buday argues of this consideration of the waste lands, King "combines Eliot's disillusionment with the self with a Poesque tendency of paralleling the environment to the state of the character's mind and thus reinforcing the desperation, isolation, and ultimate futility of both Roland and Mid-World itself, though it is not only Mid-Word which is in jeopardy" (141). As these examples demonstrate, King engages Eliot's themes of isolation, destruction, and the connections between the individual and their world at both the macro- and microcosmic levels, with the imagery of the waste land influencing Mid-World and its countless interconnected universes, as well as reflecting the internal state of the gunslinger himself.

Another element of Eliot's "The Waste Land" that influences King's *Dark Tower* series is the central significance of a tarot reading in each. In Eliot, this reading is done by Madame Sosostris, "known to be the wisest woman in Europe, / With a wicked pack of cards" (lines 45–6). Madame Sosostris turns over cards bearing "the drowned Phoenician Sailor, the Belladonna, the man with three staves, the Wheel, and the one-eyed merchant with something on his back" (G. Miller 110), among others. She specifically notes the absence of the Hanged Man in this reading, a figure that symbolizes change and rebirth. Georgianna O. Miller explains that in pointedly "mentioning the lack of the card in her reading, Madame Sosostris is suggesting to her unnamed patron that modern society, and especially World War I, has had a negative effect on the spirituality of the world. Recovery or spiritual healing will be difficult, if not impossible, to achieve" (110). The upside-down Hanged Man is also evocative of the Fisher King, "who had to die in order to cause rebirth" (Creekmore 916). The role of this tarot reading connects both the past and future, echoing the larger themes of Eliot's "The Waste Land." As Emily Auger explains, "Much of 'The Waste Land' is about memory, including memories of the dead—as the Phoenician Sailor and the title of the first part ['The Burial of the Dead'] suggests—and the loss or absence of memory" (193). Memory plays a significant role throughout the *Dark Tower* series: Roland is informed in all he does by the memories of those he has lost, including his mother, his father, Susan Delgado, and his original *ka-tet*. However, as he gains the Dark Tower, his memory itself is lost to him as well, as he forgets the versions of the quest which have come before, in a complex and contested cycle of remembering and forgetting, where the memory of his lost friends is essential but his memories of himself and his quest are impossible to maintain. Eliot's use of the tarot in "The Waste Land" is complicated: while he is drawing on some established traditions and figures, he also creates others to suit his own purposes. For example, Betsey B. Creekmore[5] notes

1. Epic and Legend   27

that "the 'Drowned Phoenician Sailor' is not the name of a Tarot Trump in [the Rider-Waite Tarot] pack or in any other. The picture ... however, functions precisely as Waite intends: as a catalyst which evokes individualized association" (911), exploring the interconnections between the individual, his perception, and the wider world. The final card Madame Sosostris turns over is The Tower, which Creekmore argues is in this context indicative of violent regeneration, as "the things held to be of value in the Waste Land will be excised, and the protagonist will, from the ruin, from the dissolution of the doctrines and subjugation of pride, be able to be reborn. The death which must precede rebirth is total dissolution, is a violent rending of basic values and beliefs" (921). In other words, all must be destroyed—including the individual himself—in order for progress and rebirth to become possible.

Near the conclusion of King's *The Gunslinger*, when Roland has finally caught up with the Man in Black, he gets a tarot reading of his own.[6] As in Eliot, this tarot reading deviates from the norm, as the Man in Black tells Roland that his cards are "a mixture of the standard deck to which have been added a selection of my own development" (King, *The Gunslinger* 275). The first four cards he turns up are the Hanged Man, the Sailor, the Prisoner, and the Lady of Shadows, which represent Roland himself, Jake, Eddie, and Susannah, the last two of whom he has not yet met. The fifth and seventh cards are death and life, respectively, "But not for you" (King, *The Gunslinger* 278), as the Man in Black tells Roland. The sixth card is The Tower, which the Man in Black lays on top of the Hanged Man, with the Tower and his quest seeming to efface Roland completely, though the Man in Black can offer no explanation, telling Roland, "That is not for you to know now.... Or for me to know" (*ibid.*). The tarot reading in Eliot's "The Waste Land" foregrounds necessary destruction, the death that must presage rebirth. Roland's tarot reading seems potentially more promising, with the centrality of his quest for the Dark Tower serving the aim of such rebirth and its foreshadowing of the *ka-tet* with whom he will soon travel, no longer alone in his endeavors. However, his tarot reading is also indicative of the cyclical nature of Roland's quest. Auger notes that the turned cards "sum up Roland's fate to never die and to live only to find and save the Tower. That there is Death, but not for Roland, and Life, but not for Roland, returns us to Eliot's 'The Waste Land' with its descriptions of a state of being between life and death: when the narrator's 'eyes failed, I was neither / Living nor dead, and I knew nothing[...]' (ll. 39–40)" (206). The tarot readings in both Eliot and King engage the larger themes of their respective narratives, drawing connections between the individuals receiving the readings, the worlds that surround them, and the future that awaits them in the combination of death, life, rebirth, and repetition.

To effectively read Eliot demands a thorough knowledge of literature and history, with references and allusions drawn from his own life as well as a wide range of literary traditions. John J. Conlon notes the influence of the Bible, Dante, Metaphysical and French Symbolist poetry, and Elizabethan and Jacobean playwrights reflected in Eliot's work (1070) as a partial list of the authors and conventions from which Eliot drew inspiration. This intertextual engagement is similarly central to the other works of epic and legend discussed in this chapter: writers of Arthurian literature draw from, expand upon, or edit those narratives which have come before them, while the range of Rolands have similarly taken inspiration from those that preceded them, presenting a reinvented Roland for a new time, place, and audience. An understanding of the dynamic engagement between these texts and the ways in which they build upon and interact with one another is essential for a truly engaged and informed reading of each. As Conlon advises of Eliot specifically, "To come to Eliot's poetry with such a literary background is to see the phrases of other writers whom Eliot admired take on new and sometimes surprising meaning. To read Eliot's work without such a background may mean that the reader will miss both the larger and the particular allusions; but still the reader may grasp possible meanings of individual poems" (*ibid.*). Much the same could be said of King's *Dark Tower* series, in which he draws on a wide variety of genre influences, specific texts, and interconnections with his own larger body of work: one can certainly read the *Dark Tower* series without literary knowledge of the Arthurian tradition, *The Song of Roland*, or the poems of Browning and Eliot, but a familiarity with this larger context undoubtedly enriches and deepens the reading experience, opening even more doors of analysis, understanding, and meaning.

≋ 2 ≋

Fairy Tale

> "The stories we hear in childhood are the ones we remember all our lives."—Stephen King, *The Wind Through the Keyhole* (67)

King's work throughout his career has been widely influenced by fairy tales and the foundational elements of fantasy, horror, and social engagement that have made these stories so timeless, with King himself arguing that "to my mind, the stories that I write are nothing more than fairy tales for grown ups" (qtd. in Magistrale, *Second Decade* 4). Several critics have explored these fairy tale allusions, from readings of *Carrie* (1974) as a dark and modern take on the "Cinderella" story (Strengell 160; Yarbro 64–6) and *The Girl Who Loved Tom Gordon* (1999) as a variant of "Little Red Riding Hood" or "Hansel and Gretel" (Cowan 17), to the multiple and overlapping fairy tale influences evident in the narrative structure and tone of *The Shining* (1977), including the dangerous isolation of "Hansel and Gretel" and the forbidden exploration and macabre punishment of "Bluebeard" (Strengell 168–9; Curran 37–41).

Fairy tale traditions echo throughout King's *Dark Tower* series, ranging from allusion and passing reference to the central position of storytelling as individual expression, oral tradition, and a reflection of social organization and values. Similar to King's foundational engagement with epic and legend from *Le Morte Darthur* to "The Waste Land," through his engagement with fairy tale narratives, King draws from the past to create new stories and chart connections between multiple worlds, with tales and traditions echoing not just from the past to the present but also signaling points of continuity between Roland's world and the worlds of his fellow gunslingers. In addition, just as with the reverberations of epic and legend throughout the *Dark Tower* series, the inclusion of fairy tales, from specific narratives to the larger traditions of repetition and oral transmission, further contributes to the intertextuality of the series, as King draws connections between a wide variety of texts to create a rich and multilayered literary tapestry for his readers to interpret and explore.

As a result of the dramatic dissonance between the *ka-tet*'s worlds, fairy tales in the *Dark Tower* series are especially impactful in their unifying potential of sharing in a common story. Similar to the predictable patterns of myth, fairy tales have a seemingly timeless and familiar set of characteristics and narrative structures. As Andrew Teverson outlines this formula, "A fairy tale typically deals with the experiences of a youthful protagonist engaged on a journey, or in a series of tasks and trials, that has been necessitated by a change in his or her status: the death of a parent, or the loss of a magical object" (32), taking place within a magical world peopled by "strange beings and wonderful creatures" (*ibid.*) who aid or threaten the protagonist's progress. In the end, the protagonist almost always succeeds and "secures for himself or herself a more comfortable life and a more socially eminent position than seemed possible at the start of the story" (Teverson 33). Through this familiarity, Jack Zipes argues in *Fairy Tale as Myth/Myth as Fairy Tale*,

> the classical fairy tale makes it appear that we are all part of a universal community with shared values and norms, that we are all striving for the same happiness, that there are certain dreams and wishes which are irrefutable, that a particular type of behavior will produce guaranteed results, like living happily ever after with lots of gold in a marvelous castle ... [which] will forever protect us from inimical and unpredictable forces of the outside world [5].

Bruno Bettelheim similarly addresses this didactic social and cultural function of fairy tales with a psychoanalytical focus in *The Uses of Enchantment: The Meaning and Importance of Fairy Tales*, noting that these stories teach children "that a struggle against severe difficulties in life is unavoidable, is an intrinsic part of human existence—but that if one does not shy away, but steadfastly meets unexpected and often unjust hardships, one masters all obstacles and at the end emerges victorious" (8).

Fairy tales are a comforting touchstone that allow their tellers and their hearers to share in a common narrative, to avow and recommit to shared values and ideals, and to savor the reassurance of the familiar in an often unpredictable world. This is particularly true for Eddie, Susannah, and Jake, who have been pulled into Roland's Mid-World from their own disparate New York Cities: they are in a new, dangerous, and often frightening land and in being drawn between these two worlds from different times, circumstances, and personal experiences, they often lack a common frame of reference, or they may discover that the same person, place, or cultural touchstone has a completely different meaning or significance for their fellow travelers. In the face of these disparate experiences, Eddie, Susannah, and Jake soon discover—and draw great comfort from the fact—that they know the same fairy tales and can apply those tropes to articulate, process, and respond to their experiences in Mid-World, whether the point of reference is a classic like "Hansel and Gretel" or a more modern tale, such as L. Frank Baum's *The Wonderful Wizard of Oz* (1900). One example of this is in *Wolves of the Calla*, when the people of Calla Bryn Sturgis ask Roland and his *ka-tet* to protect them from the marauding Wolves that take their children, a horror that Eddie negotiates through a fairy tale framework, reflecting that "the storybook town has a fairy-tale problem.... And so the storybook people call on a band of movie-show heroes to save them from the fairy tale villains. I know it's real—people are going to die, very likely, and the blood will be real, the screams will be real, the crying afterward will be real—but at the same time there's something about it that feels no more real than stage scenery" (King 166–7). Through this rumination, Eddie reconciles the uncanny experience of finding the familiar in an unfamiliar land, the collision and conflation of the fantastic with reality, and his own newfound identity as a gunslinger and potential savior, as the residents of Calla Bryn Sturgis implore him and his friends to be, setting their hopes—and those of their children—on this redemptive potential.

In addition to drawing the narratives of Eddie, Susannah, and Jake's old worlds into this new one, the art and practice of telling fairy tales also allows them to connect to the brusque and pragmatic Roland in a more romantic and less literal way than their day-to-day interactions offer, with their primary focus on training, combat, and survival. Roland seizes every opportunity he can to hear the stories his companions can tell and as Vincent explains, Roland is "a glutton for stories, especially those that lead off with 'Once upon a time when everyone lived in the forest' or 'Once upon a bye, before your grandfather's grandfather was born,' though he usually listens to them like an anthropologist trying to figure out some strange culture by their myths and legends" (*The Dark Tower Companion* 485), absorbing not just the narrative itself but the ideological purpose it has served in the lives, societies, and psyches of his friends. These stories also offer Roland, Eddie, Susannah, and Jake the opportunity to make note of the intersections, similarities, and differences between their worlds. Through these tellings, "the four had discovered a great number of stories that were common to both worlds. Roland knew a tale called 'Diana's Dream' that was eerily close to 'The Lady or the Tiger,' which all three exiled New Yorkers had read in school. The Tale of Lord Perth was similar to the Bible story of David and Goliath" (King, *Wolves of the Calla* 39). These familiar stories seem to indicate a common foundation, a shared articulation of the universal human experience metaphorically explored through myth and fairy tale, which "are both fictitious yet true" (Strengell 109), simultaneously providing an escape from and a means of making sense of the surrounding world. Fairy tales and their telling are also instrumental in individuals finding their place within the world around them and determining their roles and relationships with others. As Zipes argues in *The Irresistible Fairy Tale: The Cultural and Social History of a Genre*, fairy tales "enabled humans to invent and reinvent their lives" (4) and in a quite literal sense, that is the challenge set before Roland and his companions, as Eddie, Susannah, and Jake must forge new lives and identities in a world very different from the ones from which they have come and as Roland relearns the habit of sharing his life with others and takes on new roles as a teacher and mentor.

King engages with a number of classic fairy tales throughout the *Dark Tower* series and these comparisons are often the way Roland's companions make sense of the challenges they must rise to face, transforming the alien and threatening into something familiar, a process of imaginative translation through which the characters can cope with, assimilate, and respond to the new realities they encounter. For example, when Roland asks Eddie to come closer to better hear him shortly after Eddie has been drawn into Roland's world, Eddie responds warily with "what big eyes you have, grandma..." (King, *The Drawing of the Three* 349), an allusion which is unfamiliar to Roland but sums up Eddie's competing feelings of unease and intrigue very effectively. In *The Waste Lands*, the Tick-Tock Man's obsession with clocks reminds Jake of *Peter Pan*, Captain Hook, and the ticking crocodile that pursues the captain (King 494). Blaine the mad monorail is likened to the awakening giant from "Jack and the Beanstalk," while a couple of the threatening inhabitants Susannah encounters in the dystopic ruins of Lud appear to her "more like Hansel and Gretel than Bonnie and Clyde; tired, frightened, confused, and lost so long in the woods that they had grown old there" (King, *The Waste Lands* 468), capturing their frailty and terror, in addition to the threat they pose to the *ka-tet* and their quest. The wilderness in particular seems easier for the erstwhile New Yorkers to conceptualize through fairy tale comparisons (King, *Wizard and Glass* 620; King, *Wolves of the Calla* 38) and the potential dangers found there make "Hansel and Gretel" a frequent touchstone. Eddie tells Roland the story of "Hansel and Gretel," bridging the gap between their two worlds as he incorporates a monstrous horror from Roland's past, "turning the wicked child-eating witch into Rhea of the Cöos almost without thinking of it" (King, *Wolves of the Calla* 39–40). The rogue Beam-Breakers have "the Gingerbread House," an internal and imagined space of safety that takes the form of a house made of candy (King, *The Dark Tower* 267–8). In *Wolves of the Calla*, the ritualistic taking of the children in Calla Bryn Sturgis is likened to the story of "The Pied Piper of Hamlin" (King, *Wolves of the Calla* 586–7). Late in the series, as Susannah and Roland approach a house, Susannah is ready for anyone from Hansel and Gretel to Little Red Riding Hood or Goldilocks (King, *The Dark Tower* 652–3).

In addition to the infusion of these familiar classic tales throughout the series, three extended engagements with fairy tale narratives and traditions are particularly significant in the *Dark Tower* books, shaping the narrative, reflecting Roland's world, and establishing productive interconnections with King's larger canon. The first of these is the frequent references to Baum's *The Wonderful Wizard of Oz*, which takes an extended central position in *Wizard and Glass* and reverberates throughout the series as a whole. The second is the figure of the Turtle, one of the Guardians of the Beam in the *Dark Tower* series, who also appears in *IT* in the mythical Turtle encountered by Bill Denbrough. Finally, King engages in the creation and telling of new fairy tales within the series itself, including the strong oral tradition highlighted in Roland's storytelling in *The Wind Through the Keyhole* and the role of children's literature through the faux children's story *Charlie the Choo-Choo*, which appears in the *Dark Tower* series and a version of which was published in 2016 as a textual artifact of King's *Dark Tower* universe.

Following the Yellow Brick Road Along the Path of the Beam

L. Frank Baum's *The Wonderful Wizard of Oz* is a distinctly American fairy tale,[1] following the adventures of industrious and independent Dorothy Gale as she makes her way through Oz, helping those she meets along the way and single-minded in her quest to return to her Kansas farm and family. In writing his Oz stories, Baum deviated significantly from the established European fairy tale tradition, remarking in his introduction to *The Wonderful Wizard of Oz* that "the time has come for a series of newer 'wonder tales' in which the stereotyped genie, dwarf and fairy are eliminated, together with all the horrible and blood-curdling incidents devised by their authors to point a fearsome moral to each tale" (Baum 3), a need he intended his book to fulfill as "a modernized fairy tale, in which the wonderment and joy are retained and the heart-aches and nightmares are left out" (*ibid.*). While critics, readers, and viewers of myriad adaptations of Oz may disagree on whether Baum succeeded in leaving out the more horrific elements of the fairy tale tradition, it is indisputable that his stories of Oz have permeated American culture and become as familiar to contemporary audiences as the traditional fairy tales of old. The lesson Dorothy learns seems initially uncomplicated: that "there's no place like home" (Baum 42). She has set out, had an adventure, decided home is better, and come back, happy to be there once again, mirroring the classic hero's journey outlined by Joseph Campbell (30). However, this conclusion strikes many readers and viewers as problematic. As Salman Rushie argues in his British Film Institute (BFI) Classics book on Victor Fleming's 1939 film adaptation, *The Wizard of Oz*, it is Oz rather than Kansas that is more appealing to readers and viewers—as well as within the larger cultural memory and discourse—regardless of how Dorothy feels about it. As a result, Oz

> *became* home; the imagined world became the actual world, as it does for us all, because the truth is that once we have left our childhood places and started out to make up our own lives, armed only with what we have and are, we understand the real secret of the ruby slippers is not that 'there's no place like home' but rather that there is no longer any such place *as* home: except, of course, for the home we make, or the homes that are made for us, in Oz, which is anywhere, and everywhere, except the place from which we began [58, emphasis original].

With this in mind, it is unsurprising that Baum's Oz resonates so powerfully within the universe of King's *Dark Tower* series. Eddie, Susannah, and Jake have literally been taken into a world other than their own. Similarly, even though Mid-World is Roland's home, it is a home that has undergone significant and traumatic change over the course of his life: as a common trope within the series states, "the world had moved on." The world in which Roland grew up, became a gunslinger, and started his quest for the Dark Tower is, in many ways, not the same world through which he and his friends now travel, and sometimes he finds himself just as much a stranger in this land as his companions do.

Baum's Oz is a frequent touchstone and allusion throughout the *Dark Tower* series but is most pronounced in *Wizard and Glass*, with its frequent appearance and permutation signaling the ways in which the fairy tale as a genre "has the quality of plural signification ... it is rich in potential meanings, and can take on diverse significances depending on how it is being used and by whom" (Teverson 6). When Roland and his companions end their journey with Blaine the monorail, they find themselves in a version of the American Midwest, surrounded by echoes of Dorothy's Kansas and King's own post-plague Nebraska of *The*

Stand. As they continue on their journey, they find their road leading them toward an emerald palace that strikes them as a combination of the Wizard's palace cobbled together from the MGM film, Baum's illustrations, and their own imaginations (King, *Wizard and Glass* 657), blurring the lines between fairy tale and reality and ushering them into the liminal space that lies between these categories. The *ka-tet* find personally tailored red shoes left for them along their path to the palace, including tiny boots for the billy-bumbler Oy, and cannot enter its gates without donning them and clicking their heels three times (King, *Wizard and Glass* 661–2). However, their audience is with an entirely different kind of Wizard: Roland's timeless nemesis Marten Broadcloak, alternately known as Randall Flagg and by a score of other names and in other guises. Rather than offering them a way home, this Wizard tempts them with peace, if only they foreswear the Dark Tower. As he tells the *ka-tet*, "Things could get easier.... No more lobstrosities, no more mad trains, no more disquieting—not to mention dangerous—trips to other worlds. All you have to do is give over this stupid and hopeless quest for the Tower.... Cry off. Turn from the Tower and go on your way" (King, *Wizard and Glass* 673). They each refuse Flagg's offer, but much as Dorothy's audience with the Wizard both draws her closer to her friends and is the first step toward their parting, Flagg threatens the *ka-tet*'s solidarity. While they all remain resolute in their continuation of the quest for the Dark Tower, Roland must finish telling them his story to enable them to move forward together. As Roland considers this pivotal moment, "the question wasn't, he saw, whether or not the five of them could find their way out of the Green Palace and recover the path of the Beam; the question was whether or not they could go on as *ka-tet*. If they were to do that, there could be nothing hidden" (King, *Wizard and Glass* 675, emphasis original). In order to move forward, Roland must tell his story and reveal himself completely to them, including his very worst act: matricide. As a young man, Roland, recently returned from Mejis, killed his mother Gabrielle, tricked into thinking she was the wicked witch Rhea of the Cöos, an action and loss further complicated by Roland's heartbreak and rage at having previously discovered that his mother had become Marten Broadcloak's lover (King, *Wizard and Glass* 677–84). Though Roland has killed countless times since and almost always with much clearer intent, the murder of his mother is a sin for which Roland can never forgive himself and he cannot conceive of anyone else offering him forgiveness or absolution for it either, so in telling his companions, he is opening himself up completely to them and putting himself entirely at the mercy of their judgment. The telling of this story—which engages some familiar tropes and is among the darkest of the stories told within the series, whether real or fairy tales—is essential and the *ka-tet* cannot move forward without it. They will stand no chance of succeeding in their quest if Roland doesn't tell it truly and completely. In the end, his friends stand with him, accept him, and forgive him, so just as the story of Oz leads them into danger and jeopardizes their union, it is Roland's own story that saves them and clears the path for them to move forward.

The Turtle

While Eddie, Susannah, and Jake tell Roland many fairy tales from their world and they collectively identify a wide range of shared narratives, Roland also introduces his friends to Mid-World stories, including those of the Guardians of the Beam. According to Mid-World children's tales and cosmological narratives, there are twelve Guardians of the Beam, who stand at opposite ends of six intersecting paths, at the nexus of which stands the Dark Tower itself. The Beams are identified by their anchoring Guardians, including Bear, Turtle, Lion, Fish, and Bat, among others (King, *The Waste Lands* 60). These figures are foundational in the mythic and fairy tale discourses of Mid-World and are also indispensable navigational markers. As Vincent explains in *The Dark Tower Companion*, "People traveling along the one of the Great Roads that follow the Beams specify their location by naming the Beam they are on and the one toward which they are headed" (313). For example, "if someone heads toward the Tower from the Turtle portal, they are said to be on the Beam of the Turtle (Maturin), Way of the Bear (also known as Shardik), whereas someone starting from the opposite side would be on the Beam of the Bear, Way of the Turtle" (*ibid.*). The Crimson King's greatest desire is to bring about the fall of the Dark Tower and the resultant destruction of the universe and to that end, he employs a team of psychically-gifted Beam-Breakers to chip away at these ley lines of power, a conflict that is central to King's book of interconnected novellas *Hearts in Atlantis* and the final book of the *Dark Tower* series, *The Dark Tower*.

Each of the Guardians of the Beam has their own narrative and characteristics (though not all are fully explored within King's *Dark Tower* series). One of the most notable of these Guardians within the series itself and within the context of King's larger canon is the figure of the Turtle. As a rhyme Mid-World children are taught in the nursery explains: "*See the TURTLE of enormous girth! / On his shell he holds the Earth. / His thought is slow but always kind; / He holds us all within his mind. / On his back all vows are made; / He sees the truth but mayn't aid. / He loves the land and loves the sea, / And even loves a child like me*" (King, *The Waste Lands* 60, emphasis original). Roland's story of the Turtle serves several purposes in its telling: it introduces Eddie, Susannah, and Jake to the cosmological constructs governing Mid-World, at a very basic and accessible level; it also provides them with a brief glimpse of Roland's childhood tales and connects Roland's world to our own, where the figure of a turtle holding up the world is a "mytheme [that] has appeared in disparate cultures across the globe for millennia" (Grundhauser). This specific role of the Turtle is echoed in the fairy tales of Roland's world, recounted in *The Wind Through the Keyhole*, as the wizard Maerlyn pledges himself and his promise "True as the Turtle that holds up the world" (King 250). The cosmic turtle can be found in Hindu mythology, as well as Chinese and Native American creation stories; this figure has been incorporated and adapted in contemporary popular culture as well, including Terry Pratchett's *Discworld* series (Grundhauser). As Eric Grundhauser reflects, "The image of the world being carried through space by an ancient, impossibly massive tortoise" resonates with many cultures and peoples, perhaps because turtles are "famously long-lived, giving them a wise, ancient quality that lends itself to mythologizing." In King's use of the Turtle specifically, as seen in both the *Dark Tower* series and *IT*, Strengell writes that "King explains that the character of the Turtle derives in part from a Native American story about a turtle holding up a man who holds up the world and in part from the myth of Atlas holding the world on his shoulder. In his view the Turtle symbolizes everything that is stable and solid in the universe" (229). Just as the protective, world-building figure of the Turtle repeats between *IT* and the *Dark Tower* series, so does chaos and destruction, as Vincent points out that "there is clearly some relationship between Pennywise and the Crimson King, both of whom have business in Derry, Maine, and share the concept of deadlights" (*Road to the Dark Tower* 195). Furthering this parallel, Strengell notes that while It "symbolizes all of King's mythical representations of evil ... the counterforce of It is the Turtle" (227), a force for stability, hope, and goodness.

In the final showdown between the Losers' Club and It in 1958, Bill Denbrough is cast out into the darkness by the monster, where he encounters "a great Turtle, its shell plated with many blazing colors. Its ancient reptilian head slowly poked out of its shell.... The eyes of the Turtle were kind. Bill thought it must be the oldest thing anyone could imagine, older by far than It, which had claimed to be eternal" (King, *IT* 1070). King's version of this world-creating turtle also draws on the African creation myth of Bumba, in which Bumba, "the first creator, the first ancestor," vomits up the universe, including the sun, the moon, the animals, and humans (Scheub), an act of creation for which the Turtle also claims responsibility, telling Bill, "*I made the universe, but please don't blame me for it; I had a bellyache*" (King, *IT* 1070, emphasis original). Bill begs the Turtle for help and while the Turtle provides advice, leading Bill back to his belief in the goodness and magic of childhood faith, it tells Bill that ultimately "*you must help yourself, son*" (King, *IT* 1071, emphasis original). In *Once Upon a Time: On the Nature of Fairy Tales*, Max Lüthi notes that "children in fairy tales are by no means helpless; many of them free themselves by their own ability and cunning. The fairy tale shows not only that children have need of care and protection, it also gives them the ingenuity to make their way and to save themselves" (65). In King's Derry, the adults—including the parents of the Losers' Club members—have turned a blind eye, refusing to see the violence right in front of them or to effectively protect the children, both in the current moment and in the repeated visits of the evil that have punctuated the town's dark history. Without adult guidance and protection to rely on, the only assistance Bill and his friends find is in the Turtle. Aside from that, like countless fairy tale children before them, they are on their own, left to rescue themselves and one another and ensure their own survival. The Turtle encourages but cannot actively intervene (or "mayn't aid") and it is Bill and his friends who temporarily defeat It, driving the monster away, ending the horrors of the summer of 1958, and forcing It into hibernation before the completion of It's anticipated feeding cycle. Even as adults, the vestiges of the Turtle remain to help them in their final conflict, as Bill discovers that "the Turtle might be dead, but whatever had invested it was not" (King, *IT* 1111), as the goodness and guidance that animated the Turtle of their childhood gives them the strength to stand against evil once more.

Tim Stoutheart and Charlie the Choo-Choo

The Wind Through the Keyhole is chronologically situated between *Wizard and Glass* and *Wolves of the Calla*, as Roland's *ka-tet* seeks shelter during a starkblast—a storm characterized by high winds, dramatic atmospheric changes, and temperatures so low and sudden that trees are felled and birds freeze in mid-air—en route to Calla Bryn Sturgis. Roland passes the time telling his companions stories of Mid-World: the first, one of his own adventures and the other, a traditional fairy tale, situated as a story told within his own story (which is in turn nested within the larger story of the *ka-tet*'s adventures together). In this telling—and the multiplicities of storytelling which take place within it—King

2. Fairy Tale

embraces the oral storytelling tradition in which, as Bettelheim agues, "a fairy tale should be heard rather than read" (150) to be its most effective. The repetition of these tellings and retellings are also central to the fairy tale tradition. Teverson explains that "as a generic form, the fairy tale is a many-tongued genre, a cultural palimpsest; because even as it speaks of the time in which it is told, it carries the memory of other times in which it has circulated and flourished. It bears the print of the hand that holds it, but under that print it carries the marks of earlier hands" (5). In this retelling, Roland is also tapping back into his former experience as a hearer of these same tales, as told to him by his mother, and while their relationship and his recollections of her are complicated to say the least, his memories of her reading him these stories at bedtime are fond and he recalls "how beautiful she had been in my early childhood, as she sat beside me on my bed in the room with the colored glass windows, reading to me" (King, *The Wind Through the Keyhole* 68). Finally, in these retellings, Roland establishes the time-honored tradition and essential skill of storytelling, connection, and meaning-making that have been essential to the role of gunslingers since time out of mind, a significant cultural role and responsibility (King, *The Wind Through the Keyhole* 106).

Roland begins by telling his friends the story of "The Skin-Man," a murderous shape-shifter[2] that he and another young gunslinger, Jamie DeCurry, are sent to stop, traveling from Gilead to the outlying town of Debaria. Shortly after their arrival in Debaria, a brutal attack leaves fifteen people dead, with a young boy named Bill Streeter now an orphan and the only possible witness to the identity of the Skin-Man. Roland and Jamie take Bill to the jail to interview him, watch over him, and keep him safe as their investigations continue, and as Roland and Bill sit together, Roland tells the young boy the story of Tim Stoutheart, a boy who ventured into the dark and dangerous woods, braving the Covenant Man,[3] a giant snake (or in Mid-World-ese, a "pooky"), a dragon, an enchanted tiger, and a starkblast to avenge the murder of his father and beg a wizard for a magical potion to restore his mother's sight, before returning victorious—as all good fairy tale heroes do—and going on to a life of adventure, valor, and honor as a gunslinger. Following the telling of this tale, Bill helps Roland determine the identity of the Skin-Man, the monster is destroyed, Roland and Jamie DeCurry return to Gilead, and Bill is left to be raised by a benevolent order of monastic women, with all ending well (or at least as well as it can with an orphaned child, which is a familiar fairy tale trope for all its trauma and tragedy).

Roland's telling occupies the space of the uncanny: simultaneously familiar and unfamiliar to his companions. Sigmund Freud explains that "the uncanny is that species of the frightening that goes back to what was once well known and had long been familiar" (Freud 124). Eddie, Susannah, and Jake are familiar with and recognize the linguistic and narrative fairy tale tradition, even though Roland's telling begins with "Once upon a bye, long before your grandfather's grandfather was born" (King, *The Wind Through the Keyhole* 109) and concludes with a mirroring bookend, rather than the standard "once upon a time" and "they lived happily ever after." This repetition establishes what Lüthi refers to as "a brief statement of fairy tale philosophy: 'Once there was, One day there will be'" (47), a constant touchstone regardless of the time and place of the story's telling. In addition to this combination of the familiar and unfamiliar, Roland's story is uncanny in that he is revealing to his companions an aspect of himself and an interlude from his life which had remained heretofore untold. In both the story and its teller, his friends are already familiar with the basic shape and meaning, but the details and insights are new and potentially revelatory. Even more significant is the purpose of and interconnections between the stories and their telling, which underscore the continued relevance of fairy tales on everyday life. Roland and his companions are sheltering from a starkblast as he tells them these stories, one of which features its own starkblast, from which Tim Stoutheart must shelter with an enchanted tiger, highlighting the timeless challenge of surviving in the face of a hostile world, particularly when faced with overwhelming forces of nature far from home, shelter, or civilization. As Roland tells his friends, "There's nothing like stories on a windy night when folks have found a warm place in a cold world" (King, *The Wind Through the Keyhole* 31). This is a comfort that has resonated with all cultures and one of the driving reasons that "humans began telling tales as soon as they developed the capacity of speech" (Zipes, *The Irresistible Fairy Tale* 2).

Similarly, fairy tales can be integral in helping children cope with and respond to challenges and trauma, whether these take the form of fear of the unknown or loss of a loved one, and Bettelheim argues that a child "can gain much better solace from a fairy tale than he can from an effort to comfort him based on adult reasoning and viewpoints. A child trusts what the fairy story tells, because its world view accords with his own" (45). In both of the stories Roland tells, "The Skin-Man" and "The Wind Through the Keyhole," young boys suffer significant trauma and loss, with Bill Streeter witnessing the murder of his father and others by the skin-man and Tim Stoutheart's loss of his father and powerlessness as he sees his mother abused by her new husband. Jake Chambers, the youngest of Roland's companions, is far from a normal young boy, having faced trials and horrors of his own, from being sacrificed by Roland

2. *Fairy Tale* 41

under the mountain in *The Gunslinger*, to doubting his own perceptions and nearly driven insane by doubled memories in *The Waste Lands*, and later in the same book, kidnapped and beaten by a plague-riddled madman in Lud. However, despite all that, Jake is still a young boy and to some extent, the fairy tale negotiation of horror appeals to and holds a potentially healing property for him as well. As these connections show, fairy tales embody several timeless characteristics, from sheltering from the weather and savoring the comfort of one's fellow humans to coping with trauma, and the story of Tim Stoutheart that Roland tells Bill Streeter is integral in Bill's grieving and survival process, just as the stories of these boys' trauma and healing are a comfort to Jake as well, and both stories provide an intangible solace to the *ka-tet* as a whole, offering reassurance as they shelter from the starkblast in a world that is still often incomprehensible, frightening, and strange to them.

Another fairy tale created within the universe of the *Dark Tower* is the children's book *Charlie the Choo-Choo* by the fictional Beryl Evans, a story which makes its first appearance when Jake stumbles across it in a used bookshop run by a man named Calvin Tower in *The Waste Lands*. Jake buys *Charlie the Choo-Choo* and a battered book of riddles (titled *Riddle-De-Dum!*) from Tower, both of which help ensure his and his friends' survival in the not-too-distant future, underscoring the interconnections and the weight of the intertextualities that resonate between and connect these worlds, another example of the myriad ways in which Roland and his companions are "*haunted* by books" (*Song of Susannah* 168, emphasis original). As Roland and his *ka-tet* discover, "fictions from their reality intrude on their adventures" (Vincent, *The Dark Tower Companion* 485) and can sometimes even be the difference between life and death. *Charlie the Choo-Choo* is the story of a sentient coal-powered locomotive and his friend Engineer Bob, who make the trip from St. Louis to Topeka for the Mid-World Railway Company before Charlie is decommissioned and replaced with a shiny new steam locomotive. Both Charlie and Engineer Bob despair but get their chance at redemption when the fancy new train won't run and the head of the railroad needs to get to his daughter's piano recital. Charlie and Bob succeed and as a reward, they are given their own happily ever after in the Mid-World Amusement Park and Fun Fair "pulling laughing children hither and thither in that world of lights and music and good, wholesome fun" (King, *The Waste Lands* 206; Evans 19). A print version of *Charlie the Choo-Choo* was published by Simon and Schuster in 2016, complete with illustrations by Ned Dameron, who illustrated the first edition of King's *The Waste Lands*, in which the story of Charlie the Choo-Choo initially appears and plays an integral role. When Jake finds

Charlie the Choo-Choo, he feels a moment of instant recognition for a world he can't quite remember through his occupation of two simultaneous realities: in one reality, he went to another world and was killed by the gunslinger, while in another his life in New York City has continued, explicable and uninterrupted. Though the spark of recognition is reassuring, it is also unsettling, as are the illustrations of Charlie himself and "Jake found that he did not trust the smile on Charlie the Choo-Choo's face. *You look happy, but I think that's just the mask you wear,* he thought" (*ibid.*, emphasis original). Similarly, while the story seems to have a traditional "happily ever after" ending, Jake is unconvinced and finds the final pages particularly terrifying, thinking that Engineer Bob's smile "looked like the grin of a lunatic … and the more Jake looked at the kids, the more he thought that their expressions looked like grimaces of terror" (King, *The Waste Lands* 207). Jake is not only remembering bits of his alternate past (Roland, Mid-World, the significance of the Dark Tower) but also getting premonitions of the future which unsettle and frighten him. *Charlie the Choo-Choo* and *Riddle-De-Dum!* both serve as precursors to the *ka-tet*'s ride on Blaine the sentient, mad monorail upon Jake's return to Mid-World, when they have to best Blaine in a riddle contest in order to survive, a collective competition in the larger tradition of "riddle fairy tales … [of] people who propound riddles and those who solve them" (Lüthi 123). Once Roland and his friends have survived Blaine's contest and disembark in Topeka, they run across the real-life Charlie the Choo-Choo in Gage Park, a horror made manifest as Charlie flashes his headlamp at Jake (King, *Wizard and Glass* 92). *Charlie the Choo-Choo* also serves as a barometer of dissonance and possible slippages between worlds, such as in *Wolves of the Calla*, when Jake and Eddie visit Tower's bookstore to discover that the author's name on the cover is no longer that of Beryl Evans, but Claudia y Inez Bachman, the letters of whose name not-so-coincidentally add up to the magic number of nineteen (King 57), a fundamental shift that alerts them to the essential nature of this version of New York and the intersecting timelines they navigate (King, *Song of Susannah* 200). This shift also aligns *Charlie the Choo-Choo* more overtly with King, as Claudia y Inez Bachman shares a surname with King's pseudonym of Richard Bachman, whose fictional wife is named Claudia Inez Bachman, though without added "y" that brings the letters in her name to nineteen (King, *Song of Susannah* 288).

Charlie the Choo-Choo makes appearances elsewhere in King's canon as well, evidencing the ways in which King's work is grounded in Roland's world well beyond those novels and stories that strictly make up or directly overlap with the *Dark Tower* series. Charlie the

2. *Fairy Tale*

Choo-Choo shows up amid some fairground attractions in King's dystopian zombie novel *Cell* (2006), in which the vast majority of the world has been driven into a violent frenzy by a cell phone transmission in "a 'Night of the Living Dead' scenario with a technological twist" (Maslin). When the survivors are fighting to escape in the aftermath of the final showdown at the Northern Counties Expo fairgrounds near Kashwakamak, Maine, "they came onto the midway between the Krazy Kups and a half-constructed kiddie ride called Charlie the Choo-Choo" (King, *Cell* 428). Another haunting though largely benevolent version of Charlie is also instrumental in *Doctor Sleep* (2013), King's sequel to *The Shining*, where a grown Danny Torrance finds himself in Frazier, New Hampshire, home of the Teenytown Railway and The Helen Rivington, "a miniature train ... [with] passenger cars that were surely too small to hold anyone larger than toddler size" (King, *Doctor Sleep* 58–9). While The Helen Rivington lacks the malevolence of Charlie and proves to be quite useful when needed, there is still something a bit unsettling about it and Abra Stone, a young girl with a "shine" similar to Danny Torrance's, once saw "ghostie people riding The Helen Rivington ... dead people riding that little train through the woods, their faces like transparent apples in the moonlight" (King, *Doctor Sleep* 170), an unsettling image that echoes the crying children at the conclusion of *Charlie the Choo-Choo*, continuing long after they wish the ride would end.

Fairy tale references infuse and inform King's *Dark Tower* series. They are familiar stories in an unfamiliar land and often serve as a lens or filter through which Roland's *ka-tet* can negotiate and articulate their Mid-World experiences. As in the most popular and best-loved fairy tales, these conflicts generally turn out "happily ever after": after their meeting with Flagg, Roland and his *ka-tet* are reaffirmed in their dedication to one another and their quest for the Dark Tower, Bill Denbrough draws on the power of the Turtle to save himself and his friends, and Tim Stoutheart survives, restores his beloved mother's sight, and rises to glory as a gunslinger. However, as the unsettling images of Charlie the Choo-Choo and the repeated references to the familiar trials of "Hansel and Gretel" make clear, heroes must persevere despite pain and loss, magic is not to be doubted, and darkness and danger are never far away.

3

Fantasy and Science Fiction

In King's combination of a wide range of genre influences and characteristics in the *Dark Tower* series, he is engaging with the time-honored fantasy tradition of what Tolkien referred to as "the 'Pot of Soup' or the 'Cauldron of a Story'" (Flieger 181). As Tolkien explains this concept in his essay "On Fairy-Stories," "By 'the soup' I mean the story as it is served up by its author or teller, and by 'the bones' its sources or material—even when (by rare luck) those can be with certainty discovered" (20). According to Tolkien, "the Pot of Soup, the Cauldron of Story, has always been boiling, and to it have continually been added new bits, dainty and undainty" (27), from the mythical to the everyday. With the *Dark Tower* series, King is both drawing from and adding to this imaginative soup, building on the base of epic, legend, and fairy tale already incorporated and further engaging with elements of fantasy, science fiction, the Western, and horror. The structure and stories of the *Dark Tower* universe embrace this hybridity, as does the world King has created within it. Roland himself seems to have little patience with arbitrary genre boundaries and classifications: when Eddie explains the concept of genre characteristics, Roland asks, "Do people in your world always want only one story-flavor at a time? ... Does no one eat stew?" (King, *Wolves of the Calla* 40). Within the universe of the *Dark Tower*, this exchange highlights such separations as unnecessary and even "kinda boring" (King, *Wolves of the Calla* 41) when it comes to telling a good story.

The foundational "what if?" question of science fiction is central to the *Dark Tower* series as well, particularly in the role of time within the series. The members of Roland's *ka-tet* are all drawn from New York Cities of different years and when they travel to the Keystone World, they do so at different points on this continuum. Similarly, time and technology are frequent points of tension in Roland's Mid-World, where the lines between magic and machinery are often blurred. Patrick

Parrinder notes that "in all science-fiction stories, scientific and technological innovation has consequential effects, causing changes at the level of social structure, of individual experience, and in the perceived nature of reality itself" (23). Roland's Mid-World is one of both past and future: characteristics of medievalism engaged by the epic tradition exist side-by-side with a wide range of technologies, many of which are familiar to the contemporary reader (like surveillance and biological weapons) while others are more traditionally futuristic (like humanistic robots). This engagement is further complicated by the fact that these technologies are firmly located in the far past of Roland's world, a nearly forgotten history that is reminiscent of the reader's imagined future set in a world that has "moved on." This dynamic negotiation typifies King's engagement with individual genres, as well as his combination of them in creating the richly magical, technological, and textually-engaged universe of the Dark Tower and its many reverberations and echoes throughout his larger body of work.

While epic, legend, and fairy tale are age-old traditions that have been continually engaged and reinvented in the intervening centuries, fantasy and science fiction arguably typify the 20th century. While the foundations of fantasy unquestionably run much deeper than this—going back to *Beowulf*, Spenser's *The Fairy Queen* (1590), and William Shakespeare's *A Midsummer Night's Dream* (1595/96), among others—it is 20th-century works like Baum's *The Wonderful Wizard of Oz*, J.M. Barrie's *Peter Pan* (1904 play; 1911 novel), C.S. Lewis's *Chronicles of Narnia* series (1950–56), and Tolkien's *The Lord of the Rings* which define the contemporary fantasy tradition and have exerted a tremendous influence on 20th and early 21st-century authors. King writes of this influence in his introduction to the revised and expanded edition of *The Gunslinger*, "On Being Nineteen (and a Few Other Things)," noting Tolkien as a touchstone and reflecting that "the *Dark Tower* books, like most long fantasy tales written by men and women of my generation (*The Chronicles of Thomas Covenant*, by Stephen Donaldson, and *The Sword of Shannara*, by Terry Brooks, are just two of many), were born out of Tolkien's" (ix). While noting the impact of Tolkien's influence, King also writes about wanting to create something new and different with the *Dark Tower* series, reflecting that in reading *Lord of the Rings* for the first time, he was drawn to "the sweep of Tolkien's imagination—to the ambition of his story—but I wanted to write my own kind of story, and had I started then, I would have written his" (King, "On Being Nineteen" x). In letting the soup simmer—to draw once more on Tolkien's metaphor—and adding his own ingredients of genre, narrative, and interconnection, King's *Dark Tower* series engages with the fantastical elements and rich traditions of Tolkien's epic quest while creating a story that is entirely King's own.

Similarly, while Mary Shelley's *Frankenstein* (1818) and the work of H.G. Wells and Jules Verne are notable examples of pre–20th science fiction and foundational to the genre, the technological preoccupation of the 20th century and beyond, from automation to weapons of war, demarcate the scope of contemporary science fiction and have influenced both the imaginations and real-world concerns of its authors and readers. The dystopian visions of Aldous Huxley's *Brave New World* (1932) and George Orwell's *1984* (1949) imagine dark futures of surveillance and control, while Orson Scott Card's *Ender* saga (1985—present) and Robert Heinlein's *Starship Troopers* (1959) envision interplanetary warfare. While clockwork beings can be traced back as far as the early 20th century, contemporary conceptions of robots are profoundly shaped by Isaac Asimov's *Robot Series* (1950–85) of short stories and novels, including his coining of the term "robotics" and his delineation of the Laws of Robotics defined in *I, Robot* ("Robot Science Fiction"). With increasing automation, the growing influence of artificial intelligence, and a range of other technological advances, the interconnection and engagement between science fiction and reality continues to be of central concern and consideration to the 21st-century audience, with responses running the gamut from enthusiasm to ambivalence and fear. As with the complex genre traditions and influences of fantasy, these various permutations and the complex negotiation of science fiction characteristics reverberate throughout King's *Dark Tower* series, in the imaginings of the readers' future worlds through the echoes of Mid-World's past.

Fantasy

While definitions of fantasy are complex and contested, the majority of definitions agree on the central position of a separate world from that of the reader's everyday reality. John Clute identifies the key defining feature of fantasy as "a self-coherent narrative. When set in this world, it tells a story which is impossible in the world as we perceive it ... [and] when set in an otherworld, that otherworld will be impossible, though stories set there may be possible in its terms" (338). Namera Tanjeem echoes this definition, identifying the key characteristic of fantasy as being "set in an alternative fictional world. It might have totally different rules from ours, yet it's nevertheless fully-functioning and consistent." Tolkien refers to this simply as a "Secondary World," distinguished from the Primary World by its "arresting strangeness" (48), which requires nonetheless believable creation in order to be effective. While there are a wide range of competing definitions, conceptions, and subsections of the fantasy genre, this basic understanding of key characteristics is well-suited for reading and engaging with fantasy genre elements in King's *Dark Tower* series.

Roland's Mid-World functions as a richly detailed and well-developed Secondary World. As Roland as his *ka-tet* travel through Mid-World, they make their way through a wide range of different geographies and civilizations. There are the homesteads and ranches of Mejis that Roland visits as a young man (as recounted in *Wizard and Glass*) and through which the *ka-tet* travels together in *Wolves of the Calla*. There are the castles of Roland's childhood, the destroyed and dystopic city of Lud, mining towns like those in the tale of "The Skin-Man" in *The Wind Through the Keyhole*, and mostly abandoned frontier towns like Tull where Roland faces a standoff in *The Gunslinger*. There's the Western Sea with its lobstrosities (*The Drawing of the Three*) and the vast forest beyond, where Roland and his friends encounter the bear Shardik (*The Waste Lands*). There is the uncanny constructed "reality" of Algul Siento, designed to keep the Crimson King's Breakers comfortable and complacent (*The Dark Tower*). There are the nightmares of End-World, Castle Discordia, and the larger domain of horror ruled over by the Crimson King. At the center of it all stands the Dark Tower itself, surrounded by its field of roses. All of the natural world which surrounds it points the way to the Tower: clouds follow along the path of the Beams and tree branches form patterns pointing toward it, much as a plant will turn toward the sun. Additionally, while this Secondary World is independent from the Keystone World, there are nevertheless connections between them, with the patterns of Mid-World repeating themselves in these other, interconnected worlds, including the various manifestations of the Dark Tower in different realities. These connections make the impossible possible, as their worlds temporarily overlap. One key example of this is Jake Chambers' crisis of perception in *The Waste Lands*: as a boy with a real life in New York City, it is impossible that he can remember dying in another world, that he can have simultaneous memories of both his New York boyhood and his Mid-World experiences, that like Schrödinger's cat, he is both alive and dead, depending on which of the worlds is real, a perception which is further complicated with his ultimate realization that both are true.

The impact of the diversity and range of this Secondary World is further emphasized by the characters' interactions with it. Roz Kaveney and David Langford note that walking is of central importance in characters' and readers' experience of fantasy's Secondary Worlds. In addition to the landscape reflecting individual internal conflict, as emphasized in many epic narratives and horror traditions, the interaction between the individual and the land is intimate and intertwined in the fantasy narrative, as "the walking pace of most fantasy journeys means that people move slowly through landscapes which often acquire moral meanings in the process; problems must be *solved* rather than merely moved away from at high speed" (Kaveney and Langford 768, emphasis original). Roland and his young friends had horses in Mejis and his mule drops dead early in *The Gunslinger*. But other than Susannah's wheelchair, their brief and terrifying ride on Blaine the monorail, and their temporary use of the loaned Calla *folken*'s horses as they move around Calla Bryn Sturgis in *Wolves of the Calla*, Roland and his *ka-tet* largely travel by foot and often find themselves sleeping outdoors, which foregrounds the significance of the setting, the individual environments, and their interactions with their surroundings and the people they encounter within them. As Roland nears the Dark Tower, he, Susannah, and Patrick Danville are offered the use of a truck, and while Roland is anxious to reach the Tower after his untold years of searching, the central role of walking sets their pace, with Roland reflecting that "I need a little more time to prepare my mind and my heart. Mayhap even my soul" (King, *The Dark Tower* 718), underscoring the interconnection of the journey and the self. This intimate connection with the land is an adjustment for Eddie, Susannah, and Jake, who are used to the urban environment and modern conveniences of New York City, though they quickly adapt, growing skilled at finding the best places to camp, protecting themselves from the threats of the wilderness, and determining what is safe to eat. In this way, Roland's companions become quickly acclimated to and interconnected with the land which surrounds them, however different it may be from their own original worlds, creating the sense of believability and immersion that Tolkien notes as so central to effective fantasy world creation. This close connection with the places through which they pass has a significant impact on characterization and their interactions with the people they encounter, from their confrontations with the citizens of Lud to the time they spend living side-by-side with the people of Calla Bryn Sturgis in *Wolves of the Calla*, becoming a temporary but integral part of that community. Given the nature of this Secondary World and the *ka-tet*'s own relationship to it as they travel, the setting shapes their every decision and profoundly impacts their daily reality. They aren't traveling above it or quickly passing through: this world embraces them, challenges them, and shapes them.

3. Fantasy and Science Fiction   49

Characters' and readers' experiences of this Secondary World are further heighted through the stories Roland shares with them, providing a rich history of Mid-World as it had once been, adding further verisimilitude and believability, details and complexity that once again elevate the various landscapes and places within All-World to much more than simply a background setting. Specific locations in Mid-World, End-World, and beyond are central to Roland and his friends' journey and their quest for the Dark Tower, but that journey is always contextualized as one moment within the sweeping scope of the history of All-World, including tales of its former glories, the passage of time, and the significance of these changes, both for the world as a whole and for Roland personally. For example, in *The Waste Lands* and *Wizard and Glass*, when Roland tells his companions of the palace riddling contests he recollects from his boyhood, his telling serves multiple purposes: he is sharing details of his own life in the time before they traveled together (a rarity) and he is telling them what Mid-World was like in that long-ago time. Roland recounts the details of the riddling contest: of riddles old and new tossed into the barrel, the contest's rules and procedures, the ceremony, its seriousness, and the stakes it carried (King, *The Waste Lands* 585; *Wizard and Glass* 8). In doing so, he not only gives them a glimpse into the life of a world that no longer properly exists, but also draws a connecting line from the traditions of that long ago time to their present predicament, with Blaine demanding a riddle contest to win safe passage, their lives won by victory and death in defeat, steeping their current peril in the larger context of a time-honored tradition. A similar moment that draws together past and present through these recollections and their lived experience is when Roland dances a traditional *commala* in Calla Bryn Sturgis, much to the delight of the Calla-*folken*, who enthusiastically engage in a ritualized call-and-response (King, *Wolves of the Calla* 229–34), an invocation of the old traditions that is integral in Roland's *ka-tet* being accepted in Calla Bryn Sturgis, as well as in Eddie, Susannah, and Jake's continuing education of Roland's world, its history, and its traditions.

Linguistics and language traditions are similarly central to fantasy and Secondary World building, and Greer Gilman argues that "any fiction—but above all a work of fantasy—is a world made of words" (134). This is a foundational truth, as Gilman goes on to note that "fairy tale and philology have been entwined since Jacob Grimm first studied both, the linguistic root-stock inextricable from Briar Rose's hedge" (134). As a philologist, Tolkien's linguistics of Middle Earth are central to *The Lord of the Rings*, defining, distinguishing, and connecting the different races of that world. Verlyn Flieger argues that Tolkien's "invented languages are a formative and important element in his fiction, contributing materially to both the fantasy and reality of his secondary world" (72). With his *Dark Tower* universe, King creates an original alphabet[1] and a unique lexicon, words that are distinctly Mid-Worldian and are essential in understanding the larger, interconnected King universes of which it is a part. One of the most significant terms that radiates throughout the *Dark Tower* series in a variety of forms and meanings is *ka*, which as Vincent explains, "has several meanings, mostly to do with destiny, purpose, or fate" (*The Dark Tower Companion* 469), the inevitable way of things. As Roland first explains it to Eddie in *The Drawing of the Three*, *ka* is "duty, or destiny, or in the vulgate, a place you must go" (King 205). To Roland's mind, the guiding force of *ka* is simple and needs no explanation or justification, as "what's past is past, and what's ahead is ahead. The second is *ka*, and takes care of itself" (King, *The Drawing of the Three* 206). When a character asks why something has happened or how things will turn out, the answer is often that it is *ka*'s will or that it will be as *ka* wills it. There are further shades of meaning and complexity added to *ka* as its understanding is passed down with some individual variation to each gunslinger from father to son and, as Roland tells Jake, "because each child's father was different, each of us emerged from our childhood with a slightly different idea of what ka is and what it does" (King, *Wolves of the Calla* 392). The notion of *ka-tet* is frequently invoked throughout the series as well and refers to a united group, with Roland explaining that "*Ka-tet* is the place where many lives are joined by fate" (King, *The Waste Lands* 90). The *ka-tet*'s collective and nearly telepathic power is *khef* and the *ka-tet*'s leader is their *dinh*. There are words to describe the dangers of a wide range of enemies, like *can-toi* (the Crimson's King's "low men") and *pookie* (a giant snake). There are words for old, dark traditions like *charyou tree*, which refers to a harvest Reaping Day human sacrifice upon the bonfire, though later the humans were replaced with representative straw men (or "stuffy guys"). The word *commala* is particularly complex, with dozens of uses and variations encompassing discourses of agriculture, community, and sex, with meanings both complementary and contradictory (King, *Wolves of the Calla* 486–7). Some of the words featured in Roland's world have different meanings in the larger King universe, both connecting and reinventing them, like *cujo*, which in the lexicon of Mejis means "sweet one" (King, *The Dark Tower* 468), in dramatic contrast to Cujo, the eponymous killer St. Bernard of King's 1981 novel of the same name, whose sweetness has been destroyed by rabies. Another, more nefarious example of this is the appearance of the Mid-World greeting "Long days and pleasant nights" appropriated by Harry Streeter in "Fair Extension" (in the 2010 *Full Dark, No Stars* collection), as Bill uses this phrase with his friend Tom Goodhugh shortly after making a deal with the devil that will destroy Tom's life, professing goodwill when his heart is filled with the exact opposite intent.

Statements that "the world has moved on" and "there are other worlds than these" are repeated throughout the series and integral in characters' understanding of the worlds around them and their interconnection with the larger *Dark Tower* universe, as well as its past, present, and future. Beyond singular words and brief phrases, there are also formal statements of great ritual and meaning, like the apology "I cry your pardon" and the penitent "I have forgotten the face of my father." The most significant of these is the foundational oath of all gunslingers, which Roland teaches his companions and which defines themselves, their nature, and their purpose:

> I do not aim with my hand; he who aims with his hand has forgotten the face of his father.
> I aim with my eye.
> I do not shoot with my hand; he who shoots with his hand has forgotten the face of his father.
> I shoot with my mind.
> I do not kill with my gun; he who kills with his gun has forgotten the face of his father.
> I kill with my heart [Vincent, *The Dark Tower Companion* 468].

Spoken in moments of both training and testing, this oath is a focusing of their will, an affirmation of their purpose, and a reflection of their identity, both individually and collectively. It also situates them within the larger context and aligns them with the rich tradition of the gunslingers who have come before and whose legacy they now continue. As with the descriptions of Roland's world and its land, history, and customs, this language is foundational in the construction of this Secondary World, immersing Roland's new friends and the reader within the fantastical world King has created, with realism, verisimilitude, and believability.

Another common fantasy genre element that is central to the *Dark Tower* series is the presence and use of magic. As Diana Wynne Jones explains, within the fantasy genre "there is a huge, tangled complex of ideas concerning magic and magical practices; many varieties of magic are depicted, several of which tend to occur together, and all of which tend to melt into one another.... The primary assumption is that magic is possible in the world of the fantasy, and the exact nature of this ambient magic strongly influences the narrative" (616). Jones also notes that there are two central concerns when it comes to the presence and use of magic within the fantasy narrative, which are the definition of the magic itself and how that magic is used by specific agents, whether for good or evil (*ibid.*). Magic is often depicted as being morally neutral: powerful, but neither inherently good or bad. It is the use of that magic and the ends to which individuals employ it that determines its impact on people and the world in which it is used, and in the universe of King's Dark Tower, "in the proper hand, any object can be magic" (King, *The Wind Through the Keyhole* 153), underscoring its accessibility and the central question of intent. Roland's father is betrayed by the palace wizard, Marten Broadcloak (one of Flagg's many personas throughout the *Dark Tower* series and King's larger body of work), who seduced Roland's mother, Gabrielle Deschain. This abuse of power by a royal sorcerer is echoed by the figure of Flagg in the *Dark Tower*-related novel *The Eyes of the Dragon* as well, where Flagg murders King Roland and frames the king's son Peter for the crime. However, not all wizards are evil and in the tale of Tim Stoutheart, related in The *Wind Through the Keyhole*, the adventuring Tim comes across a version of Merlin himself, Maerlyn of the Eld, who can transform himself into a tiger and who looks upon "Tim with kindness, but also with gravity" (King 249). Maerlyn is powerful and kind, helping Tim restore his mother's sight and the safety of his home, but he is also fallible and had been tricked into his enchanted form by the Crimson King.

Beyond good and bad users of magic, there are the magical items themselves, the most notable of which in the *Dark Tower* series are the Wizard's glass, which are orbs of great power that allow their users to see events that are occurring elsewhere and even their fellow humans' deepest secrets. In *Wizard and Glass*, Rhea of the Cöos sees the coming of Roland's *ka-tet* to Mejis in the depths of the Wizard's Glass and its through this same magic that Roland sees Susan being burned alive as part of the dark *charyou tree* ritual. Magic items abound in the fantasy genre, appearing in Tolkien's fiction as the Simarils, the Ring of Power, and the Arkenstone, for example. As Flieger argues, the central significance of a magical object in "shown far more through characters' responses to the *idea* of it than through its own powers or action" (109, emphasis original), an appeal which can quickly become all-consuming, giving way to "the danger of uncontrolled desire, covetousness grown to obsession" (Flieger 100). Rhea, Eldred Jonas, and Roland each fall victim to the thrall of the Wizard's Glass, driven by a need for possession and becoming lost in its depths. As Roland's father warns him before the *ka-tet* leaves for Mejis, in advising Roland to keep an eye out for the Wizard's Glass, the orbs of Maerlyn's Rainbow are "alive, and hungry.... One begins by using em; one ends being used *by* em" (King, *Wizard and*

Glass 457, emphasis original). This is exactly what happens to Rhea, who the ball both entrances and drains of life, and when Jonas and his men come to take the Wizard's Glass back from her, she is little more than a animated corpse, driven even further to madness and obsession than she had been before it was given to her keeping. Similarly, when Jonas takes the ball from Rhea, his only thought is one of covetous acquisition: "*Mine!* he thought, and that was all" (King, *Wizard and Glass* 566, emphasis original). Even Roland himself is drawn into the Wizard's Glass, nearly losing both his sanity and his life after seeing Susan burned alive, plunged into a state of catatonia as he and his fellow gunslingers make their way back to Gilead, beyond the reach of his friends and lost so far in the ball that "the thing which rode west with them toward Gilead was not Roland, or even a ghost of Roland.... Roland had gone" (King, *Wizard and Glass* 636). The Wizard's Glass wreaks one final act of destruction that changes the course of Roland's life and shapes the man he will become, when it triggers Roland's murder of his mother, demonstrating its lasting ability to influence those whom it has touched, even after the ball itself has left their hands.

Later in Roland's adventures with his *ka-tet*, they encounter another of these orbs, the even more powerful Black Thirteen. Callahan has secreted the glass under the floorboards of his church, hoping the Calla *folken*'s faith will keep it dormant and fearing its gaze and power. Black Thirteen does in fact seem to watch and may serve as the eye of the Crimson King himself, observing and influencing those near it. When Roland and Eddie go to remove it from Callahan's church, there is an ominous hum and the distinct sense that "somewhere close, a monster of nearly unimaginable malevolence had half-opened one sleeping eye" (King, *Wolves of the Calla* 507) before returning to rest once more. It is undeniably powerful, unlocking the door in Doorway Cave and allowing Roland and his companions to cross between worlds, but its influence in insidious and destructive. It lulls Eddie into a state of near-hypnosis as he stands watch in Doorway Cave, nearly resulting in Eddie's suicide (King, *Wolves of the Calla* 625–6) and when Jake and Callahan take Black Thirteen to New York to dispose of it, it awakens once more with its siren's song calling to Jake, Callahan, and a hotel maid, all of whom are desperate to see and possess it. Callahan is willing to throw over his hard-earned redemption for this momentary glimpse, taking the box in his hands and thinking, "Now he would open it. Now he would observe Black Thirteen in all its repellent glory.... And then die. Gratefully" (King, *Song of Susannah* 329), teetering on the edge of destruction before reawakening to himself, his faith, and his duty. Jake and Callahan stash Black Thirteen in the long-term lockers beneath one of the World

Trade Center Towers, where they are relatively assured in its safety, and when Jake wonders what would happen if the building collapsed on top of it, "Callahan laughed.... 'Never happen.... [Though] That'd be one way to take care of the nasty thing, I guess'" (King, *Song of Susannah* 338). Their choice of storage and Jake's brief uncertainty foreshadow the terrorist attack of September 11, 2001, and while King doesn't posit a direct cause and effect relationship, it is clearly established that the orbs of the Wizard's Glass are terrible and powerful, and wherever they are, tragedy and death soon find them.

King's *Dark Tower* series also falls within the specific pattern of the fantasy quest narrative, which focuses on "a series of adventures experienced by the hero and his or her companions that begins with the simplest confrontations and dangers and escalates through more threatening and perilous encounters" (Senior 190). This quest pattern takes the group on a detailed journey through the fantastical land, defines the group's moral and driving purpose, and concludes with a large-scale good vs. evil confrontation with "a Dark Lord, a satanic figure of colossal but warped power, who wishes to enslave and denature the world and its denizens" (*ibid.*). The ultimate goal of Roland and his *ka-tet*'s quest is clear: to save the Dark Tower, thus ensuring the continued existence of all the interconnected worlds and the universe of which it is the axis. To do so, they must not only find and reach the Dark Tower itself, but also battle the Crimson King and his emissaries along the way, who are working at cross-purposes to Roland's own, attempting to bring down the Tower, destroy the universe, and create chaos. Some of the Crimson King's followers are monstrous (like the *can-toi* and Mordred the were-spider), while others are human (like the Breakers), and they carry out their work for the Crimson King in multiple worlds, complicating Roland and his *ka-tet*'s quest as they must navigate between and gauge the impact of actions within these different realities on the interconnected worlds and on the Dark Tower itself. In these enormous consequences, the *Dark Tower* series also engages with the macrocosmic scope of the traditional quest narrative, in which the fate of the world depends on the success of the quest. In the case of King's *Dark Tower* series, Roland's quest takes on a variety of permutations and threatens the existence of all worlds.

At the start of his quest as a young gunslinger, Roland was accompanied by other gunslingers, his friends, who have all been lost, as "the others had died or given up, committed suicide or treachery or simply recanted the whole idea of the Tower" (King, *The Drawing of the Three* 43). When the series begins with *The Gunslinger*, Roland has been traveling alone for years, but he once more becomes part of a *ka-tet* when

3. Fantasy and Science Fiction 55

he draws Eddie, Susannah, and Jake into his world in *The Drawing of the Three* and *The Waste Lands*. Eddie, Susannah, and Jake then take up the experience of the quest narrative as well, beginning simply, as W.A. Senior notes (190), in their confrontations with themselves and their adjustment to the strange new world in which they find themselves. In this fundamental shift in their experiences, they must first determine who they will be, how they must change, and the acts of which they are capable. However, as they continue, the *ka-tet*'s focus becomes externalized as well, as they face greater challenges and more daunting adversaries, from speaking demons (which appear in *The Gunslinger, The Waste Lands*, and *Song of Susannah*) and the child-stealing Wolves of Thunderclap in *Wolves of the Calla*, to the varied, monstrous vampires Jake and Callahan encounter in *The Dark Tower*, and finally, the Crimson King himself, who is mad, undead, and locked within the upper levels of the Tower.

Quests almost invariably prove transformative, revealing strength and skill previously undetected by the individual, and this is certainly the case with Roland's companions. Eddie is a heroin addict when he is drawn from his version of New York and Jake is a capable, resilient, though sheltered boy. In their travels with Roland, they discover the best and strongest parts of themselves, the strength and ability they develop far surpassing what they would likely have achieved had their New York lives been uninterrupted. When Susannah is drawn to Roland's Mid-World, her psyche is divided between that of two women—Odetta Holmes and Detta Walker—each of whom is unaware of the other, and both of which are self-limiting and damaging in their own ways. When Susannah becomes aware of this schism, reconciles it, and chooses a new name and identity for herself, she is able to keep the strongest parts of each personality, jettison the self-destructive ones, and become her best possible self. Though he remains within his own world, Roland's metamorphosis is no less significant, as through the formation of and his quest alongside this *ka-tet*, he opens himself up once more to friendship, camaraderie, teamwork, trust, and love, a kind of sharing and interdependence that he had long ago eschewed with the loss of his friends and fellow gunslingers. This self-reflection and his new companions signal a foundational shift in Roland's approach to his quest, differentiating him from the man who slept easily after killing everyone in Tull and let the boy Jake fall to his death as the price that must be paid to catch the Man in Black in *The Gunslinger*. Roland's appreciation of the importance of these relationships, the love with which he comes to invest them, and the personal transformation they reflect may well prove integral in any successful conclusion of his quest and bringing his heretofore ceaseless repetition to a close.

Echoing the epic's *entrelacement*, Senior points out the "polysemous" nature of the quest narrative, "as individuals or small groups pursue minor quests within the overall framework" (190), which also typifies the *Dark Tower* series, particularly in later books, where the *ka-tet* must divide themselves between different paths and worlds to ensure the safety of the Dark Tower before being reunited to continue on together. Just as members are separated as they pursue these smaller journeys, they are sometimes lost altogether, and it often falls to the hero or central protagonist to face the final good vs. evil showdown alone. As Roland and his *ka-tet* near the Dark Tower, Eddie, Jake, and Oy are killed in different ways and in different worlds and following these devastating losses, Susannah chooses to leave Roland before they reach the Tower. Though she loves him, Susannah reflects that "Roland's way was death for those who rode or walked beside him.... It was all for the good ... she had no doubt of it, but Eddie still lay in his grave in one world and Jake in another" (King, *The Dark Tower* 748). After coming nearly to the quest's end with Roland, Susannah takes on a new adventure of her own, choosing to risk everything to travel between worlds in the hope of being reunited with those she loves, relegating the Dark Tower back to Roland's singular quest.

The series' conclusion complicates the pattern of the standard quest narrative and larger fantasy genre conventions, in which characters typically "lead the way through travails and reversals towards the completion of a happy ending" (Clute 339) and in the fantasy quest specifically, the end "reveals a recovery from the devastating losses that characterize this genre" (Senior 190). For Eddie, Susannah, and Jake, this positive resolution holds true: they are reunited in New York City in 1987, different people than they were before, and with these versions of Eddie and Jake having dreams but no memories of Susannah, Roland, or Mid-World, but drawn together once again, with a chance at happiness and a new life together (King, *The Dark Tower* 807–13). Roland's conclusion, on the other hand, is purgatorial and nearly unbearable. After completing his quest over decades, suffering innumerable hardships and losses, and finally facing and defeating the Crimson King to gain the Dark Tower, Roland finds himself turned back once more, sent back to his travels through the desert that comprise the opening pages of *The Gunslinger*. Looking with horror and realization, Roland wonders, "How many times had he climbed these stairs only to find himself peeled back, curved back, turned back? Not to the beginning (when things might have been changed and time's curse lifted), but to that moment in the Mohaine Desert when he had finally understood that his thoughtless, questionless quest would ultimately succeed? ... How many times *would* he travel it?" (King, *The Dark Tower* 827, emphasis original). Roland is an atypical fantasy hero, denied his resolution, but in this subversion, King employs other fantasy genre conventions, including the quest narrative's "cyclical history" (Senior 190), as well as themes of amnesia and forgetting (Kaveney and Langford 767). In gaining the Dark Tower and opening the door marked with his name, Roland temporarily remembers, is overcome by horror, and then begins his quest anew, doomed to forget once more. Like the versions of Eddie and Jake with whom Susannah is reunited, it seems likely than in time, Susannah will lose all memory of Mid-World as well. Resolution is subverted, lessons and losses must be tackled anew, and the potential for the story—and one day, perhaps a happier ending for Roland—goes on.

Science Fiction

The influence of the science fiction genre on the *Dark Tower* series is less profound that that of the fantasy tradition, though some central science fiction elements have a significant impact on Roland's world, such as the power and failure of technology, including robots. While definitions of science fiction, like those of fantasy, are complex and contested, Parrinder outlines the basic description that science fiction "is a distinct kind of popular literature telling stories that arise from actual or, more usually, hypothetical new discoveries in science and technology. The science and technology must be convincing enough to invite a certain sense of the reader's disbelief" (23), a characteristic which distinguishes contemporary science fiction from its speculative fantasy-based predecessors, like Verne and Wells.

Technology plays a central role in the *Dark Tower* series, though the boundaries between science fiction and fantasy remain permeable and there is frequent overlap. As Mia tells Susannah in *Song of Susannah*, "the magic went away," and in its absence, "they replaced the *magic* with *machines* ... and now the machines are failing" (King 110, emphasis original). Much of the technology that Roland and his *ka-tet* encounter is a holdover from the world that has moved on, which is now beginning to break down. They stumble across several examples of this technology and its deterioration in Lud. The Tick-Tock Man who terrorizes Jake is obsessed with clocks and watches, wearing a time piece around his neck that is unable to accurately keep time, and he claims Jake's similarly malfunctioning and battered watch as a prize (King, *The Waste Lands* 494, 498–500). As Roland, Jake, and Oy make their way through the city's underground to be reunited with Eddie and Susannah, they pass a wide range of technological artifacts, including television monitors, surveillance equipment, and computers "awakening from their long sleep" (King, *The Waste Lands* 534) with varying degrees of functionality and destruction, as the travelers navigate their way through a world defined by "machines and madness" (King, *The Waste Lands* 539). The failing of this technology also has an impact on the state and stability of the world as a whole, well beyond the lives of individuals or a single city. While in Lud, Roland's friends see similarities to the technologies of their own worlds. They are similarly disoriented when they travel to Keystone New York, which is familiar and yet futuristic, with inventions and technology undreamed of in their own versions of New York City. When Susannah travels to Keystone New York with Mia to give birth, for example, she is struck by the "alien" nature of the city (King, *Song of Susannah* 90), struggling to reconcile what she sees around her with her own memories, before dismissing it with her conclusion that *"never mind, it's the future.... It's science fiction, like the City of Lud. Best leave it at that"* (King, *Song of Susannah* 91, emphasis original). In the *Dark Tower* series' negotiation of time and place, both Lud and the New York City of 1999 are equally strange to Susannah, viewed and engaged with through a technologically-mediated, science fiction lens.

Along with the Guardians of the Beam, King's invocation of Richard Adams's *Shardik* (1974) bridges the gap between fantasy and science fiction. *Shardik* "is a heady piece of fantasy centred on the creation of an animal-based religion, in which a giant bear is the object of worship of a developing human society riven by territorial and ideological dispute" (Clark). As Adams describes Shardik, the bear is "a figure of terror ... standing on its hind legs more than twice as high as a man. Its shaggy feet carried great, curved claws as thick as a man's fingers ... the mouth gaped open, a steaming pit set with white stakes" (4–5). As with Adams's Shardik, the Guardian of the Beam in *The Waste Lands*, known here alternately as Shardik and Mir, makes his presence known to Roland and his *ka-tet* as he travels through the forest, pushing trees over in his wake. This bear is ancient and preternaturally intelligent. As King writes, "He was the largest creature in the forest which had once been known as the Great West Woods, and he was the oldest" (*The Waste Lands* 31). He was unwounded by the arrows of the people who once lived there and when attacked, was capable of calculated and cunning retribution. The Old People's struggle to understand and effectively respond to the Bear's rage echoes the Beklans of Adams's *Shardik*, who ascribe a wide range of intents and significance to Shardik, reading him as divine and interpreting his actions and whims as indicators of a great power's will. For the Beklans, Shardik becomes a *tabula rasa*, manipulated by men and used as both a justification and scapegoat for violence. The central role of this interpretation and projection is underscored by the fact that "Adams never reveals whether Shardik is anything other than an entirely mortal bear" (Clark), whether the Beklans' mystical belief is justified or simply an anthropomorphization that suits their own needs and acquisitive desires. This act of negotiation and meaning-making is central to the appearance of the Guardian of the Beam in *The Waste Lands* as well. Once magical in nature, the Beams and their Guardians are now mechanized and this version of Shardik is a combination of the biological and the mechanical, with both component parts beginning to break down, resulting in fear, pain, and madness.[2] Its physical point of weakness is a metal radar dish on top of its head and shooting this brings the Bear down, though when Roland, Eddie, and Susannah examine the body, they discover its hybrid nature, with wires, electronics, and subnuclear cells existing cohesively with the creature's blood, bone, and tissue (King, *The Waste Lands* 52–4).

As with Shardik, Blaine the monorail is another example of a dangerous technology which has begun to fail and descend into madness. Roland and his *ka-tet* encounter a wide range of the ghosts of technology past in their journey through the once-great city of Lud, including a massive computer with tremendous, destructive power. As the computer intelligence that animates Blaine the Mono begins to power up, "this insane and inhuman intelligence had awakened in the rooms of ruin and had begun once more, although as bodiless as any ghost, to stumble through the halls of the dead" (King, *The Waste Lands* 525). Technology in general and Blaine specifically are personified and granted awareness, desire, and agency. Just as Shardik has been driven mad by his failing technology and his ill body, Blaine has similarly gone insane, the only surviving monorail after his counterpart Patricia preceded him in madness and committed suicide, plunging headlong into destruction (King, *The Waste Lands* 575). On the way out of Lud, Blaine releases poisonous gas on the city's remaining inhabitants (King, *The Waste Lands* 564–5) and again, like Shardik, Blaine reveals the degrees to which expectation and interpretation have shaped him, telling Roland and his *ka-tet* that since the inhabitants of Lud believed he was a god, he catered to these expectations and "BECAME WHAT THEY WANTED—A GOD DISPENSING BOTH FAVOR AND PUNISHMENT ACCORDING TO WHIM ... OR RANDOM-ACCESS MEMORY, IF YOU PREFER" (King, *The Waste Lands* 575). Now, in the extremes of his madness, Blaine challenges Roland and his *ka-tet* to a riddling contest, with their lives as the prize. Blaine has the enormous power and recall of a supercomputer, coupled with the personality and sadistic drive of a psychopath, foregrounding the dangerous potential of the failure of technology.

Robots play integral roles throughout the *Dark Tower* series as well. These robots are referred to within King's series as "Asimov robots" (King, *The Dark Tower* 156), invoking the name of science fiction author Isaac Asimov, his *Robot* series of short stories and novels, and his foundational definition of the three laws of robotics. As Asimov writes, there are

> three rules that are built most deeply into a robot's positronic brain.... One, a robot may not injure a human being, or, through inaction, allow a human being to come to harm.... [Two,] a robot must obey the orders given it by human beings except where such orders would conflict with the First Law.... And three, a robot must protect its own existence as long as such protection does not conflict with the First or Second Laws [37].

Some of the robots in the *Dark Tower* series follow their original programming, catering to the needs of the humans they serve, like Dobbie, the "house elf" model robot, in a distinct reference to J.K. Rowling's *Harry Potter* series (1997–2007) and another nod that blurs the barriers between fantasy and science fiction (King, *The Dark Tower* 354).[3] Similarly, in *The Wind Through the Keyhole*, a robotic silver plate named Daria with the abilities of a sentient, talking compass guides Tim Stoutheart through many of the perils of the forest, going against its programmed directives in order to keep Tim safe, which ultimately results in its own demise. Tim thinks of Daria as a combination machine and fairy, "a good fairy to match the Covenant Man's bad one" that nearly led Tim to his death (King, *The Wind Through the Keyhole* 237). Robots with malicious intent play a particularly significant role in *Wolves of the Calla*, where Andy, the seemingly friendly neighborhood robot, is revealed to be a traitor. Similarly, though the "Wolves" who ritualistically come to take the children of Calla Bryn Sturgis are fantastical in appearance with a canine profile and concealing capes, they are actually robots, able to be swiftly dispatched like the Guardian Shardik with a shot or an Oriza plate to the metal radar dish atop their heads, concealed beneath their cloaks (King, *Wolves of the Calla* 665). Andy watches over the Calla from one of Mid-World's many dogans, where Roland and his *ka-tet* find that surveillance equipment has been deployed all throughout the Calla, similar to that which they saw in Lud, making it possible for Andy to monitor the Calla *folken*'s movements and coordinate with the Wolves who come to take the children.

Just as magic is shown to be morally neutral, capable of being put to use for both good and evil, the robots themselves are capable of varied moral alignment, whether due to their programming, a breakdown in this programming, or perhaps even some degree of free will. While Andy and the Wolves are clearly not in keeping with Asimov's three laws of robotics, Roland and his *ka-tet* encounter other robots that follow these rules more closely and prove helpful allies. One example of this is Stuttering Bill, a robot Roland and Susannah encounter in the home of the monstrous Dandelo and whose name echoes that of *IT*'s young Bill Denbrough. As Stuttering Bill tells them, "I've got a f-f-fried sir-hirkit somewhere inside. I could fix it, but he fuh-fuh-forbade me" (King, *The Dark Tower* 708), leaving Bill limited by and under the control of a cruel and destructive master. Despite these failures, Stuttering Bill is able to feel and express emotion, and once his master has been destroyed, Bill puts himself in the service of Roland, Susannah, and Dandelo's freed prisoner, Patrick Danville; he even provides them with a workaround for his code-protected actions, in giving him suggestions rather than commands, which Stuttering Bill has the free will and agency to fulfill. In direct contrast to Calla Bryn Sturgis's Andy, Bill serves as a reminder that in Roland's world the technological and the human are intertwined and subject to complex contestation and negotiation.

Another example of the blurring of boundaries between science fiction and magic is in the travel between multiple words. In some cases, this transportation is formalized and controllable, achieved through a series of technologically-developed, mechanical doorways, as in the tunnels Jake discovers after surviving the attack at the Dixie Pig in *The Dark Tower* and the nearly 600 doors that connect the Fedic Dogan to other worlds (Furth 306), though not all remain operational.[4] Travel between worlds can also be achieved fantastically, through magic doors: the doors through which Roland draws Eddie and Odetta/Detta and through which he encounters and influences Jack Mort in *The Drawing of the Three* appear magically at varying intervals along the shore of the Western Sea, as foretold by the Man in Black's tarot reading at the end of *The Gunslinger*. However, as Roland's *ka-tet* discovers when they bring Jake through into Mid-World in *The Waste Lands*, these doors can also be created, given the right place, enough daring, and keys that fit the locks. There are also "thinnies," thin spots between worlds where the barriers are weakened and permeable, though the *todash* space that lies between these worlds is fraught with danger and full of monsters. In going *todash*, Roland and his *ka-tet* can also move between worlds without doors, accompanied by a "terrible, gorgeous" sound that "although ... [it] was nothing like the sinister warble of the thinny, somehow it was" (King, *Wolves of the Calla* 48), an acoustic signal of passing between worlds and the void that lies between them, which is always fraught with peril and the possibility of being caught or lost in this liminal, dark, and deadly place.

As with King's incorporation and negotiation of other genre influences throughout the *Dark Tower* series, familiar fantasy and science fiction conventions are invoked and subverted, celebrated, critiqued, and combined. Genre patterns often give readers some indication of what to expect from the story before them: the standard fairy tale ends with a "happily ever after," for example, and a traditional fantasy quest is usually successful. However, as King's use of these conventions—both on their own and in combination with those of other genres—indicates, the genre formula is not to be trusted in the *Dark Tower* series and its twists and conclusions may confound all expectation. This is one of the distinct literary elements that sets King's *Dark Tower* apart from many other series: he draws from a wide-ranging and diverse combination of influences, savoring all the flavors of Tolkien's soup, and adding some new ones of his own, creating an epic narrative with echoes of its predecessors, but wholly unlike anything which has come before.

4

Western

King's *Dark Tower* series is deeply invested in the Western genre tradition from the opening line of *The Gunslinger* and its description of a lone hero making his way across a desolate landscape, as "the man in black fled across the desert, and the gunslinger followed" (3). In this pursuit and his larger dedication to his quest, Roland can be effectively read as a knight errant embodied in a Western-style gunslinger, in an epic tale played out across an otherworldly frontier. Many of the settings through which Roland and his *ka-tet* travel are distinctly Western in their imagery, from the dusty town of Tull to the rich agricultural community of Calla Bryn Sturgis. As Eddie remarks in *Wizard and Glass*, when Roland is preparing to tell them about his experiences as a young gunslinger in Mejis, "All Roland's stories are Westerns, when you get right down to it" (King 103), though Roland himself is unsure of this genre designation or its meaning. Drawing on tropes of black hats and white hats, the beauty and danger of the wilderness, the often insular nature of frontier communities, and the value of being the fastest draw with the sharpest aim, the *Dark Tower* series incorporates a wide range of Western genre conventions, though just as with the other genres King engages throughout the *Dark Tower* series, he fulfills some of these expectations while subverting others. The Western tradition and its stoic, gunslinging hero—who is just as often a flawed and morally complicated antihero—offers a paradigm that is ideally suited for understanding and critically analyzing Roland Deschain. Finally, in addition to the general characteristics and conventions of the Western genre that permeate the *Dark Tower* series, King also alludes to and negotiates the narrative formula of specific Western films, including *The Good, The Bad, and the Ugly* and *The Magnificent Seven*.

The Western genre has attained iconic status within popular culture, with its key characteristics almost instantly recognizable. Lee Clark Mitchell writes that "the image remains unaltered in countless versions from the genre's beginning—a lone man packing a gun, astride a horse, hat pulled close to the eyes, emerging as if by magic out of a landscape from which he seems ineluctably a part" (3). Where the hero is going, where he has been, and who he may be vary from one book or film to next, but these elements are the standard-bearers, almost always present regardless of their variations. In *Six Guns and Society: A Structural Study of the Western*, Will Wright outlines the distinct steps of the classical Western plot in which a hero comes to town, arriving as a stranger and possessing some sort of special ability, and while that hero "is given a special status ... [the townspeople] do not completely accept the hero" (48). Conflict arises, in which the group is outmatched by the villains, the hero stands against those villains and is instrumental in their defeat, and order is restored. In the end, the hero sacrifices this special status, usually leaving the community he has saved (Wright 48–9). The details of the setting may vary and there are different types of villains (Native Americans or bandits are common enemies in many traditional Westerns, reflecting anxieties, exclusions, and violence in response to racial difference and Otherness within their larger context), but the narrative structure generally follows Wright's basic pattern.

Given the epic scope of the *Dark Tower*, this Western narrative pattern is repeated multiple times over the course of the series, at times adhering quite closely to this established form and other times significantly revising or challenging it. For example, *The Gunslinger* recounts Roland's visit to the small town of Tull, a stopover in his pursuit of the Man in Black. The town itself resembles those of countless other Westerns, with a dusty main street, a saloon, and an assorted cast of townspeople, including the piano player Sheb and the barkeeper Allie, with whom Roland finds company. However, thanks to Sylvia Pittston rallying the townspeople into a mob against Roland, he finds himself not protecting them from an outside threat but instead, protecting himself from them. The people of Tull ambush Roland and "they ran at him in a reaching, vicious clot. He fired his guns empty again, lying in his own spent shells.... He missed with one shot, downed eleven with the rest" (King, *The Gunslinger* 85). When he leaves to renew his pursuit of the Man in Black, Tull is literally a ghost town, every one of its inhabitants now dead and no one saved but Roland himself as he continues his quest. There are other repetitions of this classic narrative pattern throughout the series that adhere more closely to the traditional formula. For example, when Roland and his *ka-tet* stand against the Wolves and protect the people of Calla Bryn Sturgis in *Wolves of the Calla*, the story follows the expected pattern, with additional emphasis on the community's welcoming of the gunslingers who will fight alongside them to protect their town. Similarly, in *The Dark Tower*, when the gunslingers work with Ted Brautigan and the other rogue Beam-Breakers to take down Algul Siento, they fight against nearly impossible odds and prevail, though Eddie is killed in the process. In both Calla Bryn Sturgis and Algul Siento, the gunslingers come as strangers, are briefly welcomed as allies, help fight and win, and then move on as continually wandering heroes, drawn forward by Roland's quest for the Dark Tower.

Similar to the narrative pattern Wright describes, setting is another key component of the Western, with hallmark features that characterize the wide range of novels, films, and other popular culture forms that comprise the genre. Featuring small towns, vast plains, and scorching deserts, the Western setting serves as both a backdrop to the action and an avenue of thematic consideration. Whatever the specific topography might look like, the setting acts as "a means of isolating and intensifying the drama of the frontier encounter between social order and lawlessness" (Cawelti 23). It is a land of freedom, independence, and self-sufficiency, which makes the coming of the villains and the community's inability to stand against them even more significant. In this representational function, the land almost becomes a character in its own right, epitomized by "its openness, its aridity and general inhospitality to human life, its great extremes of light and climate, and paradoxically, its grandeur and its beauty" (*ibid.*). Roland and his *ka-tet* travel extensively through Mid-World, End-World, and beyond, and rather than remaining grounded in a fixed setting that witnesses the coming and going of the Western hero in a single, epic showdown, the *Dark Tower* series follows those heroes themselves, presenting a wide variety of temporary and ever-changing settings, with Western genre traditions adding yet another layer to the role and significance of these settings. There are the farming communities of Mejis (*Wizard and Glass*) and Calla Bryn Sturgis (*Wolves of the Calla*), where livestock and agriculture are central concerns. There are small frontier towns like Tull (*The Gunslinger*) and more rural communities like River Crossing (*The Waste Lands*). There are wide plains, deep forests, and the dangerous shore of the Western sea. There is the "white and blinding and waterless" Mohaine Desert that opens *The Gunslinger* (King 3) and the field of roses which surrounds the Dark Tower itself at the series' conclusion. Each of these settings presents its own unique challenges, whether posed by the land itself or its inhabitants. The only constant, uniting factors between these diverse backdrops are the gunslingers' continued peripheral presence in the lives of the communities (sometimes as allies and even friends, but never members) and the constant need for Roland and his *ka-tet* to be always moving on. When Eddie and Jake regret leaving River Crossing behind them, Roland explains the imperative of their constant travel, telling them that "the answers are still ahead. While we were helping the twenty or thirty people left in River Crossing, twenty or thirty thousand more might be suffering or dying somewhere else" (King, *The Waste Lands* 356). Similarly, when Roland and his *ka-tet* are in Calla Bryn Sturgis, Jake has the rare opportunity to make friends with a boy his own age, Bennie Slightman, and to delight temporarily in the simple pleasures of childhood. However, as much joy as this friendship brings Jake, he comes to the realization that his identity as a gunslinger is greater still: he sees the human failing and hypocrisy in the community around them and when the time comes to fight, he acts as a true gunslinger, as he "fired the Ruger in nine steady, spaced shots ... and each time he fired, one of the Wolves either slipped backward out of its saddle or went sliding over the side to be trampled by the horses coming behind" (King, *Wolves of the Calla* 685). For better or worse, Jake is a gunslinger like Roland, rather than a boy like Bennie. The different settings and communities through which Roland and his *ka-tet* move differ as they travel and many of them invoke and engage with the themes and questions raised by traditional Western settings, but they are all temporary, a brief stop within the much larger context of the journey that leads them to the Dark Tower.

The *Dark Tower* series also subverts the ideology of the Western setting in a couple of significant ways. First of all, the Western traditionally represents its setting as a land of opportunity. As Mitchell explains, "one aspect of the landscape celebrated consistently in the Western is the opportunity for renewal, for self-transformation, for release from constraints associated with the urbanized East. Whatever else the West may be, in whatever form it is represented, it always signals freedom to achieve some truer state of humanity" (5). However, in Roland's world, being "sent west" is not an affirming opportunity, but rather a punishment and a deep shame. When a young gunslinger endures his test of manhood, he leaves the courtyard by either the east or the west gate. As King writes in *The Gunslinger*, as Roland prepares for his own early test,

> many boys had left the corridor from the east end, where the teacher always entered, as men. The east end faced the Great Hall and all the civilization and intrigue of the lighted world. Many more had slunk away, beaten and bloody, from the west end, where the boys always entered, as boys forever. The west end faced the farms and the hut-dwellers beyond the farms; beyond that, the tangled barbarian forests, beyond that, Garlan, and beyond Garlan, the Mohaine Desert [230].[1]

In both the traditional Western and the geographic significance of Roland's world, the west symbolizes the wilderness. However, while the traditional hero may go west to prove himself, a young gunslinger is sent west because he has failed to do so.² The other significant departure from the traditional Western setting in the *Dark Tower* series is epitomized in the desolate and dangerous city of Lud in *The Waste Lands*. In both the traditional Western and in *The Waste Lands*, the city is something to be avoided and escaped, left behind for the greater beauty and freedom of the frontier. However, the Eastern cities that serve as the diametric opposite of the Western wilderness in traditional narratives are nothing like Lud, which is a fully technological, contemporary urban city, with skyscrapers, subway tunnels, and a range of destructive weapons. Lud serves as a dramatic contrast to the frontier wilderness and towns through which Roland and his *ka-tet* travel, further emphasizing the dichotomy between the untamed frontier and so-called "civilization," which in Lud has proven wholly and disastrously destructive, in direct refutation of the erstwhile New Yorkers' hopes that the city may be a source of guidance and resources as they continue their journey. In addition to highlighting this contrast, the presence of Lud also signals the genre hybridity of the *Dark Tower* series: while it bears many of the hallmarks of the Western genre tradition, it is by no means bound to them, and Lud presents an apocalyptic future landscape, merging the Western formula with that of science fiction and dystopia.

One of the most significant elements of the Western tradition engaged in the *Dark Tower* series lies in the ways in which Roland fulfills and challenges the characteristics of the Western genre hero. There are a number of characteristics that have been canonically established and are common to the Western hero, including his clothing, his abilities, and his position as a "lone hero" (Biderman 13) with few friends or companions, who rides off alone in search of his next adventure. While the identification of good guys and bad guys by their white and black hats is overly simplistic and belies the complexity of characterization in the Western, the hero's clothes do "[take] on heroic significance" (Day 21), visually distinguishing him from the townspeople, villains, and other travelers he encounters, and marking him as an outsider. While townspeople tend to be dressed in rather plain, functional clothing, the hero's clothes are "paradoxically ... both more utilitarian and more artificial than those of the townspeople" (Cawelti 28). The hero's practical accoutrements, like his boots and hat, are demanded by the harsh nature of the wilderness through which he passes; however, there are also often more decorative touches to his dress, reflecting "a love of elegance for its own sake" (*ibid.*), indicating an appreciation for the well-made and refined. This can be seen in small details like the "fringes, tassles and scrollwork" (*ibid.*) that often adorn the hero's clothing or in the craftsman-like design of personal elements like the hero's hat or gun-belts. While other characters may well have hats and gun-belts of their own, none are likely to be as finely-created or well-cared for as the hero's, and the quality and remarkable nature of these elements reflect his commitment to excellence, in caring for his hat and cleaning his guns just as much as in his dedication to the quest before him. When King first introduces Roland in *The Gunslinger*, he is immediately identifiable as a Western hero by his clothing, including faded blue jeans, a worn shirt, and the gun-belts he wears. The holsters of his gun-belts are tied to his thighs and the guns themselves are meticulously cared for, "the holsters oiled too deeply for even this Philistine sun to crack" (King, *The Gunslinger* 4). As Roland draws his *ka-tet* to him, clothing becomes integral in them making this transition and claiming their identities and abilities as gunslingers. When Eddie and Susannah begin their journey with Roland, one of the first things they must learn is how to survive in the wilderness, including how to hunt and effectively utilize every part of the animals they kill, including skinning and tanning the hides to make blankets and clothes for themselves, such as deerskin shirts and moccasins (King, *Wolves of the Calla* 49). While they have already traveled far—literally from one world to another—this self-sufficiency and their newfound ability to provide for themselves, making the very clothes on their backs, empowers them and invests them in the lives they have begun in this new world. This skill is even more essential when Roland and Susannah find themselves in frigid lands beyond Castle Discordia, as they spend days hunting, skinning, tanning, making bone needles, and sewing the warm clothes they need to survive, including coats and mittens (King, *The Dark Tower* 635–44). When Roland and his *ka-tet* encounter others, they are recognized as gunslingers, not just by the guns they carry but by their appearance and their air of deadly ability and self-possession.

The skill he demonstrates is another hallmark of the Western genre hero: he is able to do things that no one else can do, whether that is in the speed of his draw, the accuracy of his shooting, or his ability to prevail when the odds are stacked against him. As Wright notes, "the society recognizes the hero as a special and different kind of person" (42), which both proves his worth and establishes him as a perennial outsider. His shooting skills, for example, are recognized as useful in standing against enemies, but he is also deadly and dangerous, a potential ally, but not a friend. While the Western hero is capable of killing very effectively, he is not a bloodthirsty barbarian and the genre's "gunfighter is bound to a moral code that does not allow him to indiscriminately shoot bystanders, even forcing him to fight 'fairly' against his enemies" (Kozackzka 95). Cawelti notes that "the most important implication of this killing procedure seems to be the qualities of reluctance, control and elegance that it associates with the hero.... Killing is an act forced upon him and he carries it out with the precision and skill of a surgeon and the careful proportions of an artist" (40). The Western hero does not take pleasure in killing but is able to do it very well and doesn't hesitate when the situation demands it. The hero's approach to killing reflects both who he is and who he is not, contrasted with the underhandedness or sadism often evidenced by his opponents, as the hero's "controlled and aesthetic mode of killing is particularly important as the supreme mark of differentiation between hero and savage" (*ibid.*). In the *Dark Tower* series, Roland's skill is exceptional, as demonstrated in his killing of every citizen in Tull when they form an angry mob to attack him (King, *The Gunslinger* 86), though he only kills when necessary, for his own survival or the safety of those he protects. He does not kill indiscriminately, as evidenced when he neutralizes rather than kills the men who stand in his way when he takes over the body of Jack Mort toward the conclusion of *The Drawing of the Three* (King 409–10, 426, 434–6).

Roland's ability to shoot is foundational to his very identity. When he loses two fingers to the lobstrosities in *The Drawing of the Three* and when he begins to feel the first stiffening of arthritis in *Wolves of the Calla*,[3] these are not only physical losses, but threats to his very sense of who he is a person. His entire long and wandering life, punctuated by loss and horror, has been built around his ability to shoot, his identity as a gunslinger, and the quest upon which it has set him. If he is no longer able to shoot—or even simply no longer able to shoot as quickly or as well—Roland is uncertain of just who he is and the meaning of his life. It is, in part, through these losses that the abilities he has passed on to his *ka-tet* come into starker relief, highlighting Roland's mentorship and their essential nature in functioning as a team. Roland trains Eddie and Susannah by having them shoot at small chips of stone, honing their attention and aim to a fine point, while also instilling in them a drive that will accept nothing less than perfection (King, *The Waste Lands* 21–7). Through the rigor of this training, Eddie, Susannah, and Jake become gunslingers that Roland can rely on and be proud to fight beside, even if they may never match his own prodigious skill. In fight after fight, they demonstrate their ability and prove themselves, against the Wolves in Calla Bryn Sturgis, the Crimson King's creatures in The Dixie Pig and Algul Siento, and Enrico Balazar's henchmen in King's Keystone Maine, among others, fighting evil on small and large scales to aid Roland in his quest and prevent the fall of the Dark Tower.

The Western hero's ability speaks for itself, which is why he is often a man of few words. This silence further underscores his isolation from the larger community and his position as an outsider, bound not by the collective but by following his own moral compass and beliefs. As Shai Biderman explains, the Western hero "doesn't speak much, and he hardly ever asks for advice or shares his thoughts (and hence his contemplation) with others.... He doesn't seek information from others, and he doesn't share information with anyone, either. We rarely know his thoughts, his feelings, or even his name" (21). Roland's taciturn nature is established in his very first conversation in the series, when Roland meets the man Brown in the desert. Brown recognizes Roland as a gunslinger:

> "Thought your kind was gone."
> "Then you see different, don't you?"
> "Did'ee come from In-World?"
> "Long ago," the gunslinger agreed.
> "Anything left there?"
> To this the gunslinger made no reply, but his face suggested this was a topic better not pursued [King, *The Gunslinger* 13].

Roland remains a man of few words when the talk turns to the Man in Black, who had also stopped at Brown's, responding to Brown's prediction "You'll never catch him" with a simple "I'll catch him" (King, *The Gunslinger* 14), with no elaboration, explanation, or debate. The exception to this rule in King's *Dark Tower* series is Roland's occasional storytelling, such as his sharing of tales of his young manhood with his *ka-tet* in *Wizard and Glass* and *The Wind Through the Keyhole*, opening up to them and perhaps even employing this storytelling as a means of self-reflection, an indication of the ways in which Roland may be challenging and moving beyond the archetypal characteristics of the isolated Western genre hero as he repeats his quest again and again, embodying its conventions even as he critiques their tenability.

Similarly, while the Western hero may agree to use his skills to help protect a community, that doesn't mean his solution is open for discussion. He is unlikely to explain or justify his course of action, and those actions are usually unilateral and decisive. *The Dark Tower*'s Roland initially fits this model and when Eddie and Susannah first join Roland, his taciturn nature infuriates them. Where they seek answers and explanations, he offers only instruction and command. There is little room for small talk when it comes to survival. However, just as Roland must adjust to once more having companions after countless years alone, he has to learn to communicate with them, explain his motivations, take them into his confidence, and work alongside them as part of a cohesive team. While Roland will never be described as loquacious, this increased communication echoes his training of the other members of his *ka-tet*: they need one another, often relying on each other for survival, and at times, talk is central to ensuring that safety and solidarity. Cawelti notes of the Western hero that "like his gun, language is a weapon the hero rarely uses, and when he does, it is with precise and powerful effectiveness" (41–2). When the hero speaks, people listen. For example, in *Wolves of the Calla*, when Roland stands before the people of Calla Bryn Sturgis to speak, they all fall silent as he asks them questions of great import and which put into motion the age-old covenant between gunslingers and the communities who call upon them, including "Do you see us for what we are, and accept what we do?" (King 230). Prior to Roland's posing of this question, the ranchers of Calla Bryn Sturgis had talked at length, questioning and debating the wisest course of action, while Roland listened and remained silent, the Calla *folken* exchanging many words that came to no real resolution. However, now when Roland speaks, it is his few words that carry the true power. Similarly, words carry tremendous weight at the end of Roland's quest, as he stands before the Dark Tower and shouts the names of those he has lost along his journey, and "those names carried clear in that strange air, as if they would echo forever" (King, *The Dark Tower* 801). With this declaration, Roland remembers and honors those he has loved and lost, and through his words he brings them with him to this final moment, including his claiming of Jake as his son (King, *The Dark Tower* 802). Though one final traveler, mute Patrick Danville, hears Roland's words, they are not spoken for Patrick, but for Roland and for the Dark Tower itself, which opens its door to him after Roland's calling of these names. Though they be few, Roland's words teach and share, forge alliances and friendships, and even speak directly to the fate of the multiple, interconnected worlds that revolve around the axis of the Dark Tower.

In the series' final moments, as Roland stands before and then enters the Dark Tower, he epitomizes the traditional Western's "lone hero" (Biderman 13). As Biderman explains, "Whether it's in the final scene, where he takes that inevitable 'lone ride' off into the sunset or in his heroic acts throughout the film, where he saves the town folk from danger, the lone hero keeps to himself" (13). This alone-ness serves as a defining feature of the protagonist: while the traditional Western hero may form alliances and work together with others to achieve a particular goal, his natural condition is to be alone. This isolated position also serves as a narrative characteristic, highlighting the hero's emergence from and then return to this state, as "First, the hero rides alone. Second, the hero faces his enemy in the final duel alone. And in between these two narrative scenes, he is usually on his own" (Biderman 18). As with many of the other characteristics of the Western genre tradition, the *Dark Tower*'s Roland both fulfills and subverts these expectations. As Biderman's pattern describes, Roland both begins and ends the series alone: he walks alone across the Mohaine Desert in pursuit of the Man in Black in *The Gunslinger*'s opening pages and when he finally enters the Dark Tower at the series' end, he does so alone. Roland's solitary quest is repeated and endless, as the Tower returns him once more to the Mohaine Desert and the journey which lies before him. However, while the beginning and end of Roland's quest—and the potentially infinite repetition of these beginnings and endings—find the gunslinger alone, Roland's companions along the quest itself shape both the narrative and his identity. In *Wizard and Glass*, as Roland recounts his experiences as a young gunslinger in Mejis, he travels with and relies on his childhood friends Alain Johns and Cuthbert Allgood, and falls in love with Susan Delgado, who is sacrificed, burned alive as part of the dark *charyou tree* ritual (King, *Wizard and Glass* 633–4). Similarly, he loses his fellow gunslingers at the Battle of Jericho Hill, where he is the sole survivor, left to continue on alone. Roland carries both grief and guilt for these losses: Susan died because she loved him and his friends died because they fought beside him. Following these devastating losses, Roland travels alone for untold years, the epitome of the Western genre's lone hero.

This changes with the drawing together of his *ka-tet*: Eddie, Susannah, Jake, and the billy-bumbler Oy. These relationships are punctuated by their own sense of loss, grief, and guilt, particularly in Roland's relationship with Jake, as Roland lets Jake fall to his death in *The Gunslinger* rather than give up his pursuit of the Man in Black (King 266), only to be reunited with Jake in *The Waste Lands*, to forge a powerful relationship and ultimately claim Jake as his "own true son" (King, *The Dark Tower* 802). In addition to disrupting the narrative expectations of the solitary hero, Roland's *ka-tet* also challenges some of the traditional Western conventions, particularly in the genre's dichotomous representation of women, where the virtuous woman is positioned in direct contrast to her darker, more passionate counterpart (Cawelti 30–1). In this paradigm, while the good woman is reliable and often heroic in her own right, Cawelti argues that "the dark girl is a feminine embodiment of the hero's savage, spontaneous side. She understands his deep passions, his savage code of honor and his need to use personal violence" (31). There are several examples of these contrasting representations throughout the *Dark Tower* series, such as the goodness of Susan Delgado contrasted with the treachery of Rhea of the Cöos and Susan's Aunt Cordelia in *Wizard and Glass*. However, in the later forming of Roland's *ka-tet*, Susannah Dean first challenges and then dismantles this dichotomy, combining the well-behaved gentility of Odetta Holmes with the savagery of Detta Walker in *The Drawing of the Three* to create a multi-faceted, complex female character that challenges the traditional Western genre convention's either/or representation of women. In addition, rather than these relationships being fleeting and momentary—an allegiance formed for a specific purpose and disbanded when that purpose has been served—Roland's *ka-tet* is transformative, as he takes on the positions of a mentor, a friend, and a father, roles that continue to shape him even after he has lost those he loves.

In the formation of this *ka-tet*, Roland has to unlearn the practices of his solitary existence: his companions demand to be taken into his confidence, requiring explanations and discussions, hearing stories of Mid-World and telling tales of their own worlds as well. In some ways, adjusting to traveling once more with companions is a sacrifice, as Roland has to alter his behavior, unable to exclusively follow his own whim, move on when he feels like it, or keep his own counsel. However, this *ka-tet* is also a blessing, both in terms of Roland's quest for the Dark Tower and in his own personal growth and healing. He comes to rely upon and love his companions, emerging from himself and his haunted past as a stronger and more complex hero as a result of these relationships. Through their combination, each member of the *ka-tet* is more powerful than any of them could be on their own, Roland included. They are brought together in an integral and intimate way, able to communicate with one another without speaking aloud and even occupying one another's lives through dreams, which Roland refers to as "sharing *khef*" (King, *The Waste Lands* 368, emphasis original). Each member of the *ka-tet* often sees or senses things the others do not and when they succeed, it is because they succeed together rather than through individual action or heroism. This *ka-tet* is central to the series as a whole and their collective power is essential, particularly from *The Drawing of the Three* onward. However, just as Roland lost Susan in Mejis and his friends in the Battle of Jericho Hill, he loses his *ka-tet* along the journey, with Eddie killed in Algul Siento, Jake dying to protect Keystone World Stephen King, and Oy killed fighting Mordred. Susannah leaves Roland as he nears the Dark Tower, choosing instead to seek a world in which she can be reunited with Eddie and Jake. While these losses are hard, within the larger pattern of the Western genre tradition, they are expected and Roland himself is well aware that "in the end I'll have to go on alone" (King, *The Dark Tower* 780). Even though he ends his quest alone, Roland carries his companions with him and as he approaches the Dark Tower, he calls out their names, including those of his father and mother, his fellow gunslingers, friends met along the way, and Roland's final *ka-tet* (King, *The Dark Tower* 801–2).

King's key deviations from the Western genre tradition frequently signal the series' genre hybridity, drawing Western characteristics together with the elements and conventions of other genres. Kirsten Day argues that the Western bears a striking similarity to the epic tradition, as "each genre is anchored in a mythic-historical period from its society's past and each presents narratives that help to delineate foundational ideologies with a particular focus on notions of heroism and masculinity" (12), impacting the narrative, characterization, and purpose of each genre's stories. The fact that "Roland's quest has macrocosmic proportions of myth" (Strengell 129) similarly connects the *Dark Tower* series to the larger epic tradition. Another significant deviation from the Western tradition is that while Roland and his *ka-tet* occasionally ride, they travel much more often on foot, challenging Cawelti's definition that "the hero is a man with a horse and the horse is his direct tie to the freedom of the wilderness, for it embodies his ability to move freely across it and to dominate and control its spirit" (38). Roland's mule dies early in *The Gunslinger* and while horses figure significantly in *Wizard and Glass*, this is in Roland's recollection of his past. With the exception of the horses they ride in Calla Bryn Sturgis, Roland and his *ka-tet* spend the majority of their quest for the Dark Tower walking—or in Susannah's case, at times being pushed in her wheelchair, towed, or carried—and in doing so, the narrative shifts from the Western tradition to that of the fantasy, where moving on foot through the landscape is integral to the genre's conventions and expectations, situating the protagonists intimately and inescapably within the fantastical lands through which they pass. Science fiction elements like robots, computers, and contemporary technology lend the Western tradition a steampunk cast in the *Dark Tower* series, as the anachronistic combination of the Western genre with science fiction elements highlights "progress, in the form of extraordinary transportation, weaponry, and invention, [which] simultaneously—and visibly—positions humanity on the brink of triumph or disaster" (Miller and Van Riper 245). In Mid-World, the technology is a remnant of the world from before it moved on, highlighting both its development and failure, and further complicating the timeline and history of Roland's world in comparison with those of the Keystone World and the levels of the Tower from which Roland draws his *ka-tet*. The employment of science fiction devices in the *Dark Tower* series also foregrounds "the machines' status as quasi-magical objects" (Miller and Van Riper 247), echoed in the blurring of lines between magic and technology throughout the series.

Finally, in keeping with King's established reputation as a horror writer, the *Dark Tower* series is a decidedly "Gothic Western" (Egan,

"*The Dark Tower*" 95), a genre hybridity which is foundational to the narrative itself, as James Egan argues that "King uses the Western and the Gothic tale to establish a framework for Roland's quest, and the two genres constantly interact and reinforce one another" ("*The Dark Tower*" 101). This combination shapes the thematic exploration of the series, as "the frontier of the conventional Western moves closer to the psychological shadowland of the Gothic tradition," and as a result, "the closure and resolution so characteristic of formulaic Westerns opens out into the ambivalence of Gothicism" (Egan, "*The Dark Tower*" 101). Egan's interpretation is particularly significant in reading the series' conclusion: the Western tradition has prepared readers for a definitive resolution, a ride off into the sunset with narrative loose ends neatly tied. However, while the *Dark Tower* series is unquestionably a Western, it is also a Gothic tale, which offers no such promises, embracing the lack of a clear resolution and taking readers further into Roland's internal landscape through the series' narrative pattern of repetition and return.

The Good, the Bad, and the Ugly *and* The Magnificent Seven

Western genre characteristics are clearly identifiable within King's *Dark Tower* series, with the Western tradition offering hallmark elements, character types, and narrative patterns. While Egan is correct in his assessment that "the formula Western [is] so pervasive that tracing King's specific sources becomes virtually impossible" ("*The Dark Tower*" 95), a few influences are particularly significant and identifiable. Roland himself shares several characteristics with Clint Eastwood's iconic Western heroes across a wide range of films, a parallel many of the series' artists have capitalized on in illustrated editions of the *Dark Tower* novels. In *The Waste Lands*, when Jake finds his memories split between two realities, New York Jake sees a movie poster for *The Good, the Bad, and the Ugly* outside a theater and his memory taps into that of Mid-World Jake; looking at Clint Eastwood's image, he thinks, "*It's not him ... but it's* almost *him. It's the eyes, mostly. The eyes are almost the same*" (King 258, emphasis original). Roland's remark about the Man in Black that "I hope he smiled when he said that" (King, *The Gunslinger* 74) directly echoes the iconic line in Owen Wister's 1902 novel *The Virginian* "when you call me that, *smile*" (24, emphasis original), which has been revised and repurposed in a wide range of Westerns and popular culture more generally throughout the 20th century. Turning to specific narrative structures and themes, two films that are overtly referenced and engaged in the *Dark Tower* series are Sergio Leone's *The Good, the Bad, and the Ugly* and John Sturges' *The Magnificent Seven*, as well as *The Magnificent Seven*'s inspiration, Akira Kurosawa's *Seven Samurai*.

In his introduction to the revised and expanded edition of *The Gunslinger*, King writes about the influence of *The Good, the Bad, and the Ugly* on his *Dark Tower* series. Reflecting on watching Leone's film on the big screen, King recalls that "before the film was even half over, I realized that what I wanted to write was a novel that contained Tolkien's sense of quest and magic but set against Leone's almost absurdly majestic backdrop" (King, "On Being Nineteen" xiv). The settings through which Eastwood and company ride are echoed in King's *Dark Tower* books, from the small frontier town of Tull to the endless vistas of plain and prairie. Roland's exhaustion in the Mohaine Desert of *The Gunslinger* recalls Blondie's (Clint Eastwood) suffering as he is being driven across the desert by Tuco (Eli Wallach), and his attendant dehydration and delirium. Blondie's recovery in the mission has echoes in the holy order in *The Wind Through the Keyhole* and Roland's convalescence in "Little Sisters of Eluria," though Blondie's is decidedly less monstrous. Blondie's taciturn nature, legendary shooting abilities, and single-minded commitment to his search for the buried gold is similar to King's characterization of Roland, drawing on Eastwood's embodiment of the quintessential Western hero, and Jason Sanders's identification of Blondie as "barely" good gestures toward the antiheroic elements of both Blondie and Roland. The *Dark Tower* series and Leone's film both embrace the near-surreal qualities of their respective narratives' landscapes as well. Though Leone's film is geographically situated in the American West, his "long-distance shots of sky-stretched panoramas ... create a disorienting, almost hyper-real landscape" (Sanders). In both *The Good, the Bad, and the Ugly* and King's *Dark Tower* series, the setting is real but fantastic, identifiable but impossible to isolate, and very nearly a character in its own right. Another element of Leone's film that King found profoundly striking was its defining "feeling of epic, apocalyptic *size*" ("On Being Nineteen" xv, emphasis original). The scope of the film—both narratively and visually—is immense, a classic Western on an epic scale, and as film critic Roger Ebert notes, "Leone's stories are a heightened dream in which everything is bigger, starker, more brutal, more dramatic, than life." *The Good, the Bad, and the Ugly* is formulaic, yet uncontainable, with Leone's imagery setting the tone and engaging viewers well beyond the narrative progression and dialogue, inviting them into Leone's imagined West. Just as *The Good, the Bad, and the Ugly* expands well beyond the traditional expectations of the Western film, King's *Dark Tower* series pushes the boundaries as well, both in terms of its narrative scope and its genre hybridity, transcending any single set of conventions.

The influence of *The Magnificent Seven*—and Kurosawa's *Seven Samurai* before it—is foundational to the structure of the *Dark Tower*'s fifth book, *Wolves of the Calla*, in which Roland and his *ka-tet* are called upon to help protect the settlement of Calla Bryn Sturgis against marauders who come and take their children. King directly references the influence of these films in the journal entries section at the end of *Song of Susannah*, in a note dated 1995, where his considered title for the fifth *Dark Tower* book is noted as "The Werewolves of End-World (or some such)" (406). Similarly, Eddie overtly comments upon the details of *The Magnificent Seven* and the mirror they serve to Roland and his *ka-tet*'s own experiences in Calla Bryn Sturgis, including the similarity between "Sturges" and "Sturgis" and the fact that in the final showdown in Calla Bryn Sturgis, seven fighters stand against the Wolves (King, *Song of Susannah* 204–5). Just as in *The Magnificent Seven*, Roland and his *ka-tet* fight beside the people of Calla Bryn Sturgis and much of the novel is devoted to their growing camaraderie with the community and training its people to fight, though in *Wolves of the Calla*, the gunslingers draw more effectively upon the expertise of the people, including the Sisters of Oriza and their deadly plates, rather than attempting to train them on unfamiliar weapons. The key role of the Sisters of Oriza privileges both the role of women in the battle—again expanding women's roles beyond those of traditional Western genre conventions—and the importance of local knowledge, as Susannah joins the women in learning how to throw the Oriza plates herself. While the men of *The Magnificent Seven* are hired guns, contracted and paid for their protection of the village, Roland is insulted by the suggestion of payment, which is an affront to the honor and age-old tradition of the gunslingers. However, Roland and his *ka-tet* enter into a contract with the people of Calla Bryn Sturgis nonetheless, this one achieved through ritualistic call and response that requires the Calla *folken* to recognize and accept the gunslingers' traditions and actions (King, *Wolves of the Calla* 230), a philosophical rather than monetary partnership. Finally, just as in *The Magnificent Seven*, there is dissent among the people of the Calla, as they debate which is worse: what the marauders take or the possibility of losing much more if they stand against their attackers. The lost crops of *The Magnificent Seven* and *The Seven Samurai* become kidnapped children in *Wolves of the Calla*, as the Wolves take one of each set of the Calla *folken*'s twins, returning them "roont" (King, *Wolves of the Calla* 2), grown large but mentally stunted. There is also betrayal: in *The Magnificent Seven* some of the villagers invite Calvera (Eli Wallach) and his men in, and Roland and his *ka-tet* similarly discover that some of the Calla *folken*, including Andy the helpful robot and Ben Slightman, the father of Jake's new friend Bennie, have been giving the Wolves information and access to the Calla. Roland and his *ka-tet* are not driven from the Calla in disgrace, as the men of *The Magnificent Seven* are before their final showdown, and while the collective group in both successfully stands against and turns back the threat, it is not without significant losses. At the conclusion of both *The Magnificent Seven* and *Wolves of the Calla*, the groups are fractured. In *The Magnificent Seven*, several of their comrades fall in the final showdown and Chico (Horst Buccholz) decides to stay in the village, while in the closing pages of *Wolves of the Calla*, Susannah has disappeared as her labor nears. Each group's decision to stand and fight has changed them significantly, both collectively and as individuals. This is particularly true of Jake, for whom this battle serves as a significant coming of age milestone, as he is torn between friendship and duty, between being a boy and being a gunslinger. However, while *The Magnificent Seven*'s Chico has now seen battle and chosen to hang up his gun belts, Jake has been disillusioned, transformed by anger and loss, but continues alongside Roland and his fellow *ka*-mates wiser and more jaded, but undeterred.

Both *The Good, the Bad, and the Ugly* and *The Magnificent Seven* are classics of the Western genre tradition, though both also expand well beyond this scope. Leone's film has elements of the epic tradition, while Darren Franich argues that *Seven Samurai* "defined a narrative structure" that *The Magnificent Seven* and countless other films have followed, that of "the misfit badasses on a mission of mercy." Beyond this narrative and thematic structure, Antoine Fuqua, director of the 2016 remake of *The Magnificent Seven*, notes that *Seven Samurai* and both versions of *The Magnificent Seven* address "the classic question of who we are as human beings. Do we step up to the plate when the time comes? The question is: When do you put your life on the line for the right reasons?" (qtd. in Beale). These questions are central to not just these specific films but to the larger Western genre tradition, storytelling in general, and the humanistic quest for identity and meaning, and these same questions, considerations, and negotiations echo throughout King's *Dark Tower* series as well.

5

Horror

King's name is synonymous with contemporary horror, from his short fiction to his novels and the myriad film and television adaptations of his work. Whether it's the reanimated dead of *Pet Sematary* (1983), *IT*'s Pennywise the Dancing Clown, or the terrifyingly human psychopaths of novels ranging from *Misery* (1987) to *Mr. Mercedes* (2014) and beyond, King is credited with fueling America's nightmares and populating its popular culture with all manner of boogeymen. While the *Dark Tower* series draws from a wide variety of genre traditions and is well-described as an Arthurian-influenced fantasy Western, the horrific remains well-represented, including supernatural evil, terrifying monsters, human failures and violence, and the cosmic horror of the universe that challenges the bounds of mankind's comprehension.

Horror is ubiquitous throughout contemporary popular culture, in literature, television, movies, and beyond. As Kevin Corstophine notes, "horror has fascinated human beings from the beginning.... Suffering is universal, but horror might well be uniquely human" (1). Despite no lack of real pain or atrocities in the world, countless readers and viewers turn to fictional narratives of horror to explore their darkest fears, exorcise those demons and, at least temporarily, contain the terror. Just as individuals' motivations in consuming horror are diverse and complex, so are the negotiations and approaches of the genre itself. Gina Wisker argues that "horror is entertaining and educational. Horror is contradictory, paradoxical; it combines opposites, destabilises, and challenges, but often does so in order to restore order, however order is culturally constituted in that particular time and place. It is social, cultural, political, psychological, emotional, spiritual, supernatural, natural, and part of the human condition" (4). King's work engages with a wide range of these horrors. These include the all-too-real horrors of sexual abuse (*Gerald's Game* [1992], *Dolores Claiborne* [1993]), domestic abuse (*Rose Madder* [1995]), violent obsession (*Misery*), and mayhem-style violence

(*Mr. Mercedes*), as well as supernatural horrors from the dark back of the closet or the furthest realms of outer space.

King also builds upon the historical Gothic tradition, with the influence of classic works and horror tropes echoing throughout and reflected in King's own work. As Indick notes of King, "References to authors and titles abound in the pages of his novels. Even more important, he has absorbed and utilized those qualities which characterize the different types of stories in the horror genre. In his own distinctive style are mirrored the major traditions he has inherited" ("King and the Literary Tradition" 15). For example, King's *Pet Sematary* and *Revival* (2014) are meditations on Mary Shelley's *Frankenstein*, with echoes of other horror classics intertextually engaged as well, in the Wendigo legends and references to W.W. Jacobs's "The Monkey's Paw" in the former and Arthur Machen and H.P. Lovecraft as resonant influences in the latter. King taps into the age-old ghost story tradition in both the representations of haunting and the inextricable interconnection of past and present in *The Shining* and *Bag of Bones* (1998). Tropes of the werewolf and the good/evil duality of Robert Louis Stevenson's *Dr. Jekyll and Mr. Hyde* (1886) play out in King's *Cycle of the Werewolf* (1985) and *The Dark Half* (1989). *'Salem's Lot* is a negotiation of Bram Stoker's *Dracula* (1897), resituated in small-town Maine, and King's novellas "The Mist"[1] and "N." are firmly situated within the cosmic terror context of H.P. Lovecraft. As these—and countless other examples—demonstrate, King is well-versed in the history of the horror genre and this larger tradition remains a cornerstone of and inspiration for his own work. This pattern of inspiration and textual engagement shapes the *Dark Tower* series as well, from the reiteration and reinvention of familiar horror figures like the vampire and the monster to the invocation of Gothic greats such as Edgar Allan Poe and Shirley Jackson. Just as King blends seemingly disparate genre traditions to create the work of the *Dark Tower*, he draws on and combines a wide range of horror tropes and conventions, creating something inventive and intertextually-engaged, while still delivering on trademark King-style scares.

In *Danse Macabre*, King's critical consideration of the horror genre in literature and popular culture, he identifies three distinct levels at which horror can effectively engage its reader or viewer. The first and least refined of these is what King calls "the gross-out" (*Danse Macabre* 3). This is the blood, the guts, the gore: images intended to shock or horrify through their graphic, violent nature. Like a horror film jump-scare, this first level is basic and straightforward, using surprise to elicit a visceral, emotional, repulsed response. The second level at which the genre works is what King specifically refers to as "horror" and as he explains, on this "more potent level, the work of horror really is a dance—a moving, rhythmic search. And what it's looking for is the place where you, the viewer or the reader, live at your most primitive level" (*Danse Macabre* 4). Rather than triggering a knee-jerk, reactive response like the "gross-out," this kind of horror ratchets up suspense and builds anticipation in an approach that both taps into and dismantles the expectations of everyday life and civilized society. As King notes, "it is on that second level of horror that we often experience that low sense of anxiety which we call 'the creeps'" (*Danse Macabre* 6). At this level, horror often taps into larger discourses, such as social anxieties and psychological disruption, which is what makes the horror genre, its products, and their reception such a fascinating barometer of their surrounding culture in each unique social and historical moment, such as the genre's commentary on nuclear fear in the "big bug" and monster movies of the 1950s or contested gender roles explored through the figure of the "Final Girl," as discussed by Carol Clover and others. While the reader or viewer may be able to shake off the "gross-out," horror tends to linger and unsettle: with its firm grounding in the surrounding culture, it can never effectively be put away, quarantined, or dismissed. Finally, at the third and highest level, is terror. King refers to this as "outside evil" (*Danse Macabre* 65): external, unavoidable, and often unexpected. Referring to H.P. Lovecraft, the master of cosmic terror, King argues that "it is the concept of outside evil that is larger, more awesome [than other kinds of horror]. Lovecraft grasped this, and it is what makes his stories of stupendous, Cyclopean evil so effective.... The best of them make us feel the size of the universe we hang suspended in, and suggest shadowy forces that could destroy us all if they so much as grunted in their sleep" (*ibid.*). This kind of cosmic terror is not only beyond humankind's power to stop—let alone a single individual's—but is also often beyond our power to even comprehend. The scale is simply too large, the stakes too high, the adversaries too overwhelming and alien to begin to understand, let alone contain.

The "Gross Out"

The instinctual shock of the "gross out" quite often derives from the spectacle of extreme violence. As Ronald Allan Lopez Cruz defines the concept of body horror, it is "a genre trope that showcases often graphic violations of the human body" (161). Gabino Iglesias breaks body horror down in more detail, noting that "mutilation, mutation, parasites, degeneration, and all other types of physical pain/torture/

transformation/etc fall under this subgenre." From cinematic "torture porn" and slasher films to the combined textual/visual approach of E.C. Comics and the novels of modern horror masters like Clive Barker, the violence that can be done to the relatively fragile human body is a core source of horror across all popular culture mediums.

Body horror is central to the Gothic tradition as well. Victor Frankenstein conducted horrific experiments using human remains and dead body parts to create and animate his "modern Prometheus" in *Frankenstein*. In its liminal occupation of the space between living and dead, the body of the zombie is one of undead disintegration and decomposition. The transformational process of the werewolf is described as physically traumatic, with bones and flesh agonizingly rearranged as human becomes wolf: George D. MacDonald describes the horror of this painful transformation in his 1905 short story "The Gray Wolf," writing that "all at once he heard the sound of a crunching of bones—not as if a creature was eating them, but as if they were ground by the teeth of rage and disappointment.... From within [the cavern] came the sounds of a mingled moaning and growling" (119), evidence of a transformation not just in temperament but of violent and painful physical change.[2] Stoker's *Dracula* is firmly grounded in concerns of the body, including the exchange of fluids, the lack of control one might have over their own body, and the horrific consequences that may follow. In the staking of the creature that was once Lucy Westenra, Stoker engages this body horror in significant detail: "The body shook and quivered and twisted in wild contortions. The sharp white teeth champed together till the lips were cut, and the mouth was smeared with a crimson foam. But Arthur never faltered ... driving deeper and deeper the mercy-bearing stake, whilst the blood from the pierced heart welled and spurted up around it" (222). These Gothic monsters may strike terror in their audiences, but the violence enacted on the human (or once-human) body is even more gruesome and horrifying, the self becoming alien, monstrous, and uncontrollable.

Influenced by both the Gothic tradition and horror in popular culture, King's work features a wide variety of approaches to body horror, including in the *Dark Tower* series. As part of Roland's youthful test of manhood, he sets his hawk David on his teacher Cort, with David shredding Cort's face, tearing off one ear, and blinding him in one eye (King, *The Gunslinger* 235–7). In *The Drawing of the Three*, Roland is attacked by "lobstrosities," which chop off and eat parts of his body, including two fingers, as "Roland saw the stumps of the first and second fingers of his right hand disappearing into the creature's jagged beak" (King, *Drawing of the Three* 18). This body horror continues as Roland takes his vengeance on the lobstrosity, smashing it with a rock "until he saw the tip of one of his own fingers in the dead thing's sour mash, saw the white dust beneath that nail from the Golgotha where he and the man in black had held their long palaver, and then he looked aside and vomited" (King, *Drawing of the Three* 21), as he is forced to recognize what had recently been part of his own body as dissociated and Other, no longer part of himself, and begins to comprehend the dire consequences of that severing. Susannah experiences a similarly traumatic physical loss in her former life as Odetta/Detta, when she is pushed in front of a subway train, which amputates both of her legs just above the knees (King, *The Drawing of the Three* 248). Tim Stoutheart witnesses the bodily horror of others when he is making his way through the Fagonard swamp in *The Wind Through the Keyhole* and encounters a benevolent group of human/plant mutants, whose bodies have become unwilling hosts, as Tim witnesses a giant spider hatch and emerge from the chest of the Helmsman, who simply continues on with his business, only briefly pausing to "reach in and scoop out a slick mass of faintly throbbing eggs" (King 208), an event that is revealed as a simple fact of life as "none of the others paid this any particular attention" (*ibid.*). Body horror can derive just as much from what goes into the body as what is removed from it, and another example of body horror in the *Dark Tower* series is Susannah/Mia's eating habits when she is pregnant with Mordred, a gestating monster who drives the unaware Susannah into the swamps at night to feed on leeches, frogs, and water rats. As Roland looks on in horror, "she squeezed and the frog popped, squirting guts and a shiny load of eggs between her fingers. Its head burst. She lifted it to her mouth and ate it greedily down while its greenish-white legs still twitched, licking the blood and shiny ropes of tissue from her knuckles" (King, *Wolves of the Calla* 84). The body is not inviolate and serves as a source of horror through violence, dismemberment, and consumption.

There are a range of other "gross-out" moments throughout the series, including the variously plague-ridden denizens of Lud in *The Waste Lands* and the thinny in *Wizard and Glass* that devours Latigo's men, as the thinny "pawed [Hendricks's] cheek and melted away the flesh, pawed his nose and tore it off, pawed at his eyes and stripped them from their sockets" (King 623). The feast of the vampires in the Dixie Pig is a horrifying revelation (King, *The Dark Tower* 10–11) and the *taheen* Finli of Algul Siento indulges himself with a taste of pimple pus, noting that he "shouldn't do it, [but] can't resist" (King, *The Dark Tower* 222). However, arguably the most high-impact "gross-out" moment comes when Flagg (now thinking of and identifying himself as Walter Padick) meets Mordred in *The Dark Tower*, the final book of the series. Walter has taken on many names and guises throughout King's work, and has proven himself resourceful, demonstrating possession of a range of preternatural powers and seeming nearly immortal both earlier in the *Dark Tower* series and in many of King's other works in which he appears, including *The Eyes of the Dragon* and *The Stand*. However, in his confrontation with Mordred, this villain who had stalked King's canon for more than two and half decades is ultimately dispatched. Powerless before Mordred's telepathic control, "the man who had sometimes called himself Marten Broadcloak, Richard Fannin, Rudin Filaro, and Randall Flagg (among a great many others), gave over all hope except the hope of dying well" (King, *The Dark Tower* 184). Mordred commands Flagg to pull out his own eyes and tongue to feed the monster, who then devours Roland's adversary alive (King, *The Dark Tower* 184–6), with both the bodily trauma itself and Walter's all-too-aware experience of it described in detail, embracing the gross-out tradition even as it highlights the psychological and existential trauma of one of King's greatest villains.

Horror

If the "gross-out" is, as King argues in *Danse Macabre*, a kind of lowest common denominator, horror is more subtle, pervasive, and far-reaching. Horror taps into social and cultural fears, large-scale "phobic pressure points" (King, *Danse Macabre* 4), and as a result, is much harder for the reader to dismiss. The "gross-out" may disgust and disturb the reader, but horror asks tough questions about the reality of day-to-day life, raises disconcerting possibilities, and unsettles. In his use of horror in the *Dark Tower* series, King draws on a range of classic and contemporary masters, including Edgar Allan Poe and Shirley Jackson.

Poe is a master of psychological horror, taking his readers into the fractured psyches of his most unstable characters, as in the first-person perspective of the murderous narrator of "The Tell-Tale Heart." As Indick explains, "Poe's influence lies in the psychological honesty of his writing … and in the subsequent burden of introspection which Poe gave his heroes" ("King and the Literary Tradition" 20). From this privileged internal perspective, readers are able to witness the slow unraveling of the narrator, his descriptions of his heightened sensory perceptions, and the lengths to which he goes to justify his actions and prove himself sane, demanding "why *will* you say that I am mad?" (Poe, "The Tell-Tale Heart" 799, emphasis original). Roderick Usher is another of

Poe's protagonists who sees, hears, and experiences things others cannot, losing his sanity a bit at a time as he listens to his entombed sister Madeline fighting her way out of her crypt and then climbing the stairs toward his chamber (though unlike "The Tell-Tale Heart," Usher's experience is provided from an outside perspective, filtered through the telling of his friend the narrator). Like Poe's perceptive characters, in the *Dark Tower* series Roland and his friends see the world and are aware of truths within it that are invisible to most others. In *The Waste Lands*, Jake and Roland's awareness of two different and mutually exclusive realities nearly drive them both mad. In *The Drawing of the Three* and *Song of Susannah*, Susannah's identity is fragmented and at times dissociative, divided between Odetta Holmes and Detta Walker in *The Drawing of the Three* and between Susannah and Mia in *Song of Susannah*. Odetta and Detta have remained almost entirely unaware of one another throughout their shared life, and when they come face to face there is "a brief sensation of being turned inside out ... and then a much more agonizing one. *She was being torn apart*" (King, *The Drawing of the Three* 448, emphasis original). The realization that the self and the Other are one and the same nearly destroys Odetta/Detta, and it is only through accepting and processing this perception that can she can move on to a new life as Susannah Dean. In contrast, Susannah's sharing of her self with Mia is an instance of external possession rather than internal dissociation, a separate being rather than a facet of Susannah's own personality (King, *Wolves of the Calla* 479). Finally, where others might see a series of coincidences or get a vague sense of well-being in the presence of the rose in Keystone New York's vacant lot and later in Hammarskjöld Plaza, Roland and his companions see the bigger picture, the interconnections, and the various ways in which these seemingly serendipitous moments revolve around and work to protect the Dark Tower, and all that is at stake should these protections fail, a truth that is overwhelming and inescapable in its significance and repercussions, and which shifts their very perceptions of the way the universe works and is held together.

Poe's "The Masque of the Red Death"[3] is a touchstone in *Song of Susannah*, invoked particularly when Susannah and Mia retreat from Roland and the others to give birth to "the chap" (King 62), the child of Roland and the Crimson King, eventually known as Mordred. In his analysis of "The Masque of the Red Death," Charles E. May argues that while red certainly symbolizes death in Poe's story, as evidenced by the blood and "scarlet horror" (Poe, "Red Death" 743) of the specter, it is also true that "the redness of blood is a 'sign' of life ... [and] if red is the sign of life, then life in turn *is* the sign of death" (102, emphasis original). As a result, life and death are inextricable, impossible to separate from one another. Even as Prince Prospero and his guests enjoy themselves within the castle while death is just outside in the larger kingdom, Susannah and Mia live and care for the growing "chap," doing everything possible to ensure his safe arrival, without ever being able to forget that the gestating being is a monster, whose birth could very well kill them both. Their pregnancy, preparation, and negotiation takes place within the larger context of widespread death as well. Standing on the ramparts of the Castle on the Abyss, where Mia has taken them, Mia tells Susannah that "beyond it is the village of Fedic, now deserted, all dead of the Red Death a thousand years ago and more" (King, *Song of Susannah* 105). When Susannah wonders whether this Red Death is Poe's, she readily accepts this possibility, thinking, "And why not? Hadn't they already wandered into—and then back out of—L. Frank Baum's Oz? What came next? The White Rabbit and the Red Queen?" (*ibid.*). The very universe through which Roland's *ka-tet* moves is steeped in the literature and culture of their own world, with familiar references appearing in unfamiliar places, and providing a lens through which the characters can understand and respond to the situations in which they find themselves.

Time is another dominant theme in "The Masque of the Red Death" that intersects with Susannah and Mia's experience of sharing a body and a pregnancy. Patricia H. Wheat notes that "commentaries on 'The Masque of the Red Death' often, rightly, describe the story's actions in terms of a battle" (52), with Prince Prospero edifying his palace in an attempt to keep death out. However, May explains that in "The Masque of the Red Death," while the plague itself may be kept at bay—at least temporarily—"what cannot be locked outside is the notion of time, which is embodied in the palace in the seven rooms ranging from east (sunrise) to west (sunset) and the giant ebony clock at whose chiming the 'dreams' become 'stiff-frozen'" (103). Time is unstoppable, death will come, and "not only do the inhabitants make physical preparations as they take their stand against the coming onslaught, they must also be as mentally ready as possible" (Wheat 52). In *Song of Susannah*, Susannah is able to take control of their shared body's functions and even the process of labor to some extent, with an internal control room that allows her to monitor and adjust things like "EMOTIONAL TEMP," "LABOR FORCE," and whether the "chap" is awake or sleeping (King, *Song of Susannah* 69). Just as with Prince Prospero, Susannah controls the elements she is able to, manipulating reality around and within herself in an attempt to ensure her safety and well-being, as well as that of those she loves. However, just as Prince Prospero's walls cannot keep death at bay, when Mordred's time to be born comes, there is nothing

Susannah—or anyone else—can do to stop or divert it or the horror it promises to bring.

"The Masque of the Red Death" is invoked once more as the series nears its conclusion, late in the final book, *The Dark Tower*. After a trying negotiation with the former magician of the Crimson King, this emissary casts off his glamours and issues them a final warning. As Roland and Susannah move on, King writes, "*Masks off, masks off,* [Susannah] thought tiredly. *It was a wonderful party, but now it's finished ... and the Red Death holds sway over all*" (King, *The Dark Tower* 617, emphasis original). The world through which Susannah and Roland move is largely destroyed. They have suffered nearly unbearable losses and death is a constant, invisible companion. There have been misunderstandings, misperceptions, and manipulations, but now, as they near the Dark Tower itself, there is only the truth of their quest, what it has cost them, and the certainty of their cause. While Roland would—and has, and will again—sacrifice all to gain the Dark Tower, with the guises stripped away to reveal the unvarnished truth, the overwhelming and undeniable reality is death.

Like Poe, the work of Shirley Jackson is a frequent presence in the *Dark Tower* series. Dara Downey and Darryl Jones address what they see as significant differences in the styles of these two authors, arguing that Jackson "is subtle and satirical where [King] is crude and sarcastic ... [with a] propensity to go for explicitness, 'the gag reflex of revulsion,' in powerful contradistinction to what [King] figures as Jackson's 'low, insinuating voice'" (215). While Downey and Jones are largely dismissive of King and his use of the "gross-out," in the *Dark Tower* series, as well as in his larger body of work, King has proven himself adept at combining different approaches to horror, including the more subtle horror which Downey and Jones see as a defining characteristic of Jackson's work.

One of the key narrative moments in the *Dark Tower* series that explicitly refers back to Jackson and her significant impact on the literary horror tradition is the narrative invocation of Jackson's short story "The Lottery," which garnered tremendous response following its publication in *The New Yorker* in 1948, including a slew of letters from readers, with responses ranging from horror to curiosity and questions about "where such lotteries were held, and whether they could go and watch" (Franklin 231). As Jackson biographer Ruth Franklin notes, however, "more than anything else, they wanted to know what the story *meant*" (231, emphasis added). "The Lottery" chronicles an annual ritual, in which the townsfolk draw bits of paper from a ceremonial box, narrowing the choice down first to a single family and then, upon a second drawing, a single member within that family, who is then stoned to death by their friends and neighbors. Aside from the ritual itself, one of the hallmark characteristics and most chilling elements of "The Lottery" is Jackson's matter-of-fact attention to detail, in both the history of the lottery and the its process in this particular year. As Jackson describes the traditional drawing, "the original paraphernalia for the lottery had been lost long ago, and the black box now resting on the stool had been put into use even before Old Man Warner, the oldest man in town, was born" ("The Lottery" 292). The lottery has been going on since time immemorial and serves some amorphous "civic function" (Franklin 227), foregrounding the need for sacrifice to ensure a plentiful harvest with the admonition that "lottery in June, corn be heavy soon" (Jackson, "The Lottery" 297), as well as to encourage communal identity and commitment. The lottery also emphasizes the importance of tradition, as Old Man Warner reminds his neighbors that "there's *always* been a lottery" (Jackson, "The Lottery" 297, emphasis original), curtailing any critical analysis of why they do it, when it started, and whether or not the ritual should continue.

The use of tradition and superstition to support ritualized violence is most fully realized in the *Dark Tower* series in *Wizard and Glass* and Susan Delgado's death in the *charyou tree* ritual. Though it has its foundations in human sacrifice in the hope of a bountiful harvest, in the Mejis Roland and his *ka-tet* visit, this ritual has been practiced as a symbolic one for several generations, with scarecrows ("stuffy men") with red-painted hands thrown on the bonfire instead. However, as King writes, "sometimes when the world moved on, it came back to where it had been" (*Wizard and Glass* 522). Here the sacrifice is not randomly selected, as Jonas's Big Coffin Hunters, Rhea, and Susan's Aunt Cordelia rally the town against Susan, driving them to a murderous rage through rhetoric of fear and betrayal, pinning the murder of Mejis's mayor on Roland's *ka-tet*, with Susan as their accomplice. Reverting to their most barbarous traditions, the people of Mejis pelt Susan with corn shucks, piling them around her feet, and setting her alight amid the ritualistic cries of "*Charyou TREE!*," "*COME REAP!*," and "Life for the crops, death for you" (King, *Wizard and Glass* 633, emphasis original). Just as in Jackson's lottery, people who have known Susan for her entire life, including school friends and her own aunt, turn on her, delighting in the *charyou tree* ritual and Susan's death. Where Jackson's description objectively described the townspeople and their performance of the lottery, however, King instead privileges Susan's perspective, her betrayal, and the comfort she finds in remembering Roland in the final moments of her life.

5. Horror   89

In *The Waste Lands*, when Roland and his friends come to the city of Lud, which resembles a post-apocalyptic New York City, Susannah and Eddie witness another, more modern iteration of Jackson's horror. Despite its destruction, there are still people living in Lud, though they have degenerated into a mob, reliant on ritual and violence to ensure their survival. After witnessing a public execution and trying to restore order, Susannah is reminded of "The Lottery" in her realization that the people of Lud "were living Jackson's nightmare ... not once a year, as in the story, but two or three times a day" (King, *The Waste Lands* 453, emphasis original). In Lud, Susannah and the others see the impact of Jackson's lottery taken to the extreme, enacted as a barbaric part of daily life rather than an annual tradition, and the resulting dehumanization of the individuals who must live with this reality. Many of Jackson's readers, as evidenced by the letters she received after the story's publication, wondered if the lottery could be a real thing, and in *The Waste Lands*, King gives readers a post-apocalyptic glimpse of what that might look like. Jackson notes that throughout her work, she was focused on "the sense which I feel, of a human and not very rational order struggling inadequately to keep in check forces of great destruction, which may be the devil and may be intellectual enlightenment" (qtd. in Franklin 224). This balance is tipped in "The Lottery," *Wizard and Glass*, and *The Waste Lands*, removing the bounds of humanity and showing the reader a glimpse of the horrors which lay beyond.

The Waste Lands also evokes notes of Jackson's *The Haunting of Hill House*, through the largely deserted and ominous Otherness Roland and his companions encounter in Lud. In *The Haunting of Hill House*, Jackson begins and ends with an evocative description of the house and its true nature. As Jackson writes, "No live organism can continue for long to exist sanely under conditions of absolute reality; even larks and katydids are supposed, by some, to dream.... Hill House, not sane, stood by itself against its hills, holding darkness within; it had stood so for eighty years and might stand for eighty more ... and whatever walked there, walked alone" (*Haunting* 1). At first glance, Hill House and Lud have little in common: Hill House is an isolated haunted house of the traditional Gothic cast, while Lud is a deteriorating futuristic city, largely kept running by supercomputers and mechanized technology. However, both places share a tense silence, a sense of waiting and barely restrained malevolence, a feeling of being watched by something other than human eyes. While Hill House has its ghosts and its dark past, Lud is haunted by its technology, and King's description of this madness distinctly echoes Jackson's opening lines in both style and content. As King writes,

> Certainly there had been an intelligence left in the ancient computers below the city, a single living organism which had long ago ceased to exist sanely under conditions that, within its merciless dipolar circuits, could only be absolute reality. It had held its increasingly alien logic within its banks of memory for eight hundred years and might have held them for eight hundred more, if not for the arrival of Roland and his friends; yet this *mens non corpus* had brooded and grown even more insane with each passing year; even in its increasing periods of sleep it could be said to dream, and these dreams grew steadily more abnormal as the world moved on [*The Waste Lands* 525].

The haunting of Lud has taken a science fiction twist, with nightmares coursing through the circuits of a slowly degenerating computer, expanding the danger to transcend the scope of a single house and encompass an entire city and perhaps beyond, as its ripples are felt in the larger world and its increasing chaos as it "moved on." However, despite these significant differences in genre, scope, and style, there are resonances between Jackson's Hill House and King's Lud, through their hauntings, their potential for untold destruction, and the ways in which each place both mirrors and shapes the souls and lives of their inhabitants.

Beyond engagement with specific Gothic authors and works, another key characteristic of Gothic horror that is central to King's *Dark Tower* series is repetition. As David Punter and Glennis Byron explain, "repetition is … a feature of many Gothic works" (284), from general narrative structure to the reflection on repetition and the intrusion of the past on the present that is central to the ghost story tradition. Andrea Juranovszky refers to this as the "Gothic loop," a narrative pattern in which "Gothic texts progress as if through a series of flashbacks, always revising deeds of the past in order to point out a problem, which, however strongly rooted in some ancient heritage, prevails in the present and calls for immediate resolution." In this way, the past is never entirely contained or separate from the present and the influence of the past on the present, as well as the ways in which it often shapes the future, are recursive and often traumatic. With this central feature in mind, the conclusion of King's *Dark Tower* series is undeniably Gothic, returning Roland to his starting point in the Mohaine Desert, making him a ghost that haunts his own past and one who has been—at least so far—unable to change himself, his present, or the future to which it leads. In this return to and reenactment of the traumas of the past, Roland's gaining of the Dark Tower aligns seamlessly with Juranovszky's definition of the Gothic loop "as a discursive element, a fictional time and space of various suspensions when/where certain past or present traumas must be continuously re-experienced and finally resolved—with horror and suffering involved on the part of the protagonists—in order to produce an improved (re)starting point in the narrative." This understanding of the Gothic loop encompasses the complexity of time, space, multiple universes, and interconnection central to King's *Dark Tower* series, as well as Roland's need to endure it all again, to try to get it right this time and gain some sort of rest and redemption.

Another indicator of the role of Gothic repetition in the Dark Tower series as a whole are the corresponding values assigned to each through subtitling, beginning with King's introduction to *Wolves of the Calla* in 2003. As King outlines there, the subtitle of *The Gunslinger* is "resumption," while *The Drawing of the Three* is "renewal" and *The Waste Lands* is "redemption." *Wizard and Glass* is subtitled "regard" and *Wolves of the Calla* is "resistance" (King, "The Final Argument" xi-xvi). In *Song of Susannah*, the subtitle of "reproduction" refers to the birth of Mordred, as well as the telling and continuation of the *ka-tet*'s story, as Roland and Eddie go visit King himself. Each of these subtitles indicate the roles of the gunslinger and his *ka-tet* within their journey, as well as their position within the recursive Gothic loop, returning Roland to where he started in the opening pages of *The Gunslinger* and underscoring both his victories—renewal in the drawing of his *ka-tet* and redemption in his reunion with Jake, for example—as well as the struggles and repetition he is doomed to suffer. The final book of the series, *The Dark Tower*, is the most complex in this role, closing the Gothic loop and returning it once more to its starting point with its pronouncement of "reproduction," "revelation," "redemption," and "resumption." The Dark Tower itself also bears the name of "Can Calyx, the Hall of Resumption" (King, *Song of Susannah* 109). In this litany of designations and in the Dark Tower's position as both end and beginning, Roland's repetitive quest is underscored in both its horror and the potential for redemption, not yet achieved but seemingly still possible, though only in the continuing repetition demanded by the structure of the Gothic loop.

In King's use of horror and his evocation of Gothic masters like Poe and Jackson, as well as his complex engagement with the larger Gothic tradition, he moves well beyond the "gross-out" to disturb and unsettle. The horrors of the *Dark Tower* series—and the inspirations upon which they draw—ask readers to consider central, fundamental questions: What might happen when society breaks down and the world has moved on? What is the true nature of humanity? What lies hidden in the depths of the self? By what are we haunted and is there any way to quiet those ghosts? Poe, Jackson, and others in the pantheon of horror offer little reassurance in response to these questions. Horror offers its readers visions of madness, betrayal, and destruction, and while these things are present in—and even central to—King's *Dark Tower* series, there are also friendship, love, loyalty, and perseverance in the face of likely insurmountable odds.

Cosmic Terror

While Roland and his companions can stand against and endure the overwhelming horrors they encounter, cosmic terror is a whole different level, and one against which humanity is largely defenseless. Lovecraft is the undisputed master of cosmic terror and S.T. Joshi defines Lovecraft's "cosmicism" as "the central principle in his fiction, involving the suggestion of vast gulfs of space and time and the consequent triviality of the human race" (14). As Lovecraft argues in his seminal essay "Supernatural Horror in Literature," in true weird fiction, "a certain atmosphere of breathless and unexplainable dread of outer, unknown forces must be present ... [and] that most terrible conception of the human brain—a malign and particular suspension or defeat of those fixed laws of Nature which are our only safeguard against the assaults of chaos and the daemons of unplumbed space" (28). As with Poe and Jackson, the influence of Lovecraft can be seen throughout King's canon, including in the otherworldly monsters and the permeable membrane between worlds explored in King's "The Mist" and "N."

This Lovecraftian influence of cosmic terror is foundational to King's *Dark Tower* series, engaging overtly with a horror multiverse that intersects with and informs a wide range of King's other works. The interconnections and passageways between worlds are a frequent point of consideration and conflict throughout the series, and the gaps between—or *todash* space, in the *Dark Tower* lexicon—are inhabited by monsters that threaten to destroy or drive an individual to madness, reminiscent of Lovecraft's visions of unimaginable destruction from which mankind is but thinly separated, "listening ... for the beating of black wings or the scratching of outside shapes and entities on the known universe's utmost rim" (Lovecraft, "Supernatural Horror" 28). Roland and his *ka-tet* are well aware of the thin barrier between their world(s) and the dark chaos of the *todash* space, and Jake considers its potential failure, wondering "How long before everything ended? And *how* would it end? ... Would the sky tear open like a flimsy piece of cloth, spilling out the monstrosities that lived in the todash darkness?" (King, *Song of Susannah* 18, emphasis original). As Mia tells Susannah, the Crimson King's greatest enemies are exiled to this *todash* space, "thrown into a darkness where they may exist—blind, wandering, insane—for years. But in the end, something always finds them and devours them. Monsters beyond the ability of such minds as ours to bear thought of" (King, *Song of Susannah* 249). Aside from its use as one of the cruel punishments of the Crimson King, this *todash* space must be braved to cross from one world to another, such as from Roland's world to the various New York Cities from which he has drawn his companions and the Keystone World where they find themselves drawn time and again to take care of the *ka-tet*'s business and ensure the safety of the Dark Tower across multiple realities. Ideally, these trips are brief and uneventful, but when the door between worlds is opened, there is no telling what may come through it, making the venture inherently dangerous and even life-threatening. For example, when Roland, Eddie, and Susannah bring Jake through a door between Mid-World and his version of New York City, they have to face not only the resident demon of the speaking ring, but a monster that guards the *todash* space between the worlds, which is all too aware of them. As Eddie tells Roland and Susannah just before they open the door, there is "something between the doors—between the *worlds*. Something that waits. *And it's opening its eyes*" (King, *The Waste Lands* 270, emphasis original). On Jake's side of the door, it takes the form of an enormous humanoid shape, literally made from the wood and hardware of the derelict house through which he must pass to find his way back to Roland, a sentient monster which intends to catch and eat Jake Chambers before he can make his way back to Mid-World.[4] In this instance, Roland, Eddie, and Susannah (with a bit of help from Detta Walker) successfully work together to take on both the doorkeeper of the *todash* space and the demon of the speaking ring to bring Jake through and complete their *ka-tet*.

While this thin spot between the worlds is of particular use and significance to Roland and his *ka-tet*, there are others that can be found and used by anyone sensitive enough to detect them and desperate enough to enter them. Buday describes these thinnies as "transparent and permeable membranes between realities and ... gateways to other worlds" (136). A thinny can be detected, in part, by the nearly electrical charge in the air and a low, vibratory humming sound.[5] These places are, as Roland notes, simultaneously attractive and dangerous, drawing individuals toward them and often, to their own destruction. Roland and his original *ka-tet* encounter a thinny in Mejis, in Eyebolt Canyon, which hums, beckons, and devours, pulling birds from the air (King, *Wizard and Glass* 288) and consuming Latigo's men (King, *Wizard and Glass* 623–5). The thinny also insidiously calls to Roland and his *ka-tet*, tempting them to lay aside their worries and responsibilities, to embrace the destructive oblivion it offers, to "*just jump in and let all these cares cease*" (King, *Wizard and Glass* 288, emphasis original), in a seductive voice is simultaneously that of the enemy and the gunslingers' own self-destructive impulses. Roland, Jake, Eddie, Susannah, and Oy travel through a thinny in a post–Captain Trips version of Topeka as well, though its call here is more of a nuisance than a temptation, a portal which signals a major transition in the course of their journey and their quest for the Dark Tower. Another such thin place is in Doorway Cave in *Wolves of the Calla*. Considered a place of spiritual significance and great danger by the Manni of Calla Bryn Sturgis, the cave is a place of clamoring voices that speak the listening individual's innermost truths and fears, a powerful site for meditation, self-reflection, and a potential catalyst of *todash* travel. With Callahan's arrival, however, a door appeared and with its presence, the cave serves as a fixed portal between the Calla and other wheres and whens.

Another element of Lovecraftian cosmic terror that informs King's *Dark Tower* series is the belief that there are some things that humans are not meant to know, realities their minds cannot comprehend and remain sane. This type of maddening knowledge permeates Lovecraft's fiction, including his story "The Call of Cthulhu," which the narrator begins with his observation that "the most merciful thing in the world, I think, is the inability of the human mind to correlate all its contents. We live on a placid island of ignorance in the midst of black seas of infinity, and it was not meant that we should voyage far" (139). However, in spite of this pronouncement, the constant tension of the human condition seems to be an overwhelming curiosity and desire for knowledge, however destructive it may prove. After all, the narrator of "The Call of Cthulhu" seeks answers and once he has learned the truth, feels compelled to chronicle it, leaving behind a written record; he declares his hope "that it meets no other eye" (Lovecraft 169), but must know all too well the effect curiosity is likely to have on the next person who finds his written record. Similarly, as Mia notes in *Song of Susannah*, there are monsters in the *todash* space that will drive a person mad (King 249) and many of the creatures Roland his *ka-tet* encounter defy the imagination and push the limits of their perception. Borne through the waste lands outside of Lud by Blaine the Mono, for example, Roland and his friends see monstrous, unclassifiable beings, which are "in their exquisite hatefulness, almost impossible to look at" (King, *The Waste Lands* 571).

An even more direct challenge to Roland's perception is the scope of the universe that he is forced to face head-on that punctuates his journey. When he finally catches up with the Man in Black toward the end of *The Gunslinger*, the Man in Black mentally casts Roland out into the depths of the universe, showing him innumerable worlds as even "the stars themselves began to shrink.... The whole universe seemed to be drawing around him" (King 281). The Man in Black offers to stop this onslaught of perception if only Roland will foreswear his quest for the Tower, an offer Roland refuses. As the Man in Black suggests, each grain of sand may hold "a trillion universes—not worlds but *universes* ... and within each universe an infinity of others" (King, *The Gunslinger* 289, emphasis original). This possibility is staggering in its scope, bordering on the incomprehensible, but is a reality that Roland must become aware of should his quest succeed, for the Dark Tower serves as the linchpin of all. While Roland perceives much, he cannot cope with the sheer vastness it implies and must ultimately turn away, as "he fled the light and the knowledge the light implied, and so came back to himself" (King, *The Gunslinger* 282). He has done well, but perhaps not well enough, and it could be the challenge of this perception, these universes, and his role within the cosmic order that in the end may be integral to his successful gaining of the Dark Tower, a challenge he has not yet conquered. Roland recalls a similar sense of the overwhelming size of the universe and the future suffering which awaits him in his loss of himself within the pink grapefruit of the Wizard's Glass, including his glimpse of Thunderclap and his realization that *"all is shade here, all is death here, this is the edge of End-World, where someday he will come, and all is death here"* (King 595, emphasis original), bearing witness to the death—both general and specific, such as Oy's final moments—which will come as a direct result of his quest, as well as the resultant guilt and responsibility he will bear. Finally, Roland faces a similar revelation at the end of *The Dark Tower*, with the realization that he must begin again, that even in his individual role within this enormous scope, his life and path have an infinite number of turnings, choices, and repercussions, as he internalizes the external awareness of the universes the Man in Black revealed to him at the edge of the Mohaine Desert and his own quest as glimpsed within the Wizard's Glass, each of which threaten to destroy Roland's sense of himself, the world(s) around him, and his role within it.

The most effective and all-encompassing use of cosmic terror in the *Dark Tower* series, however, is simply in the scope of the work itself, the wonder and horror of correlation to which Lovecraft refers in the opening lines of "The Call of Cthulhu." With the *Dark Tower*, King creates a multiverse in which everything is connected and key realities resonate within and between all worlds. In his version of New York City, Jake encounters a young Eddie and his older brother Henry, following them to the house that holds his doorway to Mid-World (King, *The Waste Lands* 261–8) and Susannah finds herself reunited with Eddie and Jake in another version of New York City after her adventure with Roland has come to an end (King, *The Dark Tower* 807–13). The dreams of one world may be the reality of another, a communication between levels of the Dark Tower rather than a standard dream. In *The Drawing of the Three*, Enrico Balazar's nightclub is called The Leaning Tower and late in the series, a man named Calvin Tower becomes an unlikely ally in helping Roland and his *ka-tet* ensure the safety of the Tower itself. The conclusion of *Song of Susannah* includes a news story from a reality in which Stephen King was killed, rather than gravely injured, when he was struck by a van in June of 1999 (King 410–1). Characters and realities from King's non–*Dark Tower* novels are drawn into the *Dark Tower* series, establishing a pattern of connections and correlations that expand throughout King's larger body of work, an overwhelming web of impact and interconnection that is staggering its reach. The series and its interconnections require the reader to comprehend these multiple, overlapping realities and their potential impacts on one another, even when their truths prove contradictory or mutually exclusive. Just as Lovecraft challenges his readers to consider the monsters that lie beyond the realm of human perception, King's *Dark Tower* series demands the reader's recognition of a multiverse of staggering scope and complexity, to comprehend and negotiate the lines that connect them and realities that unite them, the coincidences that aren't really coincidences, and the nightmares that are reality on another level of the Dark Tower. This challenge of perception is central to the *Dark Tower* series, both for the characters and the readers, and nowhere is this challenge of perception, repetition, and the interconnection of multiple worlds more evident than in the series' conclusion. As Roland at last gains the Dark Tower, climbs the stairs, and opens the door with his name upon it, his realization is horrific, as he finds himself back in the desert at the start of *The Gunslinger* and his pursuit of the Man in Black. With this final realization, Roland's perception is all-encompassing and nearly unbearable, as he goes back, knowing that he will once again forget, will tackle his quest anew. Every choice he makes following this particular moment, every possible reality that has been raised throughout the series is new again, demanding the reader perceive the limitless possibilities that lie once more before Roland. The scope of this reality and its ultimate denial are a purgatory for Roland, but they are also a promise that next time things might end differently. While the reality of his world—and all the others with which it intersects and overlaps—is often malleable and in flux, Roland himself, his quest, and the beliefs which drive him forward are the only certain truth.

6

'Salem's Lot

In addition to the wide range of genre influences and specific textual inspirations that resonate throughout the *Dark Tower* books, the series is also fundamentally intertwined with King's larger canon, with the world of the Dark Tower serving as a common touchstone throughout King's career and as the axis of his fictional universe. Some of these interconnections are overt and extended—such as places in the larger King universe that Roland and his friends visit or characters from another novel who show up again in the *ka-tet*'s journeys—while others are more subtle, like a passing allusion or the quick glimpse of a familiar face out of the corner of one's eye. As Vincent notes in *The Road to the Dark Tower: Exploring Stephen King's Magnum Opus*, such "interconnections within Stephen King's books are not a recent phenomenon. As early as *The Dead Zone* [1979], characters in his novels referred to other King novels ... [and] Characters and events from previous books recur, as in the Castle Rock novels" (194). These intertextual connections link King's works to one another and, in their engagement with the *Dark Tower* series, establish Roland's Mid-World as the center of that universe.

King's second novel, *'Salem's Lot*, is a 20th-century take on the familiar vampire story and, in many ways, is a small-town Maine reworking of Bram Stoker's classic *Dracula*, with an E.C. Comics flair (King, *Danse Macabre* 26). As King explains this inspiration, *'Salem's Lot* "bears an intentional similarity to Bram Stoker's *Dracula*" in a kind of "game of literary racquet-ball: *'Salem's Lot* itself was the ball and *Dracula* was the wall I kept hitting it against, watching to see how and where it would bounce, so I could hit it again" (*ibid.*). Dracula wasn't the first but is certainly one of the most iconic and recognizable literary vampires, and Stoker's Count has served as inspiration for more than a century's worth of literary and popular culture vampires. However, despite its seemingly perennial appeal, a vampire story is never just about a vampire. As Nina Auerbach explains in *Our Vampires, Ourselves*, there are innumerable permutations of the vampire and "each feeds on his age distinctively because he embodies that age" (1), adapting and reflecting the specific historical and cultural moment in which it appears, as vampires "blend into the changing cultures they inhabit" (6). As a result, while Stoker's vampires were a supernatural negotiation of sexual repression, increasing global mobility, and the potentially threatening Eastern stranger (among other anxieties), *'Salem's Lot* is rooted firmly in the cultural and political context of the 1970s moment of governmental mistrust and "specific American and mid–1970s senses of the difficulties of ascertaining a singular 'truth' or 'main plot' in comprehending political and historical complexities" (Sears 36). Strengell similarly explores this connection, noting that in this 20th-century *Dracula* story, "King reworks traditional material and uses the horror formula to depict American social reality. Although the vampire provides supernatural thrills and fun, King reveals familial discord, violence, and other social illnesses for what they are in *'Salem's Lot*" (Strengell 159–60). Set against the backdrop of seemingly idyllic small-town life, as well engaging with the ways in which appearance often belies reality and the horrors that occur behind closed doors, when the vampire threat comes to Jerusalem's Lot and begins to insidiously infect its inhabitants and take over the town, it is in part their refusal to see, recognize, and respond to horror, whether of the supernatural or everyday variety, that is the cause of their destruction. However, there are a handful of people who believe and in doing so, see the truth: Ben Mears, Susan Norton, Mark Petrie, Jimmy Cody, Matt Burke, and Father Donald Callahan. They are a mismatched group of unlikely vampire hunters, though they succeed in uncovering and briefly standing against the head vampire Kurt Barlow when the rest of the town refuses to see the truth or move to stop him. This belief is the cornerstone of their success and without that belief, they falter and fail.

This question of religious belief specifically is a driving force for Father Donald Callahan, the disillusioned priest of Jerusalem's Lot, who finds himself longing for a challenge, wanting to "see EVIL with its cerements of deception cast aside, with every feature of its visage clear. He wanted to slug it out toe to toe with EVIL, like Muhammad Ali against Joe Frazier, the Celtics against the Knicks, Jacob against the Angel" (King, *'Salem's Lot* 232). As he stands side by side with his companions against the vampire threat, Callahan rediscovers some of his passion and purpose, though in his final showdown with Barlow, when Father Callahan must rely on his faith alone to see him safely through, that faith falters and Callahan is cursed (King, *'Salem's Lot* 519–27). Callahan relies on the crucifix as an externalized symbol rather than on his own internal faith in God, depending on the crucifix as a means of "talismanic protection" (Cowan 29), an externalization that transfers faith to "the physical sign and symbol of a power we believe greater than the one that threatens us" (Cowan 33). Without Callahan's authentic religious faith to back up this belief in the cross's protection, however, that power is eroded, undercut, and ultimately incapable of standing. Callahan is forced to drink Barlow's blood, he is rejected by his own church, and as Vincent sums up Callahan's fate at the end of *'Salem's Lot*, he "was one of King's tragic figures, last seen riding out of town in shame like a failed gunslinger sent into exile, on a self-destructive path" (*The Road to the Dark Tower* 250). The mystery of where Callahan went is brought to light in the final three books of the *Dark Tower* series, when Roland and his *ka-tet* find Callahan living in Calla Bryn Sturgis, hear his story, and fight alongside him. Callahan's reappearance also coincides with the appearance of vampires in the *Dark Tower* series, in this case in their service to the Crimson King and his goal of bringing down the Tower. Finally, another significant intertextual connection between Roland's and Callahan's worlds is the appearance of King's novel *'Salem's Lot*, which turns up as an artifact and a work of fiction within the *Dark Tower* universe, interrogating the lines between fiction and reality, and plunging Callahan into an existential dilemma.

Religion, Interconnection and Redemption

When Callahan reappears in Calla Bryn Sturgis (whose very name echoes his own), he has given up his formal title and Catholic affiliation, referred to by the people of the Calla as Pere Callahan or more often, simply as "The Old Fella." However, while he may no longer be a priest, he is still driven by his foundational religious beliefs and his life—however wayward it may have been between the Lot and the Calla—has been guided by some of the core foundational values of Christianity, including selflessness, sacrifice, and caring for others. Callahan's faith and its attendant beliefs serve as his light in the darkness, having seen him through a number of dangerous situations, the crossings between multiple worlds, and even his own death. When Roland and his *ka-tet* find Callahan, "he no longer considers himself a priest, but rather a man of God" (Vincent, *The Road to the Dark Tower* 249). Serving as a religious leader in Calla Bryn Sturgis, Callahan tells Roland "God has taken me back ... although I think only on what might be called a 'trial basis'" (King, *Wolves of the Calla* 314).

King's representations and negotiations of religion throughout his canon are diverse and complex, ranging from the almost metaphysical belief of David Carver in *Desperation*, who hears and converses with a small, quiet voice of the divine and works his own loaves and fishes-style miracle, to Margaret White in *Carrie*, whose maniacal belief in a vengeful God assures her of her rightness in locking her "sinning" daughter in a closet adorned with images of hellfire and suffering, or Mrs. Carmody's fervor for sacrifice in "The Mist," which drives her to lead her fellow captives to inhuman action in the name of repentance and salvation. This complexity and contradiction is at the heart of King's representations of religion and as Douglas E. Cowan argues in *America's Dark Theologian: The Religious Imagination of Stephen King*, when religion appears in King's work, it "invite[s] no equivalent attempt to create a coherent or consistent theology. Rather, his novels and short stories continually confront the answers we have been given and often hold to as gospel" (7). Following this argument, to some extent, religion is what each character makes of it, grounded in the ways in which those individuals actively use religious belief and its attendant philosophies to understand and make sense of the world around them, to guide their lives, or to determine their individual and ultimate purpose. This role of personal self-determination is reflected in Callahan and the various permutations and performances of his faith in *'Salem's Lot* and the *Dark Tower* series, as King charts the highs and lows of Callahan's individual spiritual journey, from a young and idealistic priest who wants to save the world to a man going through the motions and invested in the symbols rather than the bedrock truth of his belief. Finally, in Calla Bryn Sturgis, Callahan discovers and lives a rich spiritual life that combines his own individual truth and experiences with those elements of the Catholic faith that still resonate with him, while he has jettisoned others and put a clear and uncomplicated trust in the divine at the center of his personal cosmology.

In the *Dark Tower* series, the notion of religion also expands significantly beyond individual faith or any singular faith tradition or denominational dogma. There is a belief in a creator (called Gan), though the more driving spiritual belief system of the series operates on a larger scale, in a cosmic force of good referred to as the White, which not only empowers Roland and his *ka-tet* to fight the evils that threaten the Tower, but animates the benevolent potential of the universe to help things turn out right, whether achieved through a random act of kindness, a decisive moral stand, or even just the seemingly sheer coincidence that puts the right person in the right place at the right time to do good and enact a positive change in the world. In the *Dark Tower* series and throughout much of King's larger canon, "the power of the White" refers to a foundational and "elemental good" (Strengell 234), the force needed to stand against overwhelming and absolute evil. The White cannot ensure that everything will turn out well—it wields *influence* rather than *control*—but Roland and his *ka-tet* feel that influence throughout their journey and this faith is one that Callahan is able to reconcile with his own, more traditionally Christian beliefs, calling on the power of the White as well as that of God in his moment of crisis (King, *The Dark Tower* 12).

Similarly, Roland, his *ka-tet*, and all of Mid-World and its interconnected universes are shaped by *ka*, a cosmic force akin to destiny. *Ka* guides Roland forward and brings those he needs into his life, uniting them with this common drive, and it clears a path before him, outlining the way just as palpably as the natural elements that follow the Path of the Beam. *Ka* serves another purpose as well in that "the spin of *ka* always brings us back to the same place, to face and reface our mistakes and defeats until we can learn from them. When we learn from the past, the wheel continues to move forward, towards growth and evolution. When we don't, the wheel spins backward and we are given another chance. If once more we squander the opportunity, the wheel continues its rotation towards devolution, or destruction" (Vincent, *The Road to the Dark Tower* 5, emphasis original). In this way, the individual and the cosmic are inextricably intertwined, intimately connected in a way that transcends the notion of a personified deity. This notion of *ka* is both larger than the self and an integral part of the self, in a dynamic engagement that links the *Dark Tower* series to the Tibetan Buddhist tradition of *citta-matra* (or "mind only"), through which in death "whatever we believe will happen determines what does happen" (Cowan 87). Following this line of belief, Roland's discovery within the Dark Tower and the end of his quest can be read as a revelation of both *ka* and Roland himself: he is taken back to the beginning of his journey, forced to struggle and fight and suffer losses all over again, both because he hasn't quite gotten it right just yet and because he doesn't *believe* he has succeeded, or perhaps even that he *deserves* to succeed. So *ka* takes him back and he is doomed to try again, both in gaining the Tower and in refining his beliefs, identity, and vision, confronting his own guilt over those who have traveled with him and been lost. There is even the chance that he could change his story altogether, making different choices that allow him to reach the Dark Tower with a friend (or friends) at his side rather than alone, though since *ka* only resets him to his pursuit of the Man in Black across the Mohaine Desert, there are some losses he will carry with him always, such as those of his mother, Susan Delgado, and his fellow gunslingers at Jericho Hill.

Callahan, his negotiation of his previous life as a priest, his ongoing engagement with and embodiment of his spiritual faith, and his own desperate need for *ka* to give him another chance, are all situated within the larger context of this complex vision of faith, belief, and a higher power that impacts and guides the lives of individuals. Callahan is a deeply flawed man and his years between Jerusalem's Lot and Calla Bryn Sturgis are punctuated by drinking and running, in a futile attempt to escape from his memories of the Lot and his own cursed nature. He builds relationships and helps people, working in homeless shelters in New York City and Detroit, but once again suffers losses as the man with whom he has fallen is love is infected with AIDS by the vampires and another friend is tortured and beaten by paid goons of the Crimson King, dying as a result of those injuries. Callahan does his best to help others and for a time, even becomes a crusading vampire hunter, but mostly he keeps to himself, just surviving, drinking, and trying to evade the attentions of the vampires and other emissaries of the Crimson King, including the low men. He hits rock bottom in Topeka—a version of which Roland and his *ka-tet* discover early in *Wizard and Glass*, another of those not quite coincidental echoes between multiple worlds and overlapping journeys—and recommits himself to doing good. He moves on to work at The Lighthouse shelter in Detroit, where the vampires and low men catch up to him once more, luring Callahan and his friends with offers of charitable funding for the shelter. Echoing his final curse by Barlow in Jerusalem's Lot, the vampires don't plan to kill Callahan but rather to infect him with AIDS, marking him and leaving him to suffer through the rest of his life. Though he is outnumbered and doesn't stand a chance of resisting his attackers, "Callahan won't let the vampires taint him again. He calls on God for the first time since his encounter with Barlow, and decides to kill himself by jumping through the window" (Vincent, *The Road to the Dark Tower* 249). This is an ultimate act of desperation and refusal, as Callahan gains his release only through suicide, an "escape [that] comes about by way of an action in direct opposition to his faith and belief" (McAleer 134). Callahan's religious belief is a site of contestation and dynamic negotiation in both *'Salem's Lot* and the *Dark Tower* series and this unfixed state is underscored by his position in the Calla as a man of God, but not a priest. Through his experiences, as well as his personal and religious struggles, Callahan seems to have come to an individual philosophy and embodiment of his own faith rather than a denominationally-imposed dogma, and within this framework, Callahan determines that being defiled by vampires is a fate worse than death and surrender to their evil a sin worse than suicide. Callahan's death is the portal that takes him from his world to Roland's Mid-World and Calla Bryn Sturgis, with a quick stopover at the way-station where Walter bestows Black Thirteen upon him and sets Callahan on an intersecting path with Roland's own, with the brief glimpse of Roland and Jake's retreating figures establishing Callahan's position much earlier in the *Dark Tower* series, present but unseen in *The Gunslinger*.[1]

In addition to *'Salem's Lot* and Callahan's way-station intersection with the earlier *Dark Tower* series narrative, Callahan's experience bears similarities to several other *Dark Tower*-connected King works. Much like Ralph Roberts in *Insomnia*, Callahan can see auras around people, which in this case let him know that they have been fed on by the vampires, connecting Callahan to a reality that others cannot see and of which they remain blissfully unaware. When Callahan travels, whether he is on the run or hiding from the Crimson King's low men, he often makes his way along the secret highways of King and Straub's *The Talisman* and *Black House*, a world and story in which Roland and his friends are also mentioned. Jack Sawyer, the protagonist of *The Talisman* and *Black House*, knows these hidden roads and their attractions well, a draw that Callahan discovers with his own growing awareness of and access to "a great, possibly endless, confluence of worlds ... [and] there are highways which lead through them" (King, *Wolves of the Calla* 298–9). Finally, the low men who pursue Callahan are the same as those who search for escaped Beam-Breaker Ted Brautigan in *Hearts in Atlantis*, using the same underground communication tactics of chalk graffiti and lost pet posters to close in on their targets. These low men appear throughout many other King works that are either adjacent to or overlap with the *Dark Tower* series, including *From a Buick 8* and the novellas "Ur" and "Mile 81." In his journeys through the multiple Americas he discovers through the hidden highways and in Callahan's appearance and key role in Mid-World and Calla Bryn Sturgis, Callahan is the site of a rich confluence of intersections and interconnections that extend throughout much of King's canon, from Callahan's first appearance in *'Salem's Lot* to his fate in *The Dark Tower*, though that position is even further complicated by the *ka-tet*'s discovery of *'Salem's Lot* the novel as a fiction within their own reality.

While Callahan sets his goal as one of atonement rather than redemption, his role in the *Dark Tower* series affords him the opportunity to stand and fight rather than run, to draw on all the power of his faith and to sacrifice himself for his friends, just as he failed to do in Jerusalem's Lot. Callahan's final moments bear a significant resemblance to his confrontation with Barlow in the Petries' kitchen: standing against monsters, at the side of a boy he is charged to protect, with his faith as one of the few weapons he has in this final showdown. However, where Callahan failed in Jerusalem's Lot, he succeeds in the Dixie Pig, though his enemy is even more overwhelming and monstrous. This time, when Callahan is dared to put away the symbols of his faith and rely on belief alone, he doesn't falter. Callahan's faith is stronger that it was in Jerusalem's Lot and in keeping with his own increasingly complex spiritual journey, in which he has drawn on his own experiences and foundational beliefs rather than a singular and prescribed dogma, he has greater and more diverse stores of strength at the ready, both in resisting the call of Black Thirteen and in standing with Jake against their monstrous enemies in the Dixie Pig. In addition to calling on divine power and the symbol of the cross, Callahan also draws on his belief in goodness, both in microcosmic and macrocosmic form, as he adjures his monstrous foes that "the ka of Mid-World commands you! *The power of the White commands you!*" (King, *The Dark Tower* 12, emphasis original). Similarly, much as Callahan holds up his cross to drive back and destroy some of his enemies, he also wields the power of the Turtle, carrying its might into battle in the form of a small "scrimshaw turtle made of ivory" (King, *The Dark Tower* 3), and tapping into the Turtle's profound significance in the cosmologies of Mid-World and beyond. Unlike in Jerusalem's Lot, in these final moments, Callahan's "faith is greater than any talisman—the power of God and the White radiates through him" (Vincent, *The Road to the Dark Tower* 250) and he "need[s] no sigul" (King, *Song of Susannah* 331). Callahan stands firm where he faltered before and goes out on his own terms, once more committing suicide to take himself beyond the reach of the vampires and the *taheen*, raising his own gun to his head as he salutes Roland, and finally achieving the peace he has so long sought.

Vampires

Throughout his career, King's works of horror have built upon the larger traditions and canonical texts of the genre, offering revisions and reinventions of familiar tropes. For example, just as *'Salem's Lot* is a reimagined *Dracula*, *The Dark Half* can be productively read as a modern *Dr. Jekyll and Mr. Hyde*, and *Revival* engages with Lovecraft's visions of cosmic horrors, Shelley's *Frankenstein*, and Arthur Machen's *The Great God Pan* (1890; revised in 1894). Just as changing times, places, and social contexts allow dynamic reframing of these familiar stories, King also recontextualizes and reimagines the horrific figures which populate these narratives. With *'Salem's Lot* and Callahan's further adventures, King adds to and expands the literary and popular culture figure of the vampire.[2]

The vampires of *'Salem's Lot* have many of the traditional features of the monster as established by Stoker and others, "serv[ing] as a virtual *catalog* of vampirism and kindred horrors" (Herron 81, emphasis original). In large part, it is these characteristics that make the threat recognizable to those who believe, including Mark Petrie and Matt Burke. As Douglas Winter explains, "King vests his undead with the trappings of traditional vampire myth: blood-lusting creatures unable to function in sunlight, repulsed by garlic, and vulnerable to the sign of the cross" (40). However, in the vampires that Callahan encounters—and occasionally hunts—as his travels along America's secret highways, King complicates the vampire myth, creating a monstrous hierarchy that Callahan learns to recognize and effectively navigate in order to survive. Callahan defines these vampires as Type One, Type Two, and Type Three vampires. Type One vampires are the ones with the real power and are often referred to as "Grandfathers," in acknowledgment of their long lives, prodigious strength, and elevated position among those who serve the Crimson King. These Type One vampires are particularly monstrous in both their appetites and their appearance, eating human flesh in addition to drinking blood and "their lips ... burst back from great croggled bouquets of teeth; the days when any of these monstrosities could close their mouths were long gone. Their eyes were black and oozing with some sort of noisome tarry stuff from the corners. The skin was yellow, scaled with teeth, and covered with patches of diseased-looking fur" (King, *Song of Susannah* 372). As Callahan explains to Roland and his *ka-tet*, "Type Ones are rare. Barlow was a Type One. They live very long lives, and may spend extended periods—fifty years, a hundred, maybe two hundred—in deep hibernation. When they're active, they're capable of making new vampires, what we call the undead. These undead are Type Twos" (King, *Wolves of the Calla* 269). As Callahan goes on to delineate their differences, it becomes clear that Type Two vampires are closest to the traditional vampire characteristics familiar from literature and popular culture: reliant on blood, unable to go out in sunlight, and so on. In drawing this distinction, Callahan is also demarcating the boundaries between a powerful head vampire—like Barlow or Stoker's Dracula—and those the head vampire infects, who may be dangerous and numerous, but are also largely expendable, with short lives and comparatively little power. Type Two vampires do have the ability to create vampires of their own, though their abilities and distinguishing characteristics continue to be diluted, as Type Three vampires largely live and eat as humans, feeding on their victims and consuming blood for pleasure rather than sustenance, and are able to go out in daylight. Type Three vampires are the end of the generative line, unable to create more vampires, and described by Callahan as "like mosquitos" (King, *Wolves of the Calla* 270). The Type Three vampires can be dispatched fairly easily, with no superhuman strength to contend with or special weapons required: Callahan kills one with a cleaver to the head (King, *Wolves of the Calla* 277) and takes out others by stabbing them in the back of the neck (King, *Wolves of the Calla* 302). After Callahan and his friends' disastrous attempt to stand against Barlow in Jerusalem's Lot, this ease is a welcome change, though Callahan also soon learns that his vampire-hunting is making little difference: like mosquitos, more Type 3 vampires keep appearing to take their place and given their wide-spread and almost completely unremarked proliferation, Callahan is fighting a battle he will never be able to win, regardless of his individual successes. The vampires will never stop multiplying, the threat will never be recognized on any large scale, and they will never be contained, derailing the familiar and heroic vampire-hunter narrative.

The vampire mythos is further complicated in the *Dark Tower* series in the engagement of vampires—particularly the lower order of Type Twos and Type Threes—as part of the larger, monstrous army in service to the Crimson King. Where vampires are the central and singular threat in most vampire narratives, including *'Salem's Lot*, in the *Dark Tower* series they are situated alongside low men and *taheen*, one horror among a host of others. When Callahan and his friends are lured to the Detroit high-rise from which Callahan jumps to his death, he is met by both low men and Type Three vampires, and when Callahan and Jake enter the Dixie Pig, they face low men, *taheen*, and a range of vampires, including Grandfathers, who are immune to the talismans that keep their lesser brethren at bay, once again dismantling the "one size fits all" approach to vampire-hunting and as a result, calling into question all of the rights, rituals, and symbols that are supposed to ensure safety, in an evocative echo of Callahan's own personal, spiritual journey from Jerusalem's Lot to Calla Bryn Sturgis and beyond.

While Callahan is the undisputed expert on vampires, Roland has come across these creatures earlier in his travels as well, in an encounter King describes in the long *Dark Tower* story "The Little Sisters of Eluria," first published as part of Robert Silverberg's *Legends* (1998) anthology and later reprinted in King's short fiction collection *Everything's Eventual* (2002). In terms of timeline, Roland's encounter with the Little Sisters is situated after he has lost Susan Delgado in Mejis (a story told in

Wizard and Glass), after his loss of his *ka-tet* at Jericho Hill, and before he begins his pursuit of the Man in Black that opens *The Gunslinger*. Traveling alone, Roland is attacked by a band of slow mutants and wakes to find himself in some sort of medical tent being tended by mysterious women wearing white habits, which also connects Roland's world to that of *The Talisman* and *Black House*, as this "ancient hospital with vampire nurses is the link between the worlds of Roland the Gunslinger and Jack Sawyer's Territories" (Strengell 52). Roland is unsettled by the women, who cast a glamour to appear younger and more human, though his first impression of their "antique crones' faces ... [with] skin as gray and runneled as droughted earth" (King, "Little Sisters" 194) is the true one. Surreptitiously watching them tend to his fellow patients, Roland soon learns that the sisters are vampires of a different sort, "a tribe of blood- and semen-drinking wraiths that wandered the land posing as a religious sect of healers" (Furth 188), moving on when their food supply runs low or suspicions are raised. The "little doctors" who assist them in their work, an army of insects that crawl upon and feed on patients' wounded bodies and aid in healing, are an extension of the sisters' own monstrous nature. Sister Jenna, who commands the little doctors and yearns for her lost humanity, sets the doctors on a fellow sister, proclaiming that "she's a part of their medicine, now" (King, "Little Sisters" 241), as the other woman is consumed by the little doctors' collective self. Jenna suffers a similar fate when she attempts to leave the sisterhood to which she is sworn, as Roland wakes to an anguished scream in the early morning to find Jenna's clothes empty, her body gone, and a flock of the insects in her place, who "began to sing, and to Roland it sounded as if they were singing his name" (King, "Little Sisters" 251). Though "The Little Sisters of Eluria" is a brief vignette in the larger epic of the *Dark Tower* series and one Roland endures alone, the characteristics explored in this story—consumption of multiple bodily fluids, the symbiotic relationship between the sisters and the insects, Jenna's stubborn humanity, and the wages of rebellion and desertion—add yet another dimension to the monstrous figure of the vampire and its engagement throughout the *Dark Tower* series and King's larger canon.

'Salem's Lot in Mid-World

In the later books of the *Dark Tower* series, the lines between the real and fictional worlds become porous, as they grow increasingly intertwined and begin to leak into and directly influence one another. Stephen King as author becomes a character in his own books and the real-life occurrences of King's own life—including when King was struck by a van and nearly killed on June 19, 1999[3]—become narrative moments in which Roland, his companions, and his quest have a direct impact on King's life and survival as explored within the world of the *Dark Tower* series.

One example of this bleeding between the two worlds and the collision of fiction and reality is the appearance of King's novel *'Salem's Lot* as a textual artifact and work of fiction discovered within the *Dark Tower* universe, where Callahan encounters his own life and experiences as though they were those of a fictional character, in a novel written "in a universe where the town of 'Salem's Lot no longer exists on any map" (Vincent, *The Road to the Dark Tower* 250). The appearance of the novel in the *ka-tet*'s world poses an existential crisis for Callahan, who proclaims with decreasing certainty, "I *can't* be in a book.... I am *not* a fiction ... am I?" (King, *Wolves of the Calla* 709, emphasis original). The possibility that he might be a fictional character in someone else's story has an impact on the way he interprets his experiences as he is living them going forward as well, as he later "wondered if everyone in this damned story had the touch but him" (King, *Song of Susannah* 22), before once again rejecting the notion of his life as a story, a narrative controlled by someone else within which he is little more than a construction. Once he sees himself described on the pages of King's *'Salem's Lot*—including his innermost thoughts and secrets—it is impossible for Callahan to see himself, his life, or the world(s) in which he lives the same way again. While this discovery is an unpleasant and disorienting one for Callahan, Furth argues that it may have a very tangible effect on the story moving forward, turning the narrative in a direction it might otherwise not have taken, as "it is quite possible that rereading his own story reinforces Callahan's decision not to give in to doubt again" (41). His failure in Jerusalem's Lot is never far from his mind, so it isn't that Callahan needs reminded of it as he goes to face another challenge, but in reading about himself from the perspective of an external, omniscient narrator, Callahan gains a new perspective and a distance from his personal experiences that he has been heretofore unable to achieve on his own. As a result, when he faces the vampires, low men, and other monsters in the Dixie Pig, he is not only able to remember his subjective experience and the attendant emotions of his confrontation with Barlow, but is also able to draw thematic comparisons between these two conflicts and see his own role within the larger "narrative," whether he privileges that particular paradigm or not. It is not only his fate and his faith at stake, but Roland's quest for the Tower, Jake and Oy's survival, and the driving force of the *ka-tet* as a whole. In that realization,

Callahan is not alone as he uses his final actions to save Jake and Oy, as well as channel and salute Roland. Where Callahan was isolated, both personally and spiritually, when he stood against Barlow, in the Dixie Pig he is powerfully connected to his friends and a part of their larger purpose, and though Callahan dies, he is also victorious.

In addition to the recurrence of several of King's works throughout the *Dark Tower* series, including *'Salem's Lot*, King himself appears as a character in the final books of the *Dark Tower* series, an authorial intrusion that is unsettling to some readers. As Furth explains, "When King enters his own stories and his characters are shown to be just characters, it breaks the spell.... Given the world we are expected to live in, where fact is supposed to be fact and fiction is supposed to be fiction ... the events that take place in the final two books of the Dark Tower cycle are bound to confound us" (5). However, in doing so, King is entering into the liminal space so central to the horror genre with a dynamic and explosive force, not just interrogating the porous line between the real and the fantastic, the natural and the supernatural, but actually *occupying* it. The reader is also implicated in this disintegration of the barriers between fiction and reality, which may account for some of the critical responses to King's appearance in his own work, since once those previously reliable boundaries "disappear, then we can free-fall into *todash* space, that no-place between worlds where monsters lurk" (Furth 5). King's choice to insert himself into his fiction also highlights the creative drive, the imaginative construction of worlds, and the intimate relationship between an author and his characters. As Furth explains, authors "may give birth to our characters, but our characters also change us" (5). King created Callahan in *'Salem's Lot* but left Callahan's story unfinished, making *Wolves of the Calla*, in part, "the sequel to *'Salem's Lot* that King sometimes said he'd like to write" (Vincent, *The Dark Tower Companion* 94). Similarly, King created Roland and his *ka-tet*, giving them a life, story, and purpose, but when King's life hung in the balance on the side of the road following his accident as it is imagined and represented in *The Dark Tower*, one of his own characters does the same for him, giving him a reason to live and demanding that he finish their story, with Roland telling King that "you'll live, and when you can write again, you'll listen for the Song of the Turtle, Ves'-Ka Gan, as you did before.... And this time you'll sing until the song is done" (King, *The Dark Tower* 458). Given this intimate interconnection between creator and created, it is unsurprising that King echoes through his own works, just as those texts reverberate through the world of the Dark Tower series.

7

The Stand and The Eyes of the Dragon

King is particularly well-known for writing horror, as evident in his negotiation of vampire mythology in *'Salem's Lot*. However, just as he has drawn on a wide variety of genre traditions in crafting the *Dark Tower* series, his oeuvre expands well beyond the horror genre, including poetry, fantasy, science fiction, and the detective stories of *The Colorado Kid*[1] and the *Bill Hodges* trilogy (*Mr. Mercedes, Finders Keepers* [2015], and *End of Watch* [2016]). Two *Dark Tower*-related novels in which King engages genre traditions well outside the realm of horror are *The Stand* and *The Eyes of the Dragon*. While there are decidedly horrific elements in both books—particularly in the description of the effects of Captain Trips[2] and its terrifying plausibility in *The Stand*— these elements are combined with other rich genre traditions and narrative formulas. Michael Collings argues that the genre of *The Stand* is "all-inclusive," as "King builds on the literature of quest-epic, apocalypse, [and] high fantasy" ("The Stand" 139). Similarly, *The Eyes of the Dragon* follows fantasy and fairy tale patterns, with "the atmosphere of a made-up bedtime story" (Tritel), written for an audience of children and young adults. As Barbara Tritel explains of these conventions, "from the book's first words—'Once in a kingdom called Delain'—we know that we must suspend our disbelief just as completely as if we were listening to a tale by Anderson or Grimm." In these novels' intersections with the *Dark Tower* series, their diverse genre traditions are highlighted and employed in carrying forth the narrative of Roland's quest, underscoring both King's genre hybridity and the interconnection of the *Dark Tower* series with his larger body of work.

The Stand in particular showcases a range of literary characteristics that are also central to the *Dark Tower* series. First of all, the sheer scope of *The Stand* prefigures the enormous context of and multiple

7. The Stand *and* The Eyes of the Dragon

storylines occurring within the *Dark Tower* series. *The Stand* is epic, in both its narrative and its size, with the uncut trade paperback edition running over 1,100 pages. *The Stand* includes several characteristics of the epic tradition evident in the *Dark Tower* series as well, including its vast scope, representative heroes, the central role of the quest and its required journey, and the interconnection of human concerns and supernatural forces. Conversely, while the scale of the Captain Trips virus and the resulting good and evil showdown are massive, in *The Stand*, King also demonstrates his incredible ability to bring minor characters into sharp relief with just a few key details, populating the novel with a core cast of individuals on each side, but surrounding them with dozens of peripheral but still richly-textured characters. As Edwin F. Casebeer writes, "One of [King's] true talents is the sketch: he is able to populate novels like *'Salem's Lot, The Stand,* and *The Tommyknockers* with hundreds of briefly executed, vivid characters—each efficiently caught in a telling and representative moment that is often grotesque and generally memorable" (45). For example, in Chapter 38 of *The Stand*, King presents a series of vignettes of the non-flu-related deaths of a range of characters who pass into and out of the narrative over the space of a few paragraphs—or in some cases, a few lines—providing the broadstrokes of characterization, emotion, and meaning in their brief appearances. There is five-year-old Sam Tauber, who falls down a dry well; Irma Fayette, who dies when the ancient gun she is using to protect herself explodes in her hands; and Eileen Drummond, who passes out drunk with a cigarette and burns down most of Clewiston, Florida (King, *The Stand* 339–43). In these brief glimpses, King invests these characters with identity, fear, and pain, highlighting the human scope and countless horrors that are occurring alongside of or under the larger dominant narrative of the superflu. Over the course of the eight-book *Dark Tower* series, King's Constant Readers are introduced to an enormous cast of characters, both friend and foe, along Roland's path toward the Dark Tower. From Allie in Tull and the man Brown in the Mohaine Desert of *The Gunslinger* to *Insomnia*'s Patrick Danville, who is rediscovered and freed in *The Dark Tower*, from the allies of Roland's *ka-tet* to the emissaries of the Crimson King who would thwart them at all costs, these individual characters and interactions remind Roland, his *ka-tet*, and the reader that while the gunslinger's quest for the Dark Tower is macrocosmic in scope, it has repercussions for every single person whose path he crosses, in all of the interconnected worlds. These characters serve not just as a narrative impetus or personification of conflict, but a reminder that Roland's quest is not all-consuming: the good and bad deeds, the struggles and victories, and the daily lives of individual people carry great import of their own, and while some of these may directly impact the Dark Tower and Roland's quest, they are also significant in and of themselves, in their very assertion of the importance of humanity and the lives of one's fellow men. Characters who pass in and out of the narrative may be gone, but are not forgotten, as demonstrated by Roland's calling of a litany of their names as he stands before the Dark Tower at the series' end (King, *The Dark Tower* 801–2).

In *The Eyes of the Dragon*, King employs a stylistic technique that is integral to the *Dark Tower* series as well, in the novel's direct-address storytelling approach. In *The Eyes of the Dragon*, King takes on "the mantle of the elder and oral narrator" (Badley 171), drawing on fairy tale narrative traditions. As Collings explains, "In a narrative voice that suggests the lyricism and deceptively simple-seeming power of folk epic and the oral traditions of storytelling, he weaves a tale originally designed for a listening audience" ("The Eyes of the Dragon" 239). While much of the *Dark Tower* series maintains a traditional third-person omniscient narrative perspective, there are occasional moments when the authorial narrator makes himself known, directly addressing the reader. For example, in *The Dark Tower*, as Roland and his friends go into what will be their final battle as *ka-tet*, King says "I'd have you see them like this; I'd have you see them very well. Will you?" (383). King also punctuates the *Dark Tower* series with specific direct-address patterns, asking the reader "*do you not kennit*" (King, *The Dark Tower* 439, emphasis original), instructing readers that "you must mark" specific details (King, *The Dark Tower* 777), expressing gratefulness with "say thankya" (King, *The Dark Tower* 813), and offering apologies or regret with "Say sorry" (King, *The Dark Tower* 383). While the audiences are different, with *The Eyes of the Dragon* conceived as a story for children and young adults and the *Dark Tower* series for adult readers, this engaging and intimate approach to storytelling resonates and casts a spell, inviting King's readers to put aside the everyday, enter the imaginative world, and take in a story.

In addition to these considerations of genre and literary style, there are two particularly important connections between these novels and King's *Dark Tower* series. First, the character of Randall Flagg[3] is central to and connects *The Stand*, *The Eyes of the Dragon*, and the *Dark Tower* series. He goes by many names and takes on many forms, but his abilities and his penchant for mayhem and destruction are common characteristics between these novels. And second, there are significant overlaps and intersections between the worlds of these novels, such as mention of *Eyes*' kingdoms of Garlan and Delain in the *Dark Tower* series, Roland's *ka-tet*'s glimpse of the aftermath of Captain Trips

7. The Stand *and* The Eyes of the Dragon

in *Wizard and Glass*, and the crossing of Roland's path with that of Thomas and Dennis, the two young men who set out to pursue Flagg at the end of *The Eyes of the Dragon*.

Flagg

Randall Flagg is an ageless evil, able to jump from one world to the next to continue his campaign of destruction. As Winter argues, Flagg is "the epitome of the Gothic villain: his appearance is indistinct, malleable, a collection of masks" (60). He has lived for at least fifteen hundred years (King, *The Dark Tower* 186) and has appeared in a variety of different forms under countless names, including Marten Broadcloak, Walter o' Dim, Walter Padick, Richard Fannin, the Man in Black, the Dark Man, and the Walkin' Dude, among others.[4] He is ultimately unnamable and uncontainable: in *The Stand*, Mother Abagail reflects that "He [has] no name" (King 641), while Glen Bateman gives him a full roll call of names drawn from mythological and cosmic horrors, saying, "Call him Beelzebub, because that's his name too. Call him Nyarlahotep and Ahaz and Astaroth. Call him R'yelah and Seti and Anubis. His name is legion and he's an apostate of hell" (King 1050).[5] He is Marten Broadcloak, the wizard of Roland's father and lover of his mother, spurring Roland to an early test of manhood in *The Gunslinger*. He is a court wizard named Flagg who kills a king and frames a prince in *The Eyes of the Dragon*, and the ringleader of chaos in the aftermath of the superflu in *The Stand*, drawing the disenfranchised to him in an army of death and destruction. He seems to be everywhere and nowhere, and just when he might be defeated, he has a remarkable ability to simply disappear, showing up somewhere else with a new name, a different face, and the same evil intent.

While Flagg first appears in King's fiction in *The Stand*, King had Flagg on his mind long before this. As King explains, "Randall Flagg came to me when I wrote a poem called 'The Dark Man' when I was a junior or senior in college. It came to me out of nowhere, this guy in cowboy boots who moved around on the roads, mostly hitchhiking, at night, always wore jeans and a denim jacket" (qtd. in Wood 12).[6] This poem is a descriptive account of the Dark Man's journeys along railroad tracks, through swamps, down the highways, and through the fields of America. The Dark Man remains largely out of sight, seen from the corner of one's eye, briefly glimpsed and then forgotten, with the exception of those he preys upon, like a young girl who he rapes, kills, and leaves in a desolate field as "a savage sacrifice" (King, *The Dark Man* 74). This brief sketch formed the foundation for Flagg, whose evil walks through Gilead, Delain, and the America of *The Stand*, among other wheres and whens.

In *The Stand*, the survivors gravitate around two key figures in the aftermath of Captain Trips, setting up an epic good versus evil showdown: those who go to Mother Abagail in Hemingford Home, Nebraska, and later Boulder, Colorado, and Flagg's faction, which congregates in Las Vegas. In his first appearance in *The Stand*, with the nation on the brink of the Captain Trips epidemic, Flagg is walking down the highway, as "he knew where the roads went, and he walked them at night" (King, *The Stand* 171), much like the "dark man" in King's original poem and reminiscent of the secret highways Donald Callahan and Jack Sawyer travel, an indication of the roads' simultaneous wonder and danger. As King outlines Flagg's history, it becomes apparent that he is a nucleus for all manner of mischief and violence, a destructive force who often leaves the actual destroying of things up to those he gathers around him. Flagg writes the speeches of agitators, fueling hate and driving action, though he himself "never spoke at rallies because the microphones would scream with hysterical feedback and circuits would blow" (King, *The Stand* 175). In the apocalyptic wasteland America becomes following Captain Trips, Flagg begins to do much the same. He appears to survivors in their dreams and their nightmares, calling some to his side and working to terrify those who would stand against him. While some of these survivors who gravitate toward Flagg have violent criminal pasts, like Lloyd Henreid, others are simply outsiders, those who have existed at the fringes of society, the abused, lonely, and rejected. Flagg draws a crowd, in part because as James Smythe argues, he "has an advantage: evil is inherently stronger. It's easier" ("The Stand"). While the Free Zone community that has coalesced around Mother Abagail works and worries, rebuilding civilization from the ground up, in Flagg's Las Vegas, the lights are on, food is plentiful, and the living is easy (or at least easier). Flagg offers survivors a path of least resistance and after losing all order, certainty, or chain of command on which people can rely, the authority he wields offers reassurance. To those who serve him truly and well, Flagg gives their wildest dreams, tapping into Harold Lauder's sexual desires and sense of his own unappreciated greatness and promising the arsonist Trashcan Man "a Great Burning" (King, *The Stand* 566), ensuring their allegiance through the fulfillment of their darkest desires as Flagg "brings out everything awful in those susceptible to him" (Smythe, "The Stand").

Flagg is a terrifying and powerful adversary: he can levitate and create "a blue ball of fire" (King, *The Stand* 1067) with his fingertips. He magically opens Lloyd's cell door and he promises Nick Andros that he can give him the ability to hear and speak, if Nick will just capitulate to the Dark Man's will and swear his allegiance (King, *The Stand* 361). Flagg can command the weasels and the wolves, who take on "the eyes of their Master" (King, *The Stand* 602), like Dracula before him. Similar to Tolkien's Eye of Sauron, Flagg can send his eye out to spy on his followers and enemies alike, and he seems able to see and know all, an ability which Joseph Reino traces back to "the cosmology of Heliopolis in ancient Egypt" and Atum's "single eye, known as 'Wedjet'—representing the Egyptian Mother Goddess in her destructive aspect" (59). Flagg can transform into a crow to aid him in this surveillance, as Bobby Terry finds to his horror when botches the Dark Man's assignment, hearing the rush of bootheels on the road and turning just in time to see Flagg coming "like some terrible horror monster out of the scariest picture ever made ... [with] shiny black crowfeathers fluttering from his hair" (King, *The Stand* 929–30). Flagg's power and his capacity for violence terrify both his followers and his enemies. However, Flagg proves to be quite fallible in the end. As James Egan explains in "Apocalypticism in the Fiction of Stephen King," "Flagg is far from omnipotent. His evil has a half-life; he cannot create, but only destroy" (220). In *The Stand*, he is brought down by Trashcan Man, one of his mad followers, who brings Flagg a nuclear gift, leaving his master frozen in "a terror of the unknown and the unexpected" (King, *The Stand* 1068) in the moments before this dark gift is seemingly detonated by the Hand of God himself. But even before this, Flagg's followers have begun to doubt and desert him, his powers of levitation begin to wane, and he is driven to near-madness when Glen Bateman laughs at him, taunting Flagg to "touch me with your finger and stop my heart. Make the sign of the inverted cross and give me a massive brain embolism. Bring down the lightning from the overhead socket to cleave me in two" (King, *The Stand* 1056) before dissolving once more in laughter at Flagg's inability to act. In addition to the limited nature of his power, Flagg is revealed to be the pawn of a much larger evil, without even full knowledge of himself. When he tells Nadine Cross that she had been promised to him as his bride and she asks by whom, he tells her, "I have forgotten" (King, *The Stand* 974). Bits of his own history are hazy to him, though he remembers other lives, that "he had been born when times changed, and the times were going to change again" (King, *The Stand* 176). As he disappears moments before the nuclear explosion, those watching glimpse "something slumped and hunched and almost without shape—something with enormous yellow eyes slit by dark cat's pupils" (King, *The Stand* 1072). Flagg is reborn once again in the novel's coda, initially uncertain of his identity before his knowledge of his mission returns to him once more. In this continuation, Flagg "is bigger than the novel, than the world that's collapsed and torn itself apart" (Smythe, "The Stand"). As the reborn world begins moving on at the conclusion of *The Stand*, Flagg has been temporarily stopped, driven away but not defeated, free to wreak his havoc throughout the larger landscape of King's fiction.

Flagg next appears in *The Eyes of the Dragon*, as a wicked magician and advisor to Delain's King Roland, poisoning the King and pinning the murder on Roland's eldest son, Peter. In this novel, Flagg is "an evil enchanter ... capable of casting spells, versed in the ways of poisons, and proficient in the art of making himself almost invisible" (Strengell 151), or as he calls it, "*dim*" (King, *The Eyes of the Dragon* 77, emphasis original). Here, as in *The Stand*, Flagg's presence in Delain is but one of the many lives he has lived there, and "he came under a different name each time, but always with the same load of woe and misery and death" (King, *The Eyes of the Dragon* 61). He is again able to summon blue fire with his hands and appears in others' dreams, or more aptly, in their nightmares. Another similarity in Flagg's characterization between *The Stand* and *The Eyes of the Dragon* is that he is never the public face of power, but rather a malignant influence in the shadows. Whether as a magician, executioner, or confidante of the monarch, Flagg comes, wreaks destruction, and then takes his leave until "when the rebuilding was complete and there was again something worth destroying, Flagg would appear once more" (King, *The Eyes of the Dragon* 63). As Peter learns from the note left behind by another wrongfully convicted prisoner, Flagg has been sowing discord and destruction in Delain for at least four hundred years (King, *The Eyes of the Dragon* 234), though Flagg's appearance remains unaltered and unaged, a characteristic similarly shared by another of Flagg's embodiments as the Covenant Man in the *Dark Tower* novel *The Wind Through the Keyhole* (King 141). Just as with those who come to gather around him in Las Vegas in *The Stand*, Flagg preys on the weaknesses and desires of those he would ally to himself, buying young Thomas's silence and complicity with a sympathetic ear, unfettered and secret access to spy on King Roland, and Flagg's support of Thomas, rather than the far more popular Peter, as the King of Delain. Thomas is weak and desperate for approval, though King's narrator argues that "he was not a really bad boy" (King, *The Eyes of the Dragon* 54). Flagg meticulously plans King Roland's murder and Peter's imprisonment, paying great attention to detail and casting suspicion and resentment wherever it might serve most useful. However, as before, Flagg is not omnipotent: though his own dreams and his magic crystal alert him to Peter's impending escape, this knowledge comes too late for him to do anything to prevent it. As always, Flagg is thwarted by a better and greater power than his own: in this case, Peter's ingenuity, the loyalty of his friends, and the love of his brother Thomas. Just as at the end of *The Stand*, in *The Eyes of the Dragon* Flagg disappears before he can be truly defeated, though Thomas manages to injure him with an arrow through the eye, which drips with "some stinking black fluid ... most assuredly not blood" (King, *The Eyes of the Dragon* 375). In both novels, Flagg's departure is so rapid and complete that his clothes are left standing on their own for a moment (King, *The Stand* 1072; *Eyes of the Dragon* 375), and in both, this horror was just a single stop in Flagg's long, destructive journey.

Flagg bears many of these same powers and characteristics in his appearances throughout the *Dark Tower* series: he first appears as Marten Broadcloak, a Gilead palace wizard and advisor to Roland's father, Steven Deschain, though Flagg/Marten's treachery here is both political and personal, working his will on Gilead and taking Gabrielle Deschain as his lover, splintering Roland's family with this personal betrayal as well. Marten's manipulation of and Roland's horror at discovering his mother's infidelity have far-reaching repercussions. Roland is driven by his rage into an early test of manhood, which Marten fully expects him to fail and which would lead to disgraceful exile for the young man, with no possibility of ever becoming a gunslinger. Later, when Roland and his friends return from their work in Mejis, Marten's influence continues to corrupt Gabrielle, who is enlisted in a murder attempt on her husband and Roland's father, Steven Deschain (King, *Wizard and Glass* 681). The Man in Black with whom Roland palavers at the end of *The Gunslinger* is another permutation of Flagg, as is the wretched Covenant Man, who figures as a fairy-tale villain in Roland's storytelling in *The Wind Through the Keyhole*. He was known as Walter Padick long ago (King, *The Dark Tower* 184) and has also been referred to as Walter o' Dim. He has been called Richard Fannin, Rudin Filaro (King, *The Dark Tower* 184), Russell Faraday (King, *The Stand* 1141), and by a host of other names. When Roland and his *ka-tet* encounter Flagg at the conclusion of *Wizard and Glass*, Roland recognizes him as Marten, though the wizard introduces himself as "Flagg, actually.... And we've met before" (King 674), revealing his presence and observing eye in many of the steps along Roland's path toward the Dark Tower, watching Roland on the battlefield of Jericho Hill, in Mejis, and in the Mohaine Desert (King, *The Dark Tower* 174–5). Flagg has served as an organizer, manipulating evil from behind the scenes and in *The Dark Tower*, his own history and allegiances are chronicled and considered (*The Dark Tower* 174). Flagg has switched sides and served different masters in the course of his long and duplicitous life, though while he has often been the figurehead of evil in individual showdowns—in the America of *The Stand* and the Delain of *The Eyes of the Dragon*, for instance—he has always served a master and never been the most powerful evil in the fight at any given moment, a revelation that reframes Flagg's role and function throughout King's canon. The limitations of Flagg's powers and the ultimate use to which the Crimson King puts him are best revealed in his guardianship of baby Mordred, who Flagg plans to kill after using Mordred to destroy Roland (King, *The Dark Tower* 181). However, Mordred quickly and efficiently inserts himself into Flagg's mind, taking control of him, and dining on Flagg's eyes and tongue, before moving on to devour Flagg completely (King, *The Dark Tower* 182–6).

One particular element of *The Eyes of the Dragon* that is notable in the characterization of Flagg is, as Smythe notes, the storytelling format and "narrative point of view ... [which allows] us inside Flagg's head in a way that we are not permitted in his other appearances, and we see him as nearly human, confused and flawed, with just the beginnings of his malignant evil" ("The Eyes of the Dragon"). Flagg at first only has a vague sense of something amiss, not sensing Peter's escape, desperately wracking his brain in a near-panic as he paces the floor of his room, reaching for knowledge which remains just outside his grasp as he asks, "*How? When? Who helped? ... I have to know!*" (King, *The Eyes of the Dragon* 338, emphasis original). In his final appearance in *The Dark Tower*, Flagg's internal horror and fallibility are once again central to the narrative perspective. This brief glimpse into Flagg's backstory and the long journey that brought him to this point also foreground his own history of trauma and abuse, with McAleer noting that with this new knowledge, "speculations arise as to whether or not Flagg's actions are truly those of purely evil intention or those which stem from a victimized mindset that seeks a sense of equilibrium to counterbalance the atrocity he endured" (109). Following Flagg's brief reflection on his own personal history and the havoc he has wreaked throughout Mid-World and beyond, he comes face-to-face with his own overestimation of his abilities in dealing with Mordred, realizing too late that "he'd underestimated the little monster, relying too much on what it looked like and not enough on his own knowledge of what it *was*" (King, *The Dark Tower* 182, emphasis original). This is Flagg's last, fatal mistake, proving him both fallible and expendable in the large-scale conflict that surrounds the Dark Tower. While King's readers have long been familiar with and horrified by Flagg's actions in all of his many forms, in these final moments, King gives them insight into the awareness and horror of Flagg's coming death, his struggle, surrender, and suffering, achieving an intimate understanding of, if not potential empathy with, this villain who has stalked King's universe for decades.

Intersecting Worlds

In addition to Flagg's wandering the worlds of *The Stand*, *The Eyes of the Dragon*, and the *Dark Tower* series in his many names and guises, these worlds themselves also intersect in significant ways. In *Wizard and Glass*, Roland's *ka-tet* learns of *The Stand*'s Captain Trips, the superflu that decimated the human race. As they move through the now-abandoned Topeka, they see newspaper headlines chronicling the rise of the superflu, as well as graffitied messages that read "Watch for the Walkin Dude" and "All Hail the Crimson King," along with the drawn eye that serves as the Crimson King's sigul (King, *Wizard and Glass* 95). When Susannah asks Roland if any of this is familiar to him, "he shook his head, but he looked troubled, and that introspective look never left his eyes" (*ibid.*). While some things—like Topeka itself and its location in Kansas—are recognizable to Eddie, Susannah, and Jake, other details distinguish it as a world not quite the same as the ones from which they were drawn. Many of the abandoned cars are of familiar makes and models, but there are also Takuro Spirits (King, *Wizard and Glass* 88); Nozz-A-La is the soda of choice (King, *Wizard and Glass* 688) and the Kansas City baseball team is called the Monarchs, rather than the Royals or the Athletics (King, *Wizard and Glass* 88). Roland's *ka-tet* have stumbled into the realm of the uncanny, where what they see and the world through which they move are simultaneously familiar, yet alien. This approach is part of what makes *The Stand* so effectively unsettling as well. As Keith Phipps argues, the world of *The Stand* is horrifying in its familiarity, as King "recreates the world as we know it—either today or in the recent past—which makes disruptions to that world that much more terrifying." In the same way, this postapocalyptic Topeka is similar to Eddie, Susannah, and Jake's worlds, but is not of those worlds themselves. This destruction has occurred on another level of the Dark Tower, in another version of the American reality, but that does not make its horrors any less jarring for these three. Paquette argues that "readers may mourn the loss of America in *The Stand*, but they realize anew just how awful such a thing could be when they see Jake, Susannah, and Eddie try to rationalize how it couldn't be 'their' America that has been lost" (145). While *The Stand* chronicles Captain Trips and its aftermath through the eyes of its survivors, the presence of the superflu in *Wizard and Glass* takes a step back, situating this tragedy within

King's larger macroverse, a horror that came to pass in one world but was avoided in countless others.

However, just because the same fate hasn't befallen these other worlds, that doesn't mean it couldn't, because another salient characteristic shared between these worlds is the use and abuse of technology. As Egan writes, from the engineering of the superflu itself to the news coverage that chronicles it, the martial power used to suppress resistance, and the survivors' struggle to adapt to an off-the-grid society, in *The Stand*, "technology becomes synonymous with iniquity ... for technology creates a weapon it cannot control" ("Apocalypticism" 221). The Captain Trips virus exists because scientists created it, and it escaped due to the failure of a series of technology-reliant security measures. While these technologies were temporarily taken off-line with civilization's collapse, they still exist and remain usable to those who can learn and would dare to do so. There are still nuclear bombs, such as the one that the Trashcan Man brings back to Las Vegas, and there are still engineered super-viruses in labs across the country. These destructive tools are all just "lying around, waiting to be picked up" (King, *The Stand* 334). Similarly, Roland's world has a strong technological influence, though its heyday was generations ago. Despite the fact that "the world has moved on," there are still monorails, dogans, robots, and weapons scattered around Mid-World, waiting to be of use once more, to be called back to their full, destructive power. Roland's world even has its own technologically-mad Tick-Tock Man, echoing *The Stand*'s Trashcan Man. Just as the Trashcan Man wanders into the deserts surrounding Las Vegas and returns bearing deadly gifts for Flagg, the Tick-Tock Man is obsessed with Lud's computers and the destructive potential of which they are capable (King, *The Waste Lands* 516). Also like the Trashcan Man, the Tick-Tock Man finds his life saved by Flagg (here calling himself Richard Fannin), who requires the familiar oath of "My life for you" (King, *The Waste Lands* 547). While in each case, the weapons are dangerous enough on their own, in the hands of madmen they become even more volatile, unpredictable, and capable of tremendous violence at a moment's notice, with no warning or reason. While the Topeka ravaged by the Captain Trips virus is not that of Eddie, Susannah, or Jake's worlds, the power and abuse of their worlds' technologies means that it very well could have been, that a disaster such of this was only narrowly averted, or is perhaps waiting just around the corner.

Just as the *Dark Tower* universe frequently overlaps with different versions of Eddie, Susannah, and Jake's own worlds, there are direct connections between Roland's world and the kingdom of Delain, the setting of *The Eyes of the Dragon*. Delain is located in Mid-World's Eastar'd Barony (Furth 215) and Roland meets residents of Delain along his journey, including John Norman in "Little Sisters of Eluria" and *The Eyes of the Dragon*'s Thomas and Dennis, in the midst of their pursuit of Flagg (King, *The Drawing of the Three* 418). Roland is familiar with the stories of Delain, including a dragon that "had been slain by another king, one who was later murdered" (King, *Song of Susannah* 197), recounting the broad strokes of King Roland's hunt of Niner. In addition, as Winter explains, "*The Eyes of the Dragon* is set in the Territories, the parallel world of *The Talisman*—that mythical, medieval land of kings and queens, two-headed parrots, and magic—although it occurs in a different place and time than Jack Sawyer's quest" (168). The medieval cast of *The Eyes of the Dragon* is reflected in Roland's boyhood memories of Gilead, including the castles, courtly structure, and formal mannerisms. In *The Eyes of the Dragon*, Flagg has a two-headed parrot, much like the one Jack sees in *The Talisman* in a marketplace while traveling through the Territories, though Flagg's parrot is of a darker cast, screaming of "*Death!*" and "*Murder!*" (King, *The Eyes of the Dragon* 69, emphasis original) rather than cracking jokes. This overlapping geography spatially brings together the *Dark Tower* series with *The Eyes of the Dragon*, *The Talisman*, and *Black House*. Artifacts and familiar narratives pass between these worlds, including the telepathy-blocking "thinking cap" from *Black House* (King, *The Dark Tower* 183) that Flagg unsuccessfully attempts to use to protect his thoughts from Mordred and fight against the creature's mind control.

While technology is the uniting destructive factor between the worlds of *The Stand* and the *Dark Tower* universe, Roland is familiar with the poisons of the neighboring kingdoms, such as the dragon sand Flagg uses to murder Delain's King Roland in *The Eyes of the Dragon*, which burns the king from the inside out. As Roland recounts the attempt on his father's life in *Wizard and Glass*, he describes a poison that came from the Barony of Garlan, "so strong even the tiniest cut would cause almost instant death" (King 645). While the technological threat connects the world of the *Dark Tower* series significantly with that of *The Stand* and even the reader's own contemporary world, the threat of these mysterious poisons in *The Eyes of the Dragon* and beyond situate Roland's world—and its various interconnections and overlappings—more firmly within the context of the fantasy genre, the world of "once upon a time" and "there once as a king" that invites readers into the Secondary World of fantasy and the imaginative domain of fairy tales for a story, rather than playing on the sense of the uncanny that engages the familiar world with an unsettling twist. In combining the technological horrors of *The Stand* with the mystical poisons of *The Eyes of the Dragon*, and incorporating both into Roland's Mid-World, King underscores the genre hybridity and various influences that are engaged by the *Dark Tower* series, each with their own unique wonders and horrors.

8

Insomnia

Insomnia focuses on characters who are in many ways marginalized, unseen, or forgotten,[1] tracing the lives and intrigues of what Ralph Roberts sardonically refers to as Derry's "Old Crocks" (King, *Insomnia* 13). Much like *IT* and the experiences of children at its core, *Insomnia* not only gives voice to its marginalized characters, but privileges their perspectives, complete with the uncertainty about what is objectively real and what may be written off as imagination or hallucination. Ralph Roberts, the central protagonist of *Insomnia*, even regularly doubts himself: the more sleep deprived he becomes, the more prone he is to seeing things that aren't "there," realities he struggles to come to terms with until he can deny them no longer. However, as Collings notes, Ralph's insomnia and its revelations are accompanied by "the concomitant discovery that he is *not* insane, that his insomnia has a larger purpose beyond anything he can truly comprehend, and that he and his newfound love, Lois Chasse, have been involved in actions on the cosmic scale approached in *It* and *The Talisman*" ("Insomnia" 325, emphasis original). Like the children in *IT*, Ralph and Lois see things no one else sees and are aware of the danger facing Derry long before anyone else has begun to pick up on the signs.

King's *Insomnia* is a novel that blurs the distinctions between boundaries and whose action frequently occurs in the liminal spaces that straddle multiple worlds and ways of seeing. As John Sears explains, "*Insomnia* constructs a space in which intersections between the real and the unreal, waking and sleeping, night and day, youth and age, afford flows and unblockings of desire that redefine character relations, and return us to the question: what is it for? What can it do?" (93). While part of the horror of *Insomnia* comes from the malevolent manipulation of the Crimson King and in Ralph Roberts' showdowns with an agent of chaos named Atropos, the novel is just as firmly grounded in the horrors of domestic abuse and the fight for reproductive rights, with the clashes between the pro-life and pro-choice factions of Derry a central source of conflict, and sometimes even violence. Ralph and Lois both suffer from increasingly severe insomnia and the debilitating effects of extended sleep deprivation, but their troubles also veer into the realm of the supernatural. They begin to see things others cannot, including individualized auras around the other citizens of Derry and "little bald doctors" (King, *Insomnia* 382) in white smocks who turn up to hasten the journey of those near death, though the actions of these two beings—Clotho and Lachesis—are more benevolent and purposeful than Atropos's anarchic, destructive glee. As a result, Ralph and Lois find themselves fighting against both overwhelming supernatural evil and the all-too-human horrors of hatred and madness.

Similarly, on one hand, *Insomnia* is clearly established within King's everyday universe, set in familiar Derry, Maine, with narrative moments and details tying it back to King's other Derry-centered fictions: it is connected, for example, to *IT* in references to the flood of 1985, the sewers beneath Derry, and the Crimson King's comment to Ralph that "*shape-changing is a time-honored custom in Derry*" (King, *Insomnia* 602, emphasis original). On the other hand, *Insomnia* is squarely situated within the multiverse of the Dark Tower and "*Insomnia* asserts itself ... as a linchpin in King's quest-vision, linking itself with *The Stand*, *The Talisman*, *The Eyes of the Dragon*, and the *Dark Tower* novels as explorations of that mystic nexus of all existence whose own existence is threatened by a single action about to take place in Derry" (Collings, "Insomnia" 325). The events of *Insomnia* occur at the axis of multiple worlds and possibilities, as Ralph catches a brief glimpse of the Dark Tower, plays an integral role in the Tower's survival, and crosses paths with characters who fates are intertwined with that of the Tower, including Patrick Danville and the ultimate King antagonist, the Crimson King himself.

Finally, much like *'Salem's Lot*, *Insomnia* appears in the *Dark Tower* series as a textual artifact, a book by King that Roland comes across on his journey and which connects the two worlds. While *'Salem's Lot* accurately tells of Callahan's experiences in Jerusalem's Lot, *Insomnia* is a much more complex negotiation, with hit or miss connections, and as Roland muses in *The Dark Tower*, "it feels tricksy to me" (King 524). The Tower and Roland himself appear in *Insomnia*, as do the Crimson King and Patrick Danville, but in the case of *Insomnia*, some of the clues and information provided prove "false or incongruous" (McAleer 153). In the *Dark Tower* series, Aaron Deepneau is a friend and ally of Roland's *ka-tet*, while in *Insomnia* the major human antagonist is named Ed Deepneau, though Aaron's niece Nancy argues that the use of their family name can be productively read as simply a signal or signpost for the Tet Corporation (King, *The Dark Tower* 513). The Crimson King of *Insomnia* and the Crimson King who has ensconced himself in the Dark Tower have several characteristics that distinguish them from one another, while the prophecy made about young Patrick Danville proves problematic and is only incompletely fulfilled in *The Dark Tower*. While there are a number of overt references and connections between *Insomnia* and the *Dark Tower* series, many of them don't directly connect, coming close but falling short, raising as many questions as they provide answers.

Mythology, Freud and the Power of Three

Ralph first sees two of the "little bald doctors" (King, *Insomnia* 382) coming out of his neighbor's house in the dead of night and his first impression of them is one of unease that quickly escalates to alarm. As he and Lois get drawn further into the battle for Derry and make the acquaintance of these mysterious figures, they learn that they are called Clotho and Lachesis, along with a third rough agent of sorts, Atropos: names drawn directly from Greek mythology. Arthur Cotterell and Rachel Storm explain that these, collectively known as the Fates, are "the powers which decided what must happen to individuals.... A late idea was that the Fates spun a length of yarn which represented the allotted span for each mortal" (44). Each of the three has a particular role and significance in this collective purpose, as Clotho is "the spinner" who winds out the yarn of life, Lachesis is "the apportioner" who measures and determines the fated length, and Atropos is "the inevitable" who severs the yarn and ends the life (Cotterell and Storm 44).

Insomnia's Clotho, Lachesis, and Atropos bridge the gaps between worlds, telling Ralph and Lois that there is a distinct difference between the worlds, lives, and levels of the Tower. As Stanley Wiater, Chistopher Golden, and Hank Wagner explain, "In mapping out the forces at work in his universe, Stephen King has Clotho and Lachesis explain the four constants of existence—Life, Death, the Random, and the Purpose—and the hierarchy of short timers (normal mortals), long timers (enhanced mortals), and all timers (immortals). They also add that all are part of the same Tower of existence (to Roland, the 'Dark Tower')" (116). In addition to outlining King's cosmological structure, this explanation— and the distinction between the lives and natures of Short-Timers and Long-Timers—also echoes the traditional Greek mythology from which these Fates have been drawn, in which the concerns of humans and gods (as well as half-gods, other mythological creatures, and so on) often intersect, overlap, and influence one another. Thinking of the "little bald doctors" he had seen from his window and whom he and Lois are getting ready to encounter again in their friend's hospital room, Ralph feels a spark of recognition, putting two and two together as he tells her, "It made me think of a myth I read when I was in grade-school and couldn't get enough of gods and goddesses and Trojan Horses. The story was about three sisters—the Greek Sisters, maybe, or maybe it was the Weird Sisters.... [T]hese sisters were responsible for the course of all human life" (King, *Insomnia* 365). In this connection and in Ralph's recognition of it, King is overtly returning to what his college professor, mentor, and friend Burton Hatlen referred to as "the language-pool, the myth-pool, where we all go down to drink" (qtd. in Beahm 57). With this familiar touchstone established, King is then free to deviate from expectations, subverting the readers' sense that they know this story and the role these characters ought to serve, much as Ralph and Lois themselves experience when they see Clotho and Lachesis in action. In addition to these Fates mediating between multiple worlds, including those of Derry and the Dark Tower, they are also working at cross-purposes instead of as a united, interconnected triumvirate, as in the Greek myth. In *Insomnia*, Clothos and Lachesis are the harbingers of "good" death, ushering from life those whose natural time has come. As they stand by a man's bed, Clotho tells Ralph and Lois *"what we do, we do with love and respect ... [w]e are, in fact, the physicians of last resort"* (King, *Insomnia* 488, emphasis original). In contrast, Atropos is the avatar of senseless death, such as mayhem-style violence, freak accidents, or the death of children; he is the anarchic Random in contrast to Clotho and Lachesis' Purpose.[2] Instead of working together in a united aim, Clotho and Lachesis are at odds with Atropos, though ultimately powerless to stop him.

    This repetition of three is also significant in *The Dark Tower*, when Roland and Susannah meet a tripartite trickster figure assuming the names Feemalo, Fumalo, and Fimalo in their final approach to the Dark Tower.[3] While Clotho, Lachesis, and Atropos draw on the discourse of Greek mythology, Feemalo, Fumalo, and Fimalo engage with Freud's theory of the individual psyche as composed of the id, ego, and super-ego. As Saul McLeod explains the general components of this theory, "According to Freud's model of the psyche, the id is the primitive and instinctual part of the mind that contains sexual and aggressive drives and hidden memories, the super-ego operates as a moral conscience, and the ego is the realistic part that mediates between the desires of the id and the super-ego." Once these elements of the personality have been developed, the individual negotiates between them in his or her daily life, tempering their desires in order to make the socially acceptable choice, for example. Freud's concept of the psyche has been invoked and explored in a wide range of literature, particularly influential in horror and the Gothic, including Robert Louis Stevenson's classic novella *Dr. Jekyll and Mr. Hyde*, which continues to influence contemporary authors and is a key touchstone for the modern werewolf narrative.

Though Feemalo, Fumalo, and Fimalo are ultimately revealed to be three parts of a single magician, casting a glamour to maintain the illusion of separateness and left behind by the now un-dead Crimson King to warn off Roland and Susannah, they initially appear to be three separate and conflicting beings. As Vincent explains in *The Road to the Dark Tower*, this trickster combines Freud and the fairy tale influence— here of "Jack and the Beanstalk"—that resonates throughout the *Dark Tower* series, as "the polite one calls himself *Fee*malo, the ego. The rude one is *Fum*alo, the id, and the one behind is the superego, *Fi*malo" (176, emphasis original). These three take the form of Stephen King himself, circa 1977,[4] and palaver with Roland and Susannah: the ego offers information and explanation, the id taunts and insults them, and the superego tries to reason with Roland and Susannah and convince them to give up their quest for the Tower, while also moderating the interjections of the other two. As the superego Fimalo explains, in the larger scheme of the macrocosmic universes, Roland's goal has been effectively achieved: he has saved the Beams and by extension, the Dark Tower and all the universes it anchors. With the integrity of the Beams assured, Fimalo tells Roland that "nothing sends you further.... And you do not need to do it" (King, *The Dark Tower* 610). This may be the truth or it may be a lie planted by the Crimson King, a final attempt to get Roland to abandon his quest. Ultimately, however, the truth of Fimalo's statement is a moot point. Fimalo speaks from the "big picture" perspective of the superego, in which the grounding and impact of Roland's quest have affected multiple universes. But for Roland, this macrocosmic perspective has in many ways become inconsequential: the Tower is his Purpose and his obsession. He has come too far and lost too many to give up his quest to see and gain the Tower, even if that macrocosmic goal has been effectively achieved (and given the trickster with whom he speaks, that "if" is substantial). Feemalo, Fumalo, and Fimalo are the separated elements of personality and the psyche, but Roland is their combination: his desire to see the Tower precludes all else and he has been willing to sacrifice whatever is necessary in order to achieve it (id), his quest for the Dark Tower has been his driving motivation and sole aim for his entire adult life (ego), and he made a promise to his fallen friends and the Mid-World that was that he will not quit until he completes this quest, reaffirming the values of his world before it "moved on" (superego). In this combination, Roland and his quest transcend even the superego, who challenges Roland that "there's no prophecy of such a promise" that Roland must continue his quest, to which the gunslinger responds, "There wouldn't be. For it's one I made myself, and one I mean to keep" (King, *The Dark Tower* 610).

This separation of the psyche—and its reconciliation—is also central to the *Dark Tower* series in the figure of Susannah. When Roland first draws her into his world, she is a woman with two dramatically different and dissociative personalities: Odetta Holmes and Detta Walker. Odetta Holmes is upper-class, prim and proper, and devoted to the fight for civil rights (the superego), while Detta Walker is lower-class, crass, and violent (the id).[5] In forcing these two women to realize the existence of the other, Roland prompts a reconciliation of these identities (the ego). Near the conclusion of *The Drawing of the Three*, when a near-death Roland sees her, he asks which of her selves she is, to which she responds, "I am three women.... I who was; I who had no right to be but was; I am the woman who you have saved" (King 452). While she is no longer either Odetta or Detta, elements of each personality remain in this woman, who ultimately chooses for herself the name Susannah Dean, with the three elements fused into a single cohesive individual.

From Derry to the Dark Tower

A number of themes and characters link Derry to the Dark Tower, as evidenced in the cyclical return of evil to this small town in *IT* and Vincent's connection of Pennywise with the Crimson King (*The Road to the Dark Tower* 195).[6] These connections are even more overtly explored in *Insomnia*, which taps into the structural mythos of King's *Dark Tower* multiverse and the realities which define it. The first and most direct of these is in Ralph Roberts' glimpse of the Tower itself: "an enormous tower constructed of dark and sooty stone, standing in a field of red roses" (King, *Insomnia* 385). Ralph sees the Tower and simultaneously understands its significance, as well as the very limited nature of his comprehension of what it means and what is at stake. While some of King's "real world" characters see the Dark Tower in dreams and visions, Ralph is privy to this insight as a result of the mental projection of Clotho, as he and Lachesis draw Ralph and Lois into the almost incomprehensible conflict of which Derry is the nexus.

Clotho, Lachesis, and Atropos signify a larger and structurally-central concept of the *Dark Tower* universe: the tension and constant conflict between the Purpose and the Random. As Clotho explains to Ralph and Lois, there are four common truths that connect their world to that of the Dark Tower and *"these four constants are Life, Death, the Purpose, and the Random"* (King, *Insomnia* 393, emphasis original). Clotho draws a finer distinction in telling Ralph and Lois that at the macrocosmic level, there are things which *"might be called the Higher Purpose and the Higher Random ... or perhaps there* is *no Random beyond a certain level"* (King, *Insomnia* 405, emphasis original). As Strengell argues, through these characteristics, "in *Insomnia*, King suggests a strict cosmological determinism. If the Wheel of the Universe is in balance, good triumphs over evil, which indicates that the Wheel represents necessity or the Purpose in *Insomnia*. Both poles have their preordained destinies to fulfill, but at times the Random attempts to interfere in human events and earthly matters" (230). Clotho and Lachesis are agents of Purpose, intended to keep the trajectory of actions moving along its proper path, so that all works out as it should. The Purpose on whose behalf Clotho and Lachesis orchestrate things is not quite destiny or a predetermined outcome, but rather something akin to the *Dark Tower* universe's *ka*, which is Roland and his *ka-tet*'s driving philosophy: that what is meant to be will be and that one will succeed or fail as *ka* wills it. As Dorrance Marstellar broadly explains this concept to Ralph in *Insomnia*, "We are all bound together by the Purpose.... That's *ka-tet*, which means one made of many" (King 491, emphasis original). The Purpose works toward *ka*'s fulfillment, but there is always the Random to be contended with: the senseless, the accidental, the unexpected and disastrous. Just as Clotho and Lachesis are the agents of the Purpose in Derry, Atropos is the agent of the Random, wreaking havoc, manipulating Ed Deepneau in service of the Crimson King, and killing indiscriminately and maliciously. Ralph and Lois can see all three supernatural beings and witness the contested negotiation and tug-of-war between the Purpose and the Random, salvation and devastation. This same tension between the Purpose and the Random animates the universe of the Dark Tower, making its presence felt throughout Roland's journey, both in Mid-World and its overlapping realities, where coincidences abound and people often seem to be in just the right place at the right time.

There are several examples of the Purpose that radiate throughout the *Dark Tower* series, including the recurrence of the figures of the Turtle and the rose, as well as the existence of the Tower itself—in a multitude of forms—within and across multiple worlds. The Turtle is a cosmological being, a Guardian of the Beam, and a benevolent force for guidance and salvation in *IT*. The central significance of the

Turtle is underscored by its constant presence and repetition throughout the *Dark Tower* series, grounding far-flung and disparate worlds in the same shared sense of Purpose. In Lud, the street that coincides with path of the Beam is called The Street of the Turtle and is watched over by a stone sentinel of the Guardian (King, *The Waste Lands* 436). There is a similar statue in a New York City pocket park (King, *Song of Susannah* 57). The Turtle is a voice of creation and revelation toward the end of *Wizard and Glass*, revealing a glimpse of the future and Roland's ultimate destiny with the cry of "Light! Let there be light!" (King 596). There is a vacant lot in New York City that protects its world's version of the rose, which is an axis and point of resonance between worlds. Though a sign posted by the lot proclaims, "COMING SOON, TURTLE BAY LUXURY CONDOMINIUMS" (King, *Wolves of the Calla* 96), the lot remains undeveloped and protected, as Calvin Tower refuses to sell, guided by "the voice of the Turtle" (King, *Wolves of the Calla* 99). There are clouds shaped like turtles (King, *Wolves of the Calla* 165) and an abandoned Turtle Bay Washateria (King, *Wolves of the Calla* 434) that serves as the site of a showdown between good and evil, with unexpected heroes. A small turtle talisman has hypnotic powers (King, *Song of Susannah* 83–7) and becomes a totem of faith that gives Callahan the strength he needs to endure his final showdown with the vampires (King, *The Dark Tower* 13). A thin place between worlds in rural Maine is called Turtleback Lane (King, *Song of Susannah* 181). The figure of the Turtle is a constant presence, a signpost that Roland and his companions are on the right track or where they need to be, and it serves as an overarching symbol of the Purpose throughout these many intersecting worlds.

Similarly, the Tower itself is present in a variety of forms across the multiple universes. There is the Dark Tower itself, as it exists in both reality and in the imagination, from Roland's dreams to the drawings made by Patrick Danville in *Insomnia* and Jake Chambers in *The Waste Lands*. But it also has physical, concrete doubles in other worlds, including the Keystone version of New York City. In Keystone New York, the Dark Tower's twin is 2 Hammarskjöld Plaza, located on the lot that had originally housed and protected the rose, around which the Tet Corporation has built and dedicated a lobby garden to ensure its continued safety. As Jake first sees this rose in *The Waste Lands*, he realizes that it contains "*a sun*: a vast forge burning at the center of this rose" (King 180, emphasis original). Jake also notes voices as he looks upon the rose, raised "in a harmonic shout of triumph" (King, *The Waste Lands* 179). Irene Tassenbaum asks Roland, "Do you hear people singing? ... A chorus from somewhere?" (King, *The Dark Tower* 488) as they stand in front of 2 Hammarskjöld Plaza and the protected rose within. While the rose still holds its ethereal power, it is the building itself which shocks Roland as he realizes "it wasn't the Dark Tower, not *his* Dark Tower ... but he had no doubt that it was the Tower's representation in this Keystone World, just as the rose represented a field filled with them; the field he had seen in so many dreams" (King, *The Dark Tower* 488, emphasis original). In addition to being a touchstone between these worlds, 2 Hammerskjöld Plaza is home to the Tet Corporation, the emissaries and influence of Roland's *ka-tet* in this Keystone World.

In addition to the physical echoes of the Dark Tower, there is also a man named Calvin Tower, who is integral to the *ka-tet*'s success. Tower owns the vacant lot on which the Jake finds the rose in *The Waste Lands* and is also the owner of a used bookstore, where Jake gets his copies of *Charlie the Choo-Choo* and *Riddle-De-Dum!* Tower is a reluctant hero, though when Donald Callahan is about to be beaten to death in the abandoned Turtle Bay Washateria by a pair of neo–Nazis called the Hitler Brothers, Tower and his friend Aaron Deepneau come to the rescue, saving Callahan's life (King, *Wolves of the Calla* 438–42). An antique bookseller largely in name only, Tower often buys books then falls in love with them, unable to part with them. He even prizes his books above his own well-being, the safety of other people, or the promises he has made to them; he very nearly capitulates when Jack Andolini threatens to set Tower's rarest and most valuable books on fire if Tower doesn't agree to sell the lot to the Sombra Corporation, a Keystone World extension of the emissaries of the Crimson King (King, *Wolves of the Calla* 521–2). Tower is inconstant and unreliable: he agrees to temporarily leave New York after his encounter with Andolini but then convinces himself that it's not really necessary to do so, he is instructed to lay low and avoid detection but can't seem to help being conspicuous and noticeable, and he promises to sell the vacant lot to Roland and his *ka-tet* but goes back on his word. Tower is human and fallible; much like Roland, he is guided and controlled by his obsession, which in Tower's case is rare books rather than the Dark Tower, though his need to pursue them is just as great. However, like many of the flawed characters throughout the *Dark Tower* series as a whole, Tower proves himself heroic, saving Callahan, selling the lot to Roland's *ka-tet*, and proving a valuable resource in Roland and his companions' quest for the Dark Tower.

In *Insomnia*, while Ralph's Derry may only be adjacent to the universe of Roland's Mid-World, they are fundamentally interconnected. The outcome of Ralph and Lois's endeavor has enormous ramifications on that other world, and much more hinges on their success than the (not inconsiderable) lives of those in the Civic Center Ed Deepneau plans to destroy.⁷ This sense of Purpose and interconnection is at the heart of King's *Dark Tower* universe and resonates throughout his canon, as one individual's choices and actions may have a wealth of unintended and unforeseen consequences that have massive effects well beyond their own life, or even their own world. This type of interconnection and its impact across universes is explicitly described in *Insomnia*, when the disaster at the Civic Center is minimized, though not altogether averted. As King writes, in this moment, "upon all levels of the universe, matters both Random and Purposeful resumed their ordained courses. Worlds which had trembled for a moment in their orbits now steadied, and in one of those worlds, in a desert that was the apotheosis of all deserts, a man named Roland turned over in his bedroll and slept easily once again beneath the alien constellations" (*Insomnia* 617). With this description, King moves readers forward into the future that Ralph's actions have made possible, while also drawing them back to *The Gunslinger*, the first novel of the *Dark Tower* series, and immersing them—if only for a moment—within the larger context of Roland's endless quest.

The Crimson King and Patrick Danville

In *Insomnia*, Ralph first hears of the Crimson King when he goes to confront Ed Deepneau after Ed has beaten his wife Helen, initially dismissing it as the ravings of a madman. However, as Ralph and Lois find themselves drawn deeper into the unseen worlds of Derry and the cosmic battle that has converged around it, Ralph finds himself face-to-face with the Crimson King, whose monstrous visage keeps changing, from that of Ralph's mother to an enormous catfish to a "tall and coldly handsome [man] with his blonde hair and glaring red eyes" (King, *Insomnia* 604). After Ralph has attacked the Crimson King and driven him back, he gets one last look, with the Crimson's King's glamours and disguises seemingly cast away, as Ralph sees a being "ancient and twisted and less human than the strangest creature to ever flop or hop its way along the Short-Time level of existence" (King, *Insomnia* 606). A moment later, a portal between worlds seems to open to draw the Crimson King to itself and back into another world, stopped for now but not defeated as Ralph gets one last, overwhelming look into its *"deadlights"* (King, *Insomnia* 606, emphasis original), a feature that allies the Crimson King with Derry's monstrous Pennywise.

In the *Dark Tower* series, Roland doesn't come face-to-face with the Crimson King until the end of *The Dark Tower*, and then only briefly and at a distance, but he is a recurring presence throughout the series in the stories that are told about him, his symbols, and the prophecies in which he features. As Vincent explains, "The Crimson King is Roland's greatest enemy and has been his ancestors' foil for generations" (*The Road to the Dark Tower* 262), with his emissaries taking a variety of forms. The Crimson King is mentioned in the revised and expanded version of *The Gunslinger* (King 284) and his sigul appears in *Wizard and Glass*, the story of Roland's long-past adolescence, when Walter comes to ally himself with Jonas Eldred and the Big Coffin Hunters (King 424–5). The graffiti of the Crimson King appears in *Wolves of the Calla* and the *Dark Tower*-related novella collection *Hearts in Atlantis*, often punctuated with a "crude drawing of an eye, [and] this message: ALL HAIL THE CRIMSON KING!" (King, *Wolves of the Calla* 291). It is at this point that Callahan begins to draw several of these threads together, noting that the vampires, low men, regulators, and Big Coffin Hunters are all "soldiers of the Crimson King" (*ibid.*), united in a common aim of destruction. The Crimson King's presence grows stronger and more pronounced as Roland's *ka-tet* nears the Dark Tower. The Crimson King is frequently mentioned in *Song of Susannah* and *The Dark Tower*, and Roland and Susannah get their fullest account of their adversary from one of his abandoned minions, when they discover that like many of King's most dangerous and terrifying antagonists, the Crimson King has gone mad. As Feemalo, Fumalo, and Fimalo tell Roland and Susannah, when the Crimson King learned that Roland was drawing near, he made his servants eat poison and watched them die, before killing himself (King, *The Dark Tower* 605–7). This suicide makes the Crimson King an even more formidable foe, as Fimalo explains that "you can't kill a man who's already dead" (King, *The Dark Tower* 608, emphasis original) and Roland's guns are now powerless against him. When Roland sees the Crimson King with his own eyes, he is not disappointed as "for once in his life Roland saw exactly what he had imagined": a mad old man, an undead monster, and "Hell, incarnate" (King, *The Dark Tower* 785). From the high ground of one of the Tower's balconies, the Crimson King is able to keep Roland from gaining the Tower and though Roland's aim is as good as it ever was, as Fimalo pointed out, his guns are now useless against the Crimson King, and it is only Patrick Danville who can help Roland gain what he has sought for so long and at such great cost.

Patrick Danville is the other key character who unites the worlds of *Insomnia* and the *Dark Tower*. While the Crimson King is a supernatural being of the *Dark Tower* universe who often makes his presence known across other worlds, Patrick is the opposite: a human in the "real world" of Derry, who just happens to have preternatural insight into and knowledge of the Dark Tower and the universe which surrounds it. Four years old in *Insomnia*, Patrick is staying with his mother Sonia in the local women's shelter after she has left Patrick's abusive father.[8] Like Ralph and Lois, Patrick can see things that others cannot and he seems tapped into the supernatural undercurrents of Derry and its wider, interconnected universes. Accompanying his mother to the Civic Center, Patrick—who is a gifted artist, even at this young age—occupies himself by coloring a picture, immersed in the image and the world it represents. In this picture,

> a tower of dark, soot-colored stone rose into a blue sky dotted with fat white clouds. Surrounding it was field of roses so red they seemed almost to clamor aloud. Standing off to one side was a man dressed in faded bluejeans. A pair of gunbelts crossed his flat middle; a holster hung beneath each hip. At the very top of the tower, a man in a red robe was looking down at the gunfighter with an expression of mingled hate and fear. His hands, which were curled over the parapet, also appeared to be red [King, *Insomnia* 614].

Drawn from the imagination of a talented four-year-old, Patrick's illustration is also prescient, prefiguring the final showdown between Roland and the Crimson King untold eons in the future. Patrick is a unique child, a conduit between these two worlds, and as Ralph comes to discover, Patrick is the reason for Clotho and Lachesis' intervention in the larger order of things: if Ed Deepneau's plan to blow up the Civic Center succeeds, Patrick will be killed along with thousands of others and as Lachesis tells Ralph, "*If the child dies, the Tower of all existence will fall, and the consequences of such a fall are beyond your comprehension. And beyond ours, as well*" (King, *Insomnia* 576, emphasis original). Disaster is mitigated (though not altogether averted), Patrick is saved, and the boy becomes the central figure in a prophecy shared by Clotho: "*Eighteen years from now, just before his death, the boy is going to save the lives of two men who would otherwise die ... and one of those men must not die, if the balance between the Random and the Purpose is to be maintained*" (King, *Insomnia* 620, emphasis original).

However, just as some of other connections between *Insomnia* and the *Dark Tower* universe are unfulfilled, flawed, and "tricksy" (King, *The Dark Tower* 524), Patrick Danville's future doesn't turn out quite the way Clotho predicts. While the prophecy says eighteen years will pass before Patrick's death, when Roland and Susannah find Patrick imprisoned in the monster Dandelo's basement, Susannah guesses his age at around seventeen (King, *The Dark Tower* 699), though upon further consideration, Roland notes that Patrick "might be as old as thirty. Time was strange when the Beams were under attack, and it took strange hops and twists" (King, *The Dark Tower* 706). Patrick has been drawn from his own world into that of the Dark Tower, though the when and how are never explained, and while Patrick does save Roland and help him gain the Tower, McAleer points out that Patrick "[saves] two lives—his own and Roland's—but the [prophecy's] implication is that he would save two lives other than his own" (153). While these are notable discrepancies, they can perhaps be explained by Nancy Deepneau's theories of the Dark Tower notes in *Insomnia* as beacons or signposts that supersede exact narrative consistency. One clear resonance between the Patrick Danville of *Insomnia* and the one Roland encounters in *The Dark Tower* is his ethereal artistic ability. In *Insomnia*, young Patrick drew a world he had never seen but had dreamed of and knew was there, in another dimension or on a different level of the Tower. With his reappearance in *The Dark Tower*, Patrick's art has the ability to unmake rather than create, to subtract elements from the existing reality rather than imagine one which is unseen. Patrick erases a sore from Susannah's lip (King, *The Dark Tower* 735–6) and later, when Roland's guns prove useless in defeating the Crimson King and gaining the Dark Tower, it is Patrick's drawing—and more importantly, his erasing—which make it possible. The boundaries between dimensions have proven unable to contain the Crimson King and neither madness nor death has stopped him. Roland cannot kill him, but Patrick can remove him. After completing a drawing of the Tower reminiscent of his childhood crayon sketch in *Insomnia* and coloring the Crimson King's eyes with a paint made from Roland's blood and the Tower's own roses, then "Patrick erased everything but the eyes, and these the remaining bit of rubber would not even blur" (King, *The Dark Tower* 799), rendering the Crimson King's horror bodiless and impotent. Without Patrick and his artistic ability—one of the truest lines that connects *Insomnia* and the *Dark Tower* universe—Roland would be thwarted at the base of the Tower itself, held at bay by Crimson King's defenses, either killed or driven mad in his final attempt.

9

Desperation and *The Regulators*

In 1996, King challenged several publishing industry conventions, first by releasing *The Green Mile* as a serial novel and then, by publishing two novels on the same day. The first of these novels was *Desperation*, published under his own name; the second was *The Regulators*, released under his (by then well-known) pseudonym of Richard Bachman. The pairing of these two novels—which include characters of the same names but in different settings, situations, and relationships with one another—offers a kind of parallel universe/alternate reality engagement that echoes the complexity of time and space engaged throughout the *Dark Tower* series. As Wiater, Golden, and Wagner explain of this interconnection, "People survive the events of one novel and die in the next, expire in both, or survive in each. Some appear as children in one book and adults in the other; one book's shining hero may be somewhat tarnished in the other" (455). King's own description of this repetition of characters between the two novels is that he thought of them "like the members of a repertory company acting in two different plays" (qtd. in Wiater, Golden, and Wagner 455), taking on different roles in new narratives. With an understanding of the larger Stephen King universe in general and the central position of the *Dark Tower* series specifically, these two narratives can also be productively read as the realities that exist on different levels of the Tower. This repetition and engagement through multiple timelines extends to King himself in *The Dark Tower*, the final book of the series, and echoes through the use of King's pseudonym of Richard Bachman in his other books published under that name, as well as *The Regulators* and its direct connection with King's *Desperation*. In addition to these altered versions of people and places, *The Regulators* in particular engages with hybrid genre dynamics similar to those that influence the *Dark Tower* series as a whole, here in the combination of science fiction and Western genre traditions that confound the residents of Poplar Street. Finally, the interplay between *Desperation* and *The Regulators* underscores the interconnected nature of much of King's larger canon and the ways in which these worlds may impact and influence one another.

Levels of the Tower

In their repetition of key locations, characters, and themes, Vincent argues that "*Desperation* and *The Regulators* share a unique twinning relationship and take place in different realities—different levels of the Tower, as it were" (*The Road to the Dark Tower* 206–7). Desperation, Nevada, is the source of evil in both novels, the home of Tak, who is released to wreak havoc and destruction. In *Desperation*, the town itself remains the setting, as residents and innocent passersby are pulled into the horror unfolding there, including Desperation residents Tom Billingsley, who is a retired veterinarian, and Audrey Wyler, who works for the Desperation mining company. The Carver family (Ralph, Ellen, David, and Kirsten) and Peter and Mary Jackson are stopped and brought in by Collie Entragian, a local cop who has been taken over by Tak, as is traveling writer Johnny Marinville. Steve Ames, Marinville's road support on his cross-country tour, is drawn to Desperation looking for his boss, with hitchhiker Cynthia Smith (from King's novel *Rose Madder*)[1] along for the ride. Once Tak has this diverse cast of characters in Desperation, it makes it very difficult for them to escape, first through literal imprisonment and then by means of the many animals that serve its will, as they find snakes, scorpions, spiders, and coyotes between themselves and freedom. Compounding the horror is Tak's possession, first of Collie Entrangian and then of Ellen Carver. As Wickham Clayton explains in "Alien on the Inside: The Adaptation of Stephen King's Alien Possession Tales," in traditional horror possession narratives, "human figures act as conduits for the behaviours of other, stronger intelligences, typically demons. This is often accompanied by the deterioration, or at least transformation, of the human body's conceived 'healthy' state," as well as anomalous, self-destructive acts and behaviors, with the possessing entity seeing this body as a disposable vessel, to be discarded when its purpose has been served (179). This perfectly describes Tak's use—and abuse—of his human host bodies, the disintegration of which King describes in gory detail as Tak pushes these bodies, which are too small and weak to contain its immense power, violently beyond their physical limitations before destroying them completely. Vincent notes that Tak also bears a striking similarity to Mia's description of the monsters of the *todash* space in *Song of Susannah*, arguing that Tak's use of "the same language of the unformed used by the Little Sisters [of Eluria] and the Manni supports this notion" (*The Road to the Dark Tower* 207).

This larger cosmology of outside forces works in a couple of different directions. First, the use of the terms *can-tak* and *can-toi* connect *Desperation* with the low men of *Hearts in Atlantis* and the *Dark Tower* series, though their embodiments and powers differ significantly between these works.[2] In *Desperation*, the *can-tak* from which Tak takes its name means "big god." As David Carver attempts to explain Tak's nature, "I think it's more like a disease than a spirit, or even a demon.... Tak is the ancient one, the unformed heart" (King, *Desperation* 492). Speaking of the mine from which Tak emerged, David argues that "I'm not sure that place is on earth at all, or even in normal space. Tak is a complete outsider, so different from us that we can't even get our minds around him" (*ibid.*). Tak and the power that inhabits the small carvings (or *can tah*) strewn about Desperation are strong and otherworldly, possibly having crossed from one dimension to another through a weak spot between worlds or realities. The China Pit seems to be one of these places of power and permeability, a door or perhaps a thinny between worlds like those that are regularly discovered throughout the *Dark Tower* series. This reading is further supported by a similar narrative in the *Dark Tower* novel *The Wind Through the Keyhole*, in which a light emanating from a crevasse deep within the salt mines first calls to the miners and then turns one of them into a dangerous skin-man, who transforms into a wide range of animalistic forms to prey upon the people of Debaria (King 281–2). As one of the Debarian men remarks, this is no surprise, as relics of the Great Old Ones are buried in the ground and "everyone knows there are demons in the earth" (King, *The Wind Through the Keyhole* 64), a danger inherent in the act of exploration and mining, whether in Mid-World or the Nevada of *Desperation*.

The second contributing factor to King's cosmology in *Desperation* is the role of God and Christianity, which is largely explored through David Carver, a boy whose prayer helped heal his friend Brian and who takes on the role of a leader and prophet during the characters' time in Desperation, even performing his own loaves-and-fishes style miracle when it doesn't look as though there will be enough Ritz crackers and sardines to go around (King, *Desperation* 306–8). A *Publisher's Weekly* review of *Desperation* refers to it as "a novel of sacred horror" ("Desperation") and Grady Hendrix calls it "one of the most profound Christian novels of the second half of the 20th century." Religion is central to some of King's other horrors, most notably in *'Salem's Lot*, *The Stand*, *The*

Green Mile, and *Revival*, though it also resonates implicitly in the good vs. evil conflicts throughout his canon. In *Desperation*, God is conceived of in terms of Otherness, much like Tak himself. Cowan argues that the overpowering and even traumatic direct relationship that David Carver has with his God is a realization that "the word, the concept, is little more than a placeholder for an encounter that is so *outside* our realm of experience that it beggars description" (158, emphasis original). In *Desperation*, God is a miraculous outside force, speaking directly to David and providing him with inside information, like where and what Tak is, what has happened in Desperation, and what must happen next. David's power is undeniable—he knows things he shouldn't be able to know and is able to do things he shouldn't be able to do, like squeeze past the prison cell bars that are too narrow for his head to fit through and ensure there is enough food for the group—and his relationship with God is direct and intimate. However, this relationship does not mean that all will turn out well. As King reflected in an interview with *Time*,

> I was raised in a religious household, and I really wanted to give God his due in this book. So often, in novels of the supernatural, God is a sort of kryptonite substance, or like holy water to a vampire. You just bring on God, and you say 'in his name,' and the evil thing disappears. But God as a real force in human lives is a lot more complex than that. And I wanted to say that in *Desperation*. God doesn't always let the good guys win. I always wanted to say that you can still reconcile the idea that things are not necessarily going well without falling back on platitudes like 'God has a plan' and 'This is for the greater good.' It's possible to be in pain and still believe that there is some force for good in the universe [qtd. in G. Cruz].

David has to face this harsh reality, as he loses his entire family in Desperation and is then denied the opportunity to sacrifice himself by Johnny Marinville. Johnny tells David that "You said 'God is cruel' the way a person who's lived his whole life on Tahiti might say 'Snow is cold.' You knew, but you didn't understand.... Do you know how cruel your God can be, David? How fantastically cruel? ... Sometimes he makes us live" (King, *Desperation* 520). David experiences God's capacity for strength, guidance, miracles, and salvation, but he also becomes intimately familiar with—and likely profoundly changed by—God's cruelty as well, his demand for sacrifice. However, as King notes the complexity of the impact of God in human experience, David's faith is not destroyed by what he has endured and in *Desperation*'s final pages, he reflects that "God is love" (King 546) and finds comfort once more in prayer.

While *Desperation* is steeped in the mystique of the American Southwest and invokes a wide range of Western genre traditions, from desert towns to blowing tumbleweeds, with *The Regulators*, the setting shifts to suburban Wentworth, Ohio, identified as the home of the

Carver family in *Desperation*. *The Regulators* features "the same cast of characters in skewed, slightly different roles" (Handy), though these differences are of varying degrees. Billingsly is still a retired veterinarian, though in Ohio rather than Nevada; Marinville is still an author, though he is best known for writing a popular series of children's books rather than literary fiction. Steve Ames is still a cross-country traveler, though his backstory is altered, and Cynthia Smith is still the quirky, two-tone-haired character familiar to readers from *Rose Madder*. The Carvers' roles are dramatically flipped, with the parents becoming the children and vice versa, and the Desperation mining company employee Brad Josephson becomes a friendly neighbor, alongside his wife Belinda. Audrey Wyler, who also worked for the Desperation mining company and was an agent of Tak in *Desperation*, takes on a central, sympathetic role, held captive by Tak himself, who now inhabits her autistic nephew, Seth. *The Regulators* also features a range of new characters as well in the neighbors of Poplar Street, including the Reed twins, Jim and Dave. Just as in *Desperation*, this diverse cast of characters is thrown together in an isolated and deadly situation, as chaos descends on Poplar Street and they are cut off from the larger real world, which should theoretically be only a block away but proves unreachable.

In this permutation, Tak still escapes from Desperation's China Pit, but instead of its violence being limited to the small Nevada town, it instead jumps into the body of young Seth Garin, as he as his family stop to see the mine while on their family vacation. Seth is almost completely non-verbal, but when he sees Desperation and the China Pit, he speaks, begging to be taken to the mine (Bachman, *The Regulators* 359). Seth breaks free from the group and makes his way deep into the mine, to the *an tak* chamber from which Tak emerges, and as the mining company employee who accompanied them, Allen Symes, recalls, when he and Seth's father found Seth, "The boy was *grinning*, and it wasn't a nice grin, either. The corners of his mouth looked like they were pulled most of the way up to his ears, and I could see all his teeth. His face was so stretched that his eyes looked like they were bulging right out of his head.... He didn't hardly look like the little boy I'd first met at all" (Bachman, *The Regulators* 372–3, emphasis original). In addition to Tak's emergence from the China Pit, the actions of *Desperation*'s parallel reality occasionally reverberate through to that of *The Regulators*, including an explosion deep in the mines that closes the shaft and cuts off the *an tak*, for which "no cause [was] ever assigned" (Bachman, *The Regulators* 377), echoing Johnny Marinville's sacrifice and detonation in *Desperation*.

While God and the power of the *can-tak* are the guiding forces of *Desperation*, the threat to Poplar Street emerges from the combined

9. Desperation *and* The Regulars   141

power of Seth and Tak, as the occupying presence perverts Seth's fantasies and makes them a reality. Seth loves Westerns, particularly the iconic television series *Bonanza* (1959–73) and a fictional B-movie called *The Regulators*, which a synopsis included in Bachman's novel describes as a "below-average Western melodrama of vigilantes on the rampage ... who first appear to be supernatural beings but turn out to be post–Civil War baddies of the Capt. Quantrill stripe" (Bachman, *The Regulators* 61). Seth's other desperate love is for the animated series *MotoKops 2200*, its heroes, "their racy, spacy vans," and their enemies No Face and Countess Lili Marsh (Bachman, *The Regulators* 87). Both *The Regulators* film and *MotoKops 2200* are fictional creations, though they embody the characteristics and traditions of their genre predecessors and contemporary popular culture influences, blurring the lines between fiction and reality, just as Seth's projected imaginings do for the residents of Poplar Street. Tak draws on Seth's obsessions and energies, turning them dark and violent, as the MotoKops' Power Wagons police Poplar Street, filled with superheroes and cowboys, and even those whose fictional natures are inherently good are here transformed into destructive villains. Similarly, the Poplar Street crew are attacked by animals and settings literally drawn from Seth's imagination, including a buzzard which appears "[a]s a child might draw it" (Bachman, *The Regulators* 244), and the world around them becomes recast with tumbleweeds and "violent green cactuses, like something you'd see in an energetic first-grader's picture" (Bachman, *The Regulators* 273). This disparate combination of genre elements, in the Western influences of *The Regulators* and the science fiction adventures of *MotoKops 2200*, confound and disorient the residents of Poplar Street, who struggle to understand or logically respond to what is going on around them, even as their neighbors are gunned down and houses begin to burn. This combination of genre elements and the unpredictability that results make *The Regulators* a "story in which anything can happen, and does, including the warping of space-time and the savage deaths of much of [King's] large cast" ("The Regulators"). This confluence of genres is also reflected in the structure and form of the novel itself, which alternates between traditional chapters, a summary of and script pages from the film *The Regulators*, reviews of *MotoKops 2200* merchandising, Audrey Wyler's diary entries, and the written account of Allen Symes, who showed the Garin family around on their ill-fated stop in Desperation.

While David Carver's guiding force in *Desperation* is God, in *The Regulators*, Seth's primary influence is television, and the novel works in part as a "commentary on American consumerism" (Quigley), exploring "what happens when a mind fixated on TV ... runs amok" (Webster).

Seth watches *The Regulators* and his *MotoKops 2200* VHS tapes over and over again, with their characters, settings, mythology, and violence saturating his mind, from which Tak can then draw these elements to project into hellish, destructive life.[3] This dynamic intersection of images and reality also features in the *Dark Tower* series, in Jake and Oy's escape when they flee the Dixie Pig and encounter a "mind-trap" in the tunnels below, a combination of technology and magic that projects their fears to create horrors real enough to harm them. This mind-trap similarly echoes the central monster of *IT* in its ability to adapt, as one of Jake's pursuers notes that "whatever the boy saw will turn into what *we* fear" (King, *The Dark Tower* 106, emphasis original). The lines between imagination and reality are frequently blurred in *The Regulators*, not just in the animation of Seth's fantasies, but in his and his Aunt Audrey's escape mechanisms, through which they can imaginatively transport themselves to other, safer places. These sanctuaries also highlight the challenge of distinguishing Tak's powers from Seth's own, as it is through Seth's intervention that Audrey is able to take herself out of reality and revisit New York's Mohonk Mountain House, where she once spent a lovely vacation with her best friend and where her and Seth's spirits linger on at the novel's conclusion, united and safe. As Audrey attempts to explain the interweaving of Seth and Tak's power to her neighbors, Seth's fantasies are the conduit through which "Tak taps into Seth's powers, which complement its own. Tak.... I think Tak just likes what happens to us" (Bachman, *The Regulators* 406), feeding off of their suffering and fear, a kind of psychic vampire, like the True Knot of *Doctor Sleep* or *The Dark Tower*'s Dandelo.

Desperation and *The Regulators* explore two different realities with various intersections and overlaps. Given the cosmological construction of King's *Dark Tower* series, in its presentation of multiple realities and worlds, these two novels present an extended consideration of the ripple effect of a single event or entity—in this case Tak's escape from the China Pit in Desperation, Nevada—and how that single fixed element might engage with and impact those multiple worlds. Throughout the *Dark Tower* series, there are occasional glimpses of how individual lives and series of events might play out differently in these worlds: Jake as alive or dead, King as killed by the van that struck him rather than just terribly injured, the world spared or devastated by the superflu of *The Stand*. But these moments are usually just quick peeks, raising a tantalizing "what if?" and perhaps briefly considering that other possible reality before coming back to Roland's own to continue his quest for the Dark Tower. In *Desperation* and *The Regulators*, King is able to explore two versions of the same event in detail, fully develop two worlds and their intersecting and distinct experiences of Tak's coming, and reflect upon what such a showdown might look like on two different levels in the all-encompassing universe of the Dark Tower.

Richard Bachman

Late in the *Dark Tower* series, Stephen King becomes a character in his own creation, including a series of King's journal entries that span several decades and chart some of the influences on and his authorial thoughts regarding the *Dark Tower* series at the end of *Song of Susannah*. At the conclusion of these journal entries is a brief article from the Portland Sunday *Telegram* announcing that King was "killed by a van while walking near his summer home yesterday afternoon" (King, *Song of Susannah* 410), posing an alternate reality to his real-life accident. In *The Dark Tower*, Roland and Jake return to the Keystone World to prevent King's death and change the course of events, allowing King to finish the series and keep the Tower standing.

Another way in which the lines of authorial identity blur throughout King's work is in those books he has written under the pseudonym of Richard Bachman. King wrote four early paperback originals under the Bachman name: *Rage* (1977), *The Long Walk* (1979), *Roadwork* (1981), and *The Running Man* (1982). It was after the publication of *Thinner* as a Richard Bachman title in 1984 that his identity was outed, though by that time speculation that King and Bachman were one and the same had been circulating for years. On February 26, 1985, *The Bangor Daily News* announced, "Yes, Stephen King is indeed Richard Bachman" (qtd. in Beahm 145). Unsurprisingly, once King's identity was established, the sales of Bachman's books skyrocketed, though two of the earlier Bachman books were by then out of print (Beahm 145). In his introduction to the collected *Bachman Books*, "Why I Was Bachman," King explains the influencing factors of having more stories to tell than the then-standard one-book-a-year publishing industry could accommodate and wanting to see if his work stood on its own merit without his famous name to drive it (v-x). He also reflects that Bachman was "a fictional creation who became more real with each published book which bore his byline" (qtd. in Wiater, Golden, and Wagner 418), an echo which resonates through King's novel *The Dark Half*, in which Thad Beaumont is pursued and tormented by his own pseudonym come to life, George Stark.[4] Later, King published *Blaze* (2007) under the Bachman pseudonym, referring to it in the introduction as a newly discovered "trunk novel" (Bachman, *Blaze* 1). When King had the idea of publishing the simultaneous novels *Desperation* and *The Regulators*, Bachman was a natural choice for authorial credit, and an editor's note attributed to Chuck Verrill prefacing the novel claims that Bachman's widow, Claudia Eschelman, found the manuscript for *The Regulators* in a *"box secured by rubber bands, as if Bachman had been on the verge of sending it to his publisher when his final remission ended"* (Bachman, *The Regulators* 9, emphasis original). When *The Regulators* was published, King's identity as Bachman was already well-known, leading many reviewers to dismissively describe this dual publication as a "stunt" (Polito) or criticize is as evidence of King's "commitment to marketing gimmicks" (Hendrix). However, there are distinct differences between a book by King and a book by Bachman that extend well beyond the name on the cover that warrant consideration.

Bachman's books are significantly more pessimistic than King's own and while King's books generally build upon a belief in the essential goodness of humanity, Bachman's have more of an "abandon all hope, ye who enter here" vibe. As Linda Badley notes, "The Bachman books are unrelentingly pessimistic and often disturbing" (182). Bachman's protagonists are isolated and have little hope of redemption; they are often driven to either death or insanity. As King notes, "When I put on my Bachman hat, I feel everyone just starts at 'Go' and there's no guarantee of a happy ending…. It's tremendously liberating; Bachman doesn't have a conscience, he's not afraid to say things that I may be afraid to" (qtd. in Quinn). While body horror is central to *Desperation* in King's detailed descriptions of the breakdown of Tak's hosts, *The Regulators* is "almost unrelentingly violent, [with] the language used to describe the aftermath seeming to revel in it" (Quigley). Similarly, while the band of survivors in *Desperation* form a cohesive group, protecting one another and willing to sacrifice themselves for the greater good, the residents of Poplar Street are contentious and divided. They were isolated from one another before the supernatural mayhem descended on their street— with no one noticing Audrey Wyler's dramatic downward spiral, for instance—and rather than being brought together by the danger they face, in many ways they remain separate, preoccupied with their own struggles and survival. When Johnny asks Kim Geller if she could help with the orphaned Carver children, she refuses: "'No,' she said. No more, no less. And calm. No defiance in her gaze, no hysteria in her tone … but no fellow feeling, either" (Bachman, *The Regulators* 246). Kim has her own daughter Susi safe by her side and as far as she is concerned, there's no need to concern herself with anyone else's suffering, even that of two small children who have just seen their parents violently killed. Similarly, despite Audrey's explanation that Seth is not responsible for the

9. Desperation *and* The Regulars   145

nightmare that has descended on Poplar Street, Cammie Reed decides that the only solution is to kill the boy, shooting both Seth and Audrey, reflecting in the moments before this murder that she "is no longer sure that she is acting of her own free will, but it doesn't matter; if her will was free, this is still what she would do" (Bachman, *The Regulators* 446–7), as she kills a victimized, powerless child. While some of the people on Poplar Street work together to respond to the situation and attempt to be voices of reason amid the descending madness, most of these are notably the outsiders, whether socially or geographically: Audrey Wyler has been isolated in her home by Tak's power and abuse, Johnny Marinville is a Wentworth transplant, the Josephsons are the only black people in the neighborhood (the repressed racism of which emerges under the stress of the Regulators' attacks), Cynthia Smith has just started working at the neighborhood mini-mart, and Steve Ames is a traveler passing through, who is simply in the wrong place at the wrong time. As a result, the heroism that does occur during the siege seems like an outside force, an anomaly, rather than the idealized neighborliness of suburbia. There is no comfort of God or the love of one's fellow human beings, as at the end of *Desperation*, where the orphaned David is collectively cared for by Steve, Cynthia, and Mary, and able to fall back on the reassurance of his faith. At the end of *The Regulators*, order descends and the characters are isolated from one another once more, driven into silence and separation, unable to articulate or respond to what they have experienced.

Another similarity between *The Regulators* and the other Bachman books is the critiqued role of television and popular culture. As Magistrale notes, "*Rage*, *The Long Walk*, *Roadwork*, and *The Running Man* are intense, if sometimes overdramatized, studies of television's capacity for shaping public opinion and transforming individuals" (*The Second Decade* 49). Particularly in *The Long Walk* and *The Running Man*, television is both a contributing factor of and witness to the violence these dystopian societies make possible. The citizens of these futures watch and condone the violence they see expressed there, as both the Long Walk and the reality show featured in *The Running Man* are avidly consumed, and their contestants' suffering reveled in by their viewers, who then ultimately stand witness to contestants' usually violent deaths. In *The Regulators*, this dynamic is flipped: Seth watches and absorbs the violence of his beloved Westerns and *MotoKops 2200* and those images are then annexed and brought to life by Tak. As a *Publisher's Weekly* review of *The Regulators* notes, "The theme is the horror of TV ... when a discorporeal psychic vampire settles inside an autistic boy obsessed with TV westerns and kiddie action shows and brings screen images to demented, lethal life" ("The Regulators"). This is not an oversimplified case of popular culture violence inspiring real-world violence: Seth has no desire to hurt anyone and he has tragically lost his entire family as a result of Tak's possession. However, it does highlight popular culture's influence on and interconnection with its surrounding society and the individuals who consume it. Bachman is a darker version of King and while popular culture is lovingly and playfully invoked throughout much of King's fiction, in *The Regulators* it takes a darker cast, following Michael Collins's critique that "King offers his readers a glimpse of the true evil of popular culture … which has no design or intent, only an empty need to sustain itself" (qtd. in Webster).

The Regulators was published under the Bachman name, though at that point, fans had known that King was Bachman for more than a decade. Badley argues that the revelation and death of Bachman pose questions of both identity and perception, writing that "Bachman's demise raised the question of who 'Stephen King' really was" (171). With *The Regulators*, King once again identifies Bachman as a distinct and separate part of himself and his authorial identity. As Wiater, Golden, and Wagner note, though Bachman has been declared "dead," *The Regulators* demonstrates that "Bachman clearly still 'is' a vital part of the imagination of Stephen King" (418). However, with the dual publication of *Desperation* and *The Regulators*, the worlds of Bachman and King are drawn into overlapping connection, overtly linking and engaging these potential realities. In his use of this pseudonym, King also performs a kind of self-replication, exploring the different versions and echoes of himself throughout these works, from Bachman to the fictionalized King in the final books of the *Dark Tower* series.

The Interconnected Universe of King

In considering King's *Dark Tower* series—and his extensive body of work as a whole—the major significance of *Desperation* and *The Regulators* is in their overt engagement with interconnection that defines much of King's universe, from connections within a single world to the consideration of other possible realities. These interconnections are at the heart of the *Dark Tower* and the cosmology King constructs within the series: whether they are coincidence, fate, or the result of direct intervention, within the universe of the *Dark Tower*, all possible worlds and realities are connected.

This interconnection echoes throughout King's canon, with his characters in stories of Derry and Castle Rock creating distinct local

9. Desperation *and* The Regulars 147

histories and frequently referencing tragedies that have come before, as chronicled in earlier novels. King's fictional universe also acknowledges the author's own substantial impact on popular culture, through in-text references like King's invocation of *Christine* (1983) in "Mile 81" when Trooper Jimmy Golding reflects that he "hadn't believed in monster cars since he saw that movie *Christine* as a kid" (42). Even novels with dramatically different settings sometimes collide, establishing much of King's work as existing within a cohesive shared reality. For example, when *Rose Madder*'s Cynthia Smith appears in both *Desperation* and *The Regulators*, she recalls the horrors of that earlier novel in a conversation she has with Steve Ames in *Desperation*, telling him how "she had gone to a shelter ... even worked as a counsellor for awhile after the woman in charge had been murdered and it looked as if the place might close" (King, *Desperation* 98). *Desperation*'s Ellen Carver enjoys Paul Sheldon's *Misery* novels (King, *Desperation* 188) and so does Rose Daniels of *Rose Madder* (King, *Rose Madder* 17). *The Shining*'s Dick Hallorann served alongside Mike Hanlon's father, stationed on a base in Derry, Maine, with the two men barely surviving the racially-motivated fire that destroyed the Black Spot club there (King, *IT* 465–75). King's universes create a complex web of interconnection, situated around the axis of the Dark Tower itself. As Mike Fugere notes of Jake's existence in multiple worlds following his death in *The Gunslinger*, "Stephen King is no stranger to creating alternate realities and doppelgängers. He's had entire novels based on time travel, metaphysical nightmares, and other-worldly horrors, but what makes *The Dark Tower* special is how the existence of multiple Jakes takes a toll on the fabric of reality." Other than occasional echoes between the worlds—such as the unexplained mine explosion referenced in Allen Symes's written account in *The Regulators*—the characters in *Desperation* and *The Regulators* seems almost entirely unaware of these other possible realities, though as Fugere's discussion of Jake notes, that is not always the case, and characters' awareness of this multiplicity can be unsettling and even potentially destructive.

One contemporary example of this interconnection that channels King, popular culture, and the potential of multiple, intersecting realities in the larger tradition of the *Dark Tower* series is the no longer ongoing Hulu series *Castle Rock* (2018–2019), the first season of which chronicles protagonist Henry Deaver's (André Holland) return to his hometown. Set in one of King's most famous Maine towns, *Castle Rock* draws together characters, themes, and events from throughout King's wide-ranging body of work, as well as adding new characters and developing original stories.[5] This complex engagement with King's canon as a whole seems to have *Dark Tower* connections as well, including multiple realities and thin places between these worlds. This possibility is most overtly engaged in the penultimate episode of the first season, titled "Henry Deaver," in which The Kid (played by Bill Skarsgård) claims that he is an alternate universe Henry Deaver, outlining his family history, his personal relationships, and the inexplicable moment where he was lost in the Castle Rock woods and slipped from one reality into the next, where he is caught by Warden Dale Lacey (Terry O'Quinn), who believes The Kid to be the devil and locks him in a cage deep within the bowels of Shawshank Prison. Furthering this parallel universe logic, Holland's Henry Deaver was lost for nine days as a child and similarly crossed the barrier between the two worlds, which taps into both men's memories of disparate realities that should be mutually exclusive but somehow both exist. While the nature of The Kid and the veracity of his story is never firmly established within the Hulu series, another characteristic that points toward a *Dark Tower* series connection is the sound that plagues many of the major characters, alternately referred to as "the schisma," "the sound of the universe," and "the voice of God," and which drives both Henrys to the woods in search of its' source. Despite the multiple interpretations of and responses to this sound, as *SyFy Wire*'s Matthew Jackson notes, it "sounds an awful lot like a 'thinny,'" the portal between worlds central to King's *Dark Tower* series. As Jackson continues, the sound of a thinny "can infect the minds of those who hear it and has been known to drive people mad. If you walk into a thinny, there's also a chance you will end up in another universe." This sense of multiple realities, the permeability of the barriers between universes, and individuals whose lives and worlds are dramatically different on different levels of the Tower is central to the *Dark Tower* series as a whole and the foundational engagement of *Desperation* and *The Regulators*' parallel narratives.

10

Hearts in Atlantis and Other "Low Men"

Some of King's *Dark Tower*-related works involve direct overlap with King's other novels, like Father Callahan of *'Salem's Lot*, young Patrick Danville's vision of the Dark Tower, or Roland and his *ka-tet*'s visits to Keystone World New York City and Maine. But in other instances, unsuspecting humans cross paths with denizens of Roland's world only briefly and usually without a real understanding of what they've encountered, though these interactions make lasting and often tragic impressions. This is frequently the case with the *can-toi* or "low men," who are in service to the Crimson King. These low men appear at first glance to be human, but are actually hybrid in nature, human and *taheen*, with "hume bodies but the heads of beasts" (Furth 51), though they travel with their true natures concealed by "masks of living flesh" (King, *The Dark Tower* 236). These low men are largely tasked with the keeping and maintenance of the Beam-Breakers, with a goal of destroying the Beams that keep the Dark Tower standing and bringing down the resultant chaos and destruction. Despite the disguises that lend them a passingly human appearance, those who see them, like Bobby Garfield in the "Low Men in Yellow Coats" segment of *Hearts in Atlantis*[1] and Wesley Smith in "Ur" have a pervasive though indefinable sense that something is not quite right about them, that they're not actually "men" at all. In addition to their occasional appearance in the Keystone World of King's larger canon, the low men also leave behind artifacts—whether accidentally or intentionally with an aim of causing mischief—including the cars at the center of *From a Buick 8* and "Mile 81," and Wesley Smith's dimension-transcending Kindle e-reader.

Encounters with Low Men

In "Low Men in Yellow Coats," the first of the interconnected narratives that comprise *Hearts in Atlantis*, eleven-year-old Bobby Garfield makes the acquaintance of his mysterious new upstairs neighbor Ted Brautigan. Like many of King's other overlapping characters, including Father Callahan and Patrick Danville, Ted Brautigan knows all too well that "there are other worlds than these" (King, *The Gunslinger* 266) and has wound up in Bobby's nondescript Connecticut neighborhood on the run from one of these darker realities. When Ted enlists Bobby's help in keeping an eye out for these "low men," he tells Bobby, "I use 'low' in the Dickensian sense, meaning fellows who look rather stupid ... and rather dangerous as well" (King, *Hearts in Atlantis* 48), struggling to articulate the meanness and pervasive sense of something unnatural that typifies them. Though Ted's definition is diffuse and unspecific, Bobby understands, with "the sense that the word or phrase was exactly right even if you couldn't say just why" (*ibid.*). This initial and largely unspoken understanding establishes the intimacy of Ted and Bobby's friendship, drawing them into a powerful alliance with one another and revealing the world to Bobby in a way that few others ever experience. In addition to keeping an eye out for the low men, Ted asks Bobby to watch for signs of their presence as well, including their "loud and vulgar" cars (King, *Hearts in Atlantis* 49), lost pet posters, stars and moons drawn near hopscotch patterns, disembodied kite tails, and clocks that have lost their sense of time (King, *Hearts in Atlantis* 51–4).

The low men are described in more detail through Bobby's fleeting and terrifying glimpses of them. When Ted and Bobby go past the diner in which the low men are eating, Bobby can feel their minds searching for Ted, accompanied by "a savage itching attack behind the backs of his eyeballs ... followed by a fall of twisting black threads across his field of vision" (King, *Hearts in Atlantis* 142). While they are always searching, they intend this surveillance to be exclusively one-way, and the low men themselves wear "hats lined with wire to protect them against psychic assault" (Vincent, *The Dark Tower Companion* 99).[2] They drive obnoxiously flashy cars and they wear loud clothes, yellow coats, and the sigul of the Crimson King. Their physical forms are unfixed and when Bobby has a close encounter with one of these low men, the hand that grabs him shifts cyclically between fingers and claws (King, *Hearts in Atlantis* 222). When Bobby sees the faces of the low men, they are similarly fluid, as "their faces wouldn't stay their faces ... their cheeks and chins and hair kept trying to spread outside the lines" (King, *Hearts in Atlantis*

223). The low men are terrifying, dangerous, and impossible for Bobby to comprehend.

Through his vigilance in watching for signs of the low men for Ted, Bobby begins to see his familiar neighborhood through new eyes, constantly navigating between recognizing the potential danger around him and finding himself too young and powerless to do anything to stop it. This is a theme that resonates throughout "Low Men in Yellow Coats" well beyond the low men themselves and Bobby's friendship with Ted. Part of this comes from Bobby's realization that he can't protect the people he loves: he can't stop the older boys from Saint Gabriel's from beating Carol Gerber and breaking her arm, though he later gets some measure of revenge. Similarly, though he has flashes of insight and understanding of the horrific events, he can't prevent his mother being raped by her boss and two of his friends, nor can he help her process this trauma or heal in the aftermath. When the low men finally catch up with Ted—tipped off by Bobby's mother—Bobby valiantly tries to help his friend, braving dark and dangerous streets to find Ted, only to discover that he is powerless to make the great sacrifice needed to free Ted. As the low men get ready to take Ted away, they offer Bobby the chance to stand by his friend, asking him, "Would you like to come with us so you can be close to good old Ted?" (King, *Hearts in Atlantis* 226). They command him, "Decide, Bobby. Do it now, and knowing that what you decide is what will bide. Now and forever" (*ibid.*). But just like with Carol and his mother, Bobby is unable to save Ted or willingly accompany him. Bobby lets them take Ted, overwhelmed with a feeling of "shame because he knew what he was doing—crawling, chintzing, chickening out. All the things the good guys in the movies and books he loved never did. But the good guys in the movies or books never had to face anything like the low men in the yellow coats" (King, *Hearts in Atlantis* 227). Even more terrifying to Bobby than the creatures themselves is the possibility of more understanding and with it, greater horror yet to come. As Bobby senses, what he is seeing in this moment "was not the worst of it either. What if he saw the rest? What if the black specks drew him into a world where he saw the men in the yellow coats as they really were? What if he saw the shapes inside the ones they wore in this world?" (*ibid.*). What Bobby learns more than anything the summer after he turns eleven is that there are untold horrors in the world, some of which are almost too massive or monstrous to comprehend, and which he is powerless to stop.

This moment is also one of the most overt references in *Hearts in Atlantis* to King's *Dark Tower* series: while Bobby blames himself for not being able to rescue Ted, Ted gives himself up to save Bobby, including convincing the low men not to take Bobby with them as a prize to be given to the Crimson King. Ted dissuades them, calling the low men's attention back to the Crimson King's larger plan and telling them that "there is a gunslinger" (King, *Hearts in Atlantis* 225) working counter the Crimson King's goals and revealing that "he and his friends have reached the borderland of End-World" (*ibid.*). With this disclosure, King draws a direct narrative line between Ted's appearance in *Hearts in Atlantis* and his interactions with Roland and his *ka-tet* in the world of the Dark Tower, where Ted and his fellow Breakers play a pivotal role in the series' final book, which also draws together narrative threads from the larger series, including *Wizard and Glass* and King's other, *Dark Tower*-related novels, like *Black House*.

Countless times throughout the *Dark Tower* series—and King's fiction as a whole—enormous consequences hinge on a single moment or action. Bobby's choice not to sacrifice himself for Ted is just such a pivotal moment for him and in that decision, "his life is changed forever. His youthful spirit and faith in himself are taken away" (Wiater, Golden, and Wagner 75). His already contentious relationship with his mother becomes more fractured and toxic, with Bobby's view of her irrevocably altered once he has discovered the lies she told him about his father and that she turned Ted in to the low men for the reward money. His friendships with Carol and Sully deteriorate and Bobby is left largely alone, with his horror and disenchantment predominant in his new understanding of the world around him. The low men are part of Bobby's life for a single childhood summer and glimpsed only briefly, but their impact is enormous. However, so is Ted's: as he is being taken by the *can-toi*, Ted tells Bobby, "You shouldn't be too hard on yourself" (King, *Hearts in Atlantis* 228), forgiving Bobby and attempting to alleviate the guilt and responsibility he knows the boy will feel in his absence. Roland gets a kind of cosmic do-over for letting Jake fall to his death in *The Gunslinger* when the boy is returned to him in *The Waste Lands*. Bobby doesn't get quite this same crack at redemption and reunion, though a few years later his faith in the world is at least partially restored when he gets a message from Ted, an envelope of "rose petals of the deepest, darkest red he had ever seen" (King, *Hearts in Atlantis* 252), and his realization that "Ted was free. Not in this world and time, this time he had run in another direction, but in *some* world" (King, *Hearts in Atlantis* 253, emphasis original). This fact gives Bobby hope and allows him to begin to heal, renewed by the fact that Ted is alive, even though their paths will never again cross.[3] Just as he had earlier sensed the vastness of the universes which surrounded him and found himself powerless before them, Bobby now "senses the multiverse all spinning on the axis

10. Hearts in Atlantis *and Other "Low Men"*

of the Tower" (Vincent, *The Dark Tower Companion* 100), but instead of terror, finds himself comforted and at peace in the knowledge that Ted has once again escaped the low men.

Ted's story is told only incompletely in *Hearts in Atlantis* but Roland and his *ka-tet* find and work with Ted and his fellow Breakers in Algul Siento en route to the Dark Tower. These Breakers present a significant moment of overlap between multiple King narratives, as Roland is reunited with Sheemie Ruiz, who he knew in his tragic time with Susan Delgado in Mejis (*Wizard and Glass*). Dinky Earnshaw from the short story "Everything's Eventual" rounds out the trio.[4] These three Breakers have different powers—Ted is telepathic, Sheemie is a teleport, and Dinky is precognitive—though each man finds these powers harnessed by and corrupted in service to the Crimson King. Each is also recognized for his special ability, appreciated and given the opportunity to hone this previously repressed skill. This is an empowering and liberating shift, as Mr. Sharpton tells Dinky in "Everything's Eventual" that "we want to help you focus your talent, sharpen it" (King 288), though its use then becomes directed and corrupted. In exchange for their forced labor, the Breakers are kept comfortable and are well taken care of, while any resistance or failure to perform is harshly punished, as Ted found when he fled to Bobby Garfield's Connecticut and was dragged back to his post. However, as Ted explains to Roland and his *ka-tet*, "we are three rebels in a society of going along to get along, even if it means the end of existence ... and sooner rather than later" (King, *The Dark Tower* 271). The majority of the Breakers are complacent, not just because their needs are met but because the work itself is enjoyable in a compulsive, addictive way. As Ted tries to explain to Roland and his *ka-tet* on the tapes he has left for them, breaking is immensely gratifying (King, *The Dark Tower* 291). The Breakers know the enormous consequences of their actions, but with the exception of Ted, Sheemie, and Dinky, they are largely content to let the world fall as long as they can continue getting their fix along the way. Just as Bobby's choice to leave Ted changed the course of his life, however, Ted, Sheemie, and Dinky have decided to make a choice of their own: to eschew the satisfaction of "breaking," willing to sacrifice this pleasure and perhaps even themselves for the greater good of the Dark Tower.

While Ted and, to a lesser extent, Bobby, have a sense of who the low men are, their purpose, and the danger they pose, in "Ur" Wesley Smith is caught largely unaware, with the appearance of the low men serving as an unsettling coda to an odd interlude that has opened Wesley's eyes to the fundamental mystery of the world(s) around him. King wrote "Ur" in 2009 as an Amazon Kindle exclusive release, as part of the promotional campaign for their new model.[5] As King reflects on this experience, "I decided I would like to write a story for the Kindle, but only if I could do one *about* the Kindle. Gadgets fascinate me, particularly if I can think of a way they might get weird" ("Stephen King on the Kindle and iPad," emphasis original). When Wesley Smith orders his Kindle from Amazon, it shows up with some non-standard features: it is pink instead of the basic white of the then-current model and even more startlingly, it has access to the books of countless alternate worlds, in which "famous authors were born and died on different days and produced works beyond those that are known in our 'ur,' the name the device gives to each possible timeline or level of the Tower" (Vincent, *The Dark Tower Companion* 103). Wesley becomes captivated by the Kindle, as he explores and discovers parallel dimension Ernest Hemingways, James Cains, and Edgar Allan Poes. However, things get really complicated when Wesley discovers that the device also gives him access to future editions of his local newspaper, including coverage of a horrific bus crash which will kill the vast majority of the women's college basketball team. Along with student Robbie Henderson, Wesley sets out to change the course of events, using the ur local newspaper stories to trace the steps of the drunk driver whose path will cross with the bus if she isn't stopped.

They are successful and tragedy is averted, though Wesley returns home to his apartment to find that there are consequences for those actions. Unlike Ted and Bobby, Wesley has no context for the low men's appearance in his life, compounding his fear with confusion and incomprehension. Sensing their presence, his instinctual response is to run, anticipating the dangers posed by what he thinks of as "the Paradox Police" (King, "Ur" 260). Wesley gets a close look at the low men, noting that "they wore long mustard-colored coats … and Wesley understood, without knowing how he understood, that the coats were alive. He also understood that the men wearing them were not men at all. Their faces kept *changing*, and what lay just beneath the skin was reptilian. Or birdlike. Or both" (King, "Ur" 261, emphasis original). As in *Hearts in Atlantis*, the low men are indefinable, incomprehensible. Wesley senses what he cannot see and understands the danger in which he has found himself, though like Bobby before him, he is unable to effectively articulate or respond to it. Similarly, just as the low men's work is directly tied to the destiny of the Dark Tower, Wesley's actions have repercussions in worlds well beyond his own, as one of the low men tells him that "you have no idea what you did.... The Tower trembles; the worlds shudder in their courses. The rose feels a chill, as of winter" (King, "Ur" 261–2). In *Insomnia,* the life or death of Patrick Danville is the tipping point upon which all potential futures hinge and in "Ur," Wesley Smith has a similar power, though he remains unaware of it until it could be too late. Those potential repercussions are less finely defined in "Ur," and while the low men consider the potential disaster that could come from breaking the Paradox Laws, what that disaster might actually be remains uncertain. They tell Wesley, "We don't *know* what happens.... And since we don't, there's no chance to repair the damage, if there was damage" (King, "Ur" 263, emphasis original). As with Patrick Danville, significant potential—presumably for good as well as ill—hangs in the balance, but unlike the conclusion of *Insomnia*, in "Ur" which way the scales will tip in the end remains unknown.

Bobby struggles to make sense of his confrontation with the low men and his glimpse of the many worlds beyond his own, and Wesley seems to grapple with a similar dilemma, fighting to make meaning out of this inexplicable turn in his own life. However, while Bobby finds himself overwhelmed and powerless before this knowledge, Wesley works to contextualize it and establish his place and potential role within the grand scheme of things, including the countless worlds around him and the Dark Tower that stands at their center. When the low men tell him that "all things serve the Tower," Wesley responds with the question of "how do you know I'm not serving it, too?" (King, "Ur" 263). In this active reconceptualization of his role, Wesley recasts himself as an unwitting but powerful player, who was pulled into this conflict by destiny rather than his own free will or misadventure. After all, as he tells the low men, he didn't order that particular Kindle: "it just came" (*ibid.*). In this reframing of events, rather than being a mistake that landed a dangerous technology into the wrong hands of a random would-be consumer, Wesley was fated to the receive the Kindle, to discover the worlds, and to intervene, to play a small but integral role in the struggle surrounding the Dark Tower. By imagining—and perhaps even inventing—this power for himself, Wesley may well save his own life, as the low men take his Kindle but leave him alive and mostly well. He has to cope with the traumatic aftermath of his confrontation with the low men and adjust to his new, expansive understanding of the universe and his place within it, but others who have encountered the low men have fared far worse.

Cruising and Cosmic Chrome

While few people encounter the low men face to face, these beings occasionally leave behind artifacts of their presence, most often in the form of cars. These garish, gaudy cars are one of the signs Ted asks Bobby to keep an eye out for and one of the most reliable signs that the low men are near. Bobby sees a few of these cars, getting his closest and clearest look the night he attempts to rescue Ted. There's a DeSoto whose headlights *"blinked.* They weren't headlights at all. They were eyes" (King, Hearts in Atlantis 220, emphasis original) and a Cadillac whose "motor, he realized, was breathing" (King, Hearts in Atlantis 221). Similarly, the first sign Wesley gets that he has uninvited guests is the car parked outside of his apartment, which is "a Cadillac, and in the glow of the arc sodium beneath which it was parked, it seemed too bright" (King, "Ur" 260). Just like the low men themselves, their cars have something indefinably but fundamentally wrong. While the cars are notable but peripheral in *Hearts in Atlantis* and "Ur," they become the narrative focus of *From a Buick 8* and "Mile 81."

From a Buick 8 is told from an alternating first-person perspective, as the troopers and staff of the Pennsylvania State Police's Troop D tell young Ned Wilcox about his father's life as a trooper and the car that isn't really a car in a shed behind the barracks. The troopers come into possession of the Buick when it is abandoned at a nearby gas station by a mysterious stranger with a waxy face, a long cloak, and an "unpleasant, mucusy" voice (King, *From a Buick 8* 27), who then seems to disappear into thin air. While the car at first glance looks like a mid-century Buick Roadmaster, Sergeant Commanding Sandy Dearborn explains that it wasn't "a Buick. Or even a car. It was something else" (King, *From a Buick 8* 20). Ned's father, Curt Wilcox, is the first trooper to begin cataloging the Buick's strange anomalies, including an engine with "no distributor cap and no distributor.... No generator or alternator either," an empty radiator, and no battery (King, *From a Buick 8* 38–9). The steering wheel is enormous (King, *From a Buick 8* 28), all the dashboard controls are fake (King, *From a Buick 8* 40), and it has an uneven number of porthole windows on its sides (King, *From a Buick 8* 36). As Curt Wilcox is examining the car, it also emits a "high, steady hum ... [and] after a minute or so, that hum almost sounded like *talking*" (King, *From a Buick 8* 43, emphasis original), reminiscent of the thinnies that appear elsewhere in King's *Dark Tower* series and signal open doorways between worlds.

Once the car is tucked away in the shed behind the barracks, the troopers begin to get a sense of not just the car's odd appearance but its incredible, destructive power. Laurie Selwyn explains that it "interferes with state police radio and television reception; provides mysterious and frightening light shows; spits out strange, dead-smelling objects; and is suspected of being involved in the death or disappearance of

10. Hearts in Atlantis *and Other "Low Men"*

people, animals, and various inanimate objects" (143). Curt begins to conduct a series of experiments designed to ascertain the nature of the car, monitoring the temperature in the shed to look for corresponding changes that presage one of the car's flashing light displays. At its most active times, the car disgorges creatures and otherworldly artifacts, the first of which is a horrific bat-like creature. Nancy McNicol notes that King's descriptions of these alien beings "have the vibrancy of comic book illustrations heightened by allegorical overtones" (118), detailed and ominous. As King describes this bat-like being, "The wings were either black or a very dark mottled green. What they could see of the creature's back was a lighter green. The stomach area was a cheesy whitish shade, like the gut of a rotted stump or the throat of a decaying swamp-lily.... A bony thing that might have been a nose or a beak jutted from the eyeless face" (King, *From a Buick 8* 111). This creature—and the others that emerge from the car over its years in the barracks' shed—have a sense of the uncanny: simultaneously familiar and alien, recognizable but unsettling. The thing that first emerges from the Buick's trunk may look a bit like a bat, but as Sandy notes, "it doesn't *feel* like a bat" (King, *From a Buick 8* 118, emphasis original) and when Curt dissects it, its biological structure is nothing like that of a bat (King, *From a Buick 8* 164–9). Over the years, the car releases some other horrors, including corrosive vegetation and an enormous, alien fish creature, though the vast majority of beings that emerge from the Buick's trunk are dead or dying when they arrive, killed perhaps by the air or "maybe just the shock of finding [themselves] in our world" (King, *From a Buick 8* 119). The *Dark Tower* series is well-populated with such uncanny monsters, from the lobstrosities of *The Drawing of the Three* to the deformed creatures Roland and his *ka-tet* glimpse while crossing the Waste Lands on Blaine the monorail. One of the creatures from the Buick, sentient and vaguely humanoid, emerges alive, eliciting an overwhelming feeling of hatred and revulsion from the troopers who see it. As dispatcher Shirley Pasternak recalls, "We were more than horrified by its strangeness. Beyond the horror ... there was hate.... It woke an anger in me, an *enmity*, as well as fright and revulsion. The other things had been dead on arrival. This one wasn't, but we *wanted* it dead" (King, *From a Buick 8* 263, emphasis original). While they are able to kill the creature, the barracks' dog Mister Dillon bites it and is horrifically poisoned by its blood, burning up from the inside out, reminiscent of the effects of the deadly dragon sand in King's *The Eyes of the Dragon*. The interactions between the men and women of Troop D and the creatures that emerge from the Buick are steeped in a mix of curiosity, horror, and revulsion elicited by the otherworldly and alien, and this conduit between dimensions proves dangerous and violent.

Just as the Buick transports creatures from its own dimension into the shed behind Troop D, it also takes, and "just as the car can spew things out, it will ingest them" ("From a Buick 8" 58). This is what happens to Trooper Ennis Rafferty, who goes out to the shed to look at the Buick one afternoon and is never seen or heard from again; the same thing happens to a criminal named Brian Lippy, who escapes custody behind the barracks. Sandy later gets a brief glimpse into this other dimension, seeing the world that waits there—which is reminiscent of the Western Sea where Roland finds himself in *The Drawing of the Three*—as well as signs of the lost men, glimpsing Rafferty's hat and sidearm, as well as some of Brian Lippy's bones, from which the flesh appears to have been eaten (King, *From a Buick 8* 341). In this momentary glimpse, Sandy considers that just as the crew of Troop D have been horrified by the creatures that emerged from this other dimension, its own inhabitants may have been similarly terrified by their human interlopers, when he sees Rafferty's uniform Stetson staked to the ground, "as if Ennis Rafferty's killer had been afraid of the alien intruder even after the intruder's death, and had staked the most striking item of his clothing to make sure he wouldn't rise and walk the night like a hungry vampire" (*ibid.*). The Buick may also have played a role in Curt Wilcox's death: while Curt was hit and killed by a drunk driver during a routine traffic stop, that stop occurred right where the Buick had first appeared years before, a correlation that doesn't strike Sandy as coincidental (King, *From a Buick 8* 2) and serves as another example of the interconnectedness that radiates through the universe of the Dark Tower, where coincidence is always suspect.

From a Buick 8 offers a unique narrative perspective, as it "does not simply provide an embedded narrative within the proper narrative, but rather offers countless embedded narratives with thematic connections from various narrators presented in both 1st and 3rd person" (Perry 27–8). *From a Buick 8* also has a strong foundation in the oral tradition, with the novel taking the form of collective storytelling, with chapters alternating between "then" and "now" through a range of first-person narrators as the troopers and staff of Troop D tell Ned Wilcox about the Buick and his father, echoing the significance of storytelling, meaning, and a young man's tragic loss central to the narrative and structure of King's *Dark Tower* novel *The Wind Through the Keyhole*. Unsatisfied with the recalcitrant mystery of the Buick and striving to understand his father in the midst of his grief, Ned wants answers. As Sandy reflects as the storytelling comes to its conclusion,

10. Hearts in Atlantis *and Other "Low Men"*

Ned seemed to be saying, *"Tell me everything. But—this is important— tell me a story, one that has a beginning and a middle and an end where everything is explained. Because I deserve that. Don't shake the rattle of your ambiguity in my face. I deny its place. I repudiate its claim. I want a story"* (King, *From a Buick 8* 297, emphasis original). But Troop D has no answers and cannot provide Ned with the neat narrative closure he demands, and the reader is similarly stymied. A *Publishers Weekly* review of the novel notes that the Buick "certainly serves as a doorway between our world and ... what? Another dimension? Another galaxy? The Troopers never find out, despite their amateurish scientific investigations of it and the weird beings that occasionally emerge from the vehicle's trunk" ("From a Buick 8"). There are no answers to be given and everyone—Troop D, Ned Wilcox, and the reader—have to come to terms with the reality of the unknowable nature of this abiding mystery. As Michael Perry asks, "if we consider the sheer complexity of the fabula created, then it becomes possible to hone in on a concrete and focused story: how do we reconcile questions that have no answers?" (28). For all of the interconnections and correlations that radiate throughout King's *Dark Tower* series and his larger canon, there is also significant ambiguity: narrative lines that go nowhere, connections that prove meaningless or inconsequential, and questions that are never answered, like the stymying echoes (and dissonances) between *Insomnia* and the universe of the Dark Tower, the mystery of the Buick, and whether or not Wesley Smith's actions in "Ur" had unintended consequences. With so many overlapping worlds and interconnected universes encompassed by the *Dark Tower* series, there are connections and correlations, echoes and riddles, and sometimes there are questions that go unanswered and mysteries that remain unsolved.

While Troop D lives with the Buick for years, the appearance of the car in "Mile 81"[6] is comparatively brief, though no less dangerous or destructive. The station wagon in "Mile 81" is an anomaly in the cars of the low men: not flashy or garish, it is instead a mud-coated station wagon of indeterminate make, though it is clearly established as "a 'low man' vehicle that is actually alive and hungry" (Vincent, *The Dark Tower Companion* 104). The station wagon rolls up a rest stop exit ramp, seemingly driverless, and the front door opens, calling to the passing motorists, an invitation which several of them are helpless to refuse, whether out of concern or curiosity, as "the car reveals itself to be an unearthly predator, luring unsuspecting passersby to a hideous fate" ("Mile 81"). Good Samaritan Doug Clayton is the first to stop and when he peeks inside, he sees the interior is smeared with mud as well, including handprints on the steering wheel of which "the palm prints were awfully big ... but the finger marks were as narrow as pencils" (King, "Mile 81" 21). This unsettling realization comes too late, however, as a moment later the car begins to consume Doug, chewing his fingers, drawing him in, and leaving only artifacts of the man behind, like his wedding ring glittering on the pavement. While it might take on the outward appearance of a station wagon—like Troop D's ward looks like a Buick and Bobby sees approximations of a DeSoto and a Cadillac in *Hearts in Atlantis*—it is something else and even its shape, when not being looked at, is indeterminate. As it consumes Doug Clayton, "the station wagon lost its shape and puckered inward, like a mouth tasting something exceptionally sour ... or exceptionally sweet.... Then, with a *pouck* sound like a tennis ball being smartly struck by a racquet, it popped back into its station wagon shape" (King, "Mile 81" 22, emphasis original). Julianne Vernon meets a similar fate and when the Lussier family pulls up to the car, the parents Johnny and Carla quickly follow, leaving young Rachel and Blake on their own.

The adults fall prey to the car in "Mile 81" because they cannot accept the inexplicable nature of the car itself, only convinced of its reality as they are being consumed and too late to save themselves. But like so many of King's preternaturally aware children—*The Shining*'s Danny Torrance, *Pet Sematary*'s Ellie Creed, and *Hearts in Atlantis*'s Bobby Garfield, to name just a few—the children who see the car know immediately and instinctually that it is dangerous and not to be trusted. While the adults are busy looking for a rational explanation, Rachel and Blake Lussier are joined by Pete Simmons, who has been exploring the debauchery of the deserted rest stop, and the three of them are able to see, understand, and take on the station wagon in a way the adults are powerless to do. Rachel understands that "the car wasn't a car. It was some kind of monster" (King, "Mile 81" 34) and in understanding, immediately accepts the reality of this danger and its consequences. Rather than walking up to the car to get a better look, as all the adults before them have done, Rachel takes her little brother around it, giving the station wagon a wide berth. She remains observant and constantly vigilant, noticing when "the back tire of the station wagon, the one closest to them, was melting a little. A tentacle of what looked like liquid rubber was moving slowly across the pavement toward Blakie" (King, "Mile 81" 36), the car happy to quest and hunt for its next meal if it cannot lure it within its grasp. This fluidity is a common characteristic of the low men's cars: Bobby witnesses a similar phenomenon in *Hearts in Atlantis*, when the low men are preparing to take Ted and one of the cars sends out "a blackish-gray tentacle. It reached out, snared a cigarette wrapper, and pulled it back. A moment later the tentacle was a tire again, but the cigarette wrapper was sticking out of it like something half swallowed" (King 223). Troop D's Buick is similarly lively and elastic, spitting out bits of gravel placed in its tires' treads and healing the damage of its scratched paint (King, *From a Buick 8* 55, 78–9).

While the adults are unable to see or effectively respond to the threat posed by the station wagon that isn't really a station wagon, the children's instinctual suspension of disbelief empowers them and their ability to accept what their grown-up counterparts deem "impossible" saves their lives. While Troop D struggled to contain and observe the Buick, when Pete Simmons joins Rachel and Blake Lussier near the car, he immediately and instinctively knows that there is no way to contain the station wagon's power or convince the next adults who come of the danger it poses, and he takes matters into his own hands with a swift simplicity: training the focused light of his magnifying glass on one of the car's tentacle-ing, searching tires. While this simple kid power is not strong enough to destroy the car,[7] Pete does succeed in driving it away as the car "pulled in tighter and still tighter, becoming a fiery ball ... [and then] it shot up into the blue spring sky" (King, "Mile 81" 49). This plunges Pete into a consideration of the vast scope of cosmic horror as he finds "himself thinking of the cold darkness above the envelope of the earth's atmosphere—those endless leagues where anything might live and lurk" (*ibid.*). Like Wesley Smith in "Ur," these children's paths cross only briefly with that of the low men's car, though unlike Wesley, the consequences of this intersection are immediate and tragic, as both Lussier children are rescued but orphaned. Bobby Garfield, the men and women of Troop D, Wesley Smith, and the Lussier children are just a handful of those whose lives have been disrupted and devastated by the low men's passing presence and the overlapping of the world of the Dark Tower with their own, through disastrous incursions and interconnections that are central to the quest of Roland and his *ka-tet* in saving the Tower and restoring order across all worlds.

11

The Talisman and *Black House*

The Talisman and its sequel, *Black House*, are unique additions to King's *Dark Tower*-related canon for two key reasons. First, King co-authored these two books with fellow horror writer Peter Straub,[1] with these novels both expanding beyond the worlds of King's own creation through this collaboration and simultaneously connecting significantly back to King's interconnected *Dark Tower* universe, particularly with *Black House*. In addition, while the majority of King's other *Dark Tower*-related works—aside from the core books of the series itself—function effectively as standalone works, *Black House*'s position as a sequel to *The Talisman* complicates this. As McAleer argues, "*The Talisman*, as is the case with most stories followed by a sequel, only gathers its entire meaning and context by reading the second story, *Black House*, and vice-versa" (158). As a result, in reading *The Talisman* and *Black House* as *Dark Tower*-related novels, the reader is required to negotiate multiple and simultaneous textual engagements and interactions, including the continuing narrative that extends to *Black House* from *The Talisman*, the overt *Dark Tower* references, and the interconnection of these two novels with King and Straub's larger bodies of work, as well as the development of each author's respective style in the intervening years between *The Talisman* and *Black House*.

King and Straub's collaboration brought together two horror icons with very different writing styles and reputations. As Winter describes these differences, "In contrast to Stephen King's seemingly intuitive and colloquial storyteller's prose, the fiction of Peter Straub is deliberate, structurally complex, and above all, styled" (138). An *Esquire* magazine review following the release of *The Talisman* described King's style as "big, brassy, and bodacious," noting that King "has always expressed admiration for Straub's cooler, less emotional diction, and Straub in turn has praised the grand, 'operatic' quality of King's work" (qtd. in Beahm 227). The result of their combination in *The Talisman* is a narrative of epic proportions, encompassing multiple worlds (in this case, the real world in which young Jack Sawyer's mother is dying and the Territories, in which he has a chance to save her), and a synthesis of these two writers' styles. As Straub notes, "*The book has its own sound; it doesn't sound like me and it doesn't sound like Steve. And that's nice—that's what we wanted*" (qtd. in Winter 141, emphasis original). This amalgamation is true of *Black House* as well, though both authors' styles developed and evolved in the years between *The Talisman* and its sequel. In addition to the collaborative approach and the engagement of each author's trademark elements of horror, *Black House* also overtly dives into King's *Dark Tower* universe. As Vincent explains in *The Dark Tower Companion*, Straub suggested the *Dark Tower* connection for *Black House* because "he was curious about what the Breakers were and who the Crimson King was, and writing this book with King was one way to find those things out" (100). However, just as *Black House* expands upon and draws connections within the King universe, it does the same for Straub's larger canon as well, with Collings explaining that "implicit in *Black House* are Straub's signal accomplishments in novels as diverse as *Ghost Story*, *Shadowlands*, *Floating Dragon*, and the Blue Rose Trilogy. *Black House* fits seamlessly into the themes, the structures, and the styles of those books, those worlds, and expands upon them to give us a glimpse of a unity underlying Straub's fictions" (qtd. in Beahm 364). The result of *Black House* then, is not a *Dark Tower* story on which Straub is along for the ride, but rather "a linchpin narrative bringing together—explicitly, undeniably, and utterly—the mythic worlds King and Straub have drawn" (*ibid.*). creating a narrative that overlaps and interconnects with the larger worlds of both authors and their respective bodies of work.

The Talisman

Several critics have argued that *The Talisman*'s connection with King's *Dark Tower* universe is peripheral at best, with this inclusion relying largely—or even exclusively—on the narrative continuation in its sequel, *Black House*. Vincent describes these ties as "tenuous" (*The Dark Tower Companion* 94) and Wiater, Golden, and Wagner argue that "it is a mind-bending endeavor, attempting to incorporate *The Talisman* into the Stephen King Universe. In some ways, it should not be done at all" (63). However, in addition to serving as the narrative starting point for *Black House*, there are some significant elements that resonate between

The Talisman and King's *Dark Tower* universe, including the existence of multiple worlds (as well as their impact upon one another and the possibility of traveling between them) and the traditional quest narrative that shapes the novel.

The Territories to which twelve-year-old Jack Sawyer travels aren't quite Roland's Mid-World, though they bear some striking similarities. Vincent notes, "The Territories, where Jack Sawyer travels when he's not in America, are a borderland near Mid-World, a place akin to the region where the Callas are located" (*The Road to the Dark Tower* 215). It is easy to imagine that the Territories are a lot like what Roland's Mid-World was before that world moved on, an idyllic agrarian world with air so clear that, as Speedy Parker tells Jack, "if a man pulls a radish out of the ground, another man half a mile away will be able to smell that radish" (King and Straub, *The Talisman* 35), a distinction that grows increasingly clear to Jack as he begins to notice the smog, exhaust, and pollutants of his own world with heightened sensitivity after time spent in the Territories. The Territories also have characteristics of monarchy and feudalism, as evidenced by the dying Queen—and Jack's mother's twinner—Laura DeLoessian and the undead knights Jack has to confront in order to get and keep the Talisman, echoing recollections of Roland's childhood, the Arthurian influence that resonates throughout the *Dark Tower* series, and the setting and narrative of *The Eyes of the Dragon*, another of King's *Dark Tower*-related works. Finally, the Talisman itself is evocative of the Wizard's Glass of the *Dark Tower* series: a glowing, ethereal orb that has the power to heal Jack's mother, but it is also seductive, inviting obsession and covetousness that Jack must overcome and reject in order to fulfill his quest.

More significant than the similarities between Jack Sawyer's Territories and Roland of Gilead's Mid-World, however, is the existence of multiple worlds and the possibility for an individual to move between them, as *The Talisman* "was the place where King (with Straub) first explored in earnest the idea of infinite dimensions" (Wiater, Golden, and Wagner 64). This ability is central to Roland's narrative, both as he navigates between multiple worlds over the course of the *Dark Tower* series and as he draws his companions from their own respective worlds and timelines. Both *The Talisman* and the *Dark Tower* series also abound with "twinners," characters who have counterparts in a range of different worlds, like Jack's friend Speedy Parker/Parkus and Lily Sawyer/Laura DeLoessian in *The Talisman* and Henchick of the Manni in Calla Bryn Sturgis and the corresponding street preacher Earl Harrigan in *Song of Susannah* (King 312). These characters often play similar and profound roles in their disparate worlds—or on their different levels of the

11. The Talisman *and* Black House

Tower—and when Callahan hears the overlapping, proselytizing voices of Henchick and Harrigan from the *todash* space between the worlds, he thinks *"more twins"* (King, *Song of Susannah* 308, emphasis original), noting both their familiarity and their significance. This interconnection of worlds is also central to the importance of the Dark Tower itself: it is not the fate of Roland's world alone that hangs in the balance as the Crimson King and his forces fight to bring down the Tower, it is that of all worlds. With this interconnection also comes the fact that actions in one world can have a profound impact on other worlds. As Jack Sawyer's father Phil told Morgan Sloat, "anything major—any real changes we bring about—just might turn around and bite our asses back here. Everything has consequences, and some of those consequences might be on the uncomfortable side" (King and Straub, *The Talisman* 190). For example, as Phil notes, one of his and Morgan's trips to the Territories inadvertently results in the grisly death of their company electrician, Jerry Bledsoe (King and Straub, *The Talisman* 190) and on a more global, macrocosmic scale, a brief three-week war in the Territories coincides with Germany's 1939 invasion of Poland (King and Straub, *The Talisman* 190–1). Jack gets a personal sense of the potential impact of his own movement between the worlds when one of his flips from the Territories back to the America side inadvertently triggers an earthquake that kills five people (King and Straub, *The Talisman* 232–3). These interconnections and influences echo throughout the *Dark Tower* series as well, with Roland and his *ka-tet* working to combat threats to the Dark Tower in its many guises, such as their protection of the rose in 2 Hammarskjöld Plaza. As Strengell points out, the rose that Jake first finds in *The Waste Lands* "contains all of King's universes much in the same way as the Tower and the title object of *The Talisman*" (232). This interconnection of worlds is fundamental and potentially apocalyptic: if the Dark Tower falls in Roland's world, it is the end of all worlds, the destruction of the universe.

In this engagement with multiple universes and interconnected narratives, *The Talisman* also draws on a wide range of literary influences, the most overt of which is Mark Twain and his stories of his young protagonists, Tom Sawyer and Huckleberry Finn. Winter notes that like Twain's Huck Finn, Jack Sawyer heads West and "is, as his name implies, an amalgam of such fictional boyhood adventurers, at once steeped in their traditions and yet a wholly new and modern character" (143). Also like Huck Finn, Jack's journey is arduous and transformative: each of these protagonists "light out for the Territory" (Twain 362), and in some ways, "civilization" is just as much Jack's enemy as it was Huck's. As Magistrale points out in *Landscape of Fear*, "Sawyer, like the Huck

Finn prototype on whom he was modelled, must flee continually from violence and deceit ... [aside from Wolf and Speedy] every human being and social institution Jack encounters on his voyage to California seeks to enslave him physically or manipulate him psychologically" (101). While Twain is an overt reference invoked in Jack Sawyer's name, his quest, and his journey into the wilderness, King and Straub also draw on a wide range of other literary influences, with Beahm arguing that "*The Talisman* echoes Tolkien and C.S. Lewis, Mark Twain and *The Wizard of Oz*" (228–9), with sentient and hungry trees (King and Straub, *The Talisman* 133–4), closets that become portals to another world (King and Straub, *The Talisman* 468–70), and Jack's deep and heartsick longing for home. Wiater, Golden, and Wagner also note the echoes of Charles Dickens's *Oliver Twist* (1839) in Jack and Wolf's stay at the Sunlight Gardener Home, a Victorian influence that is notable in *Black House* as well, where Dickens's *Bleak House* (1853) is more overtly invoked.[2]

Another element that connects *The Talisman* with King's *Dark Tower* series is the central structure of the quest narrative. As John Skow points out of *The Talisman*, "The plot is the oldest in literature, a quest: confront the Minotaur, find the Holy Grail, follow the yellow brick road." In this case, Jack's quest is to travel across the country—flipping between his familiar America and the Territories—and return with the Talisman that can save his mother, who is dying of cancer.[3] Joseph Campbell explains in *The Hero with a Thousand Faces* that the hero's quest involves distinct stages of "*separation—initiation—return.... A hero ventures forth from the world of common day into a region of supernatural wonder: fabulous forces are there encountered and a decisive victory is won: the hero comes back from this mysterious adventure with the power to bestow boons on his fellow man*" (30, emphasis original). Following this traditional trajectory, Jack sets out, encounters strangers both friendly and threatening, rises to overcome challenges, resists temptation, gains his prize, and returns transformed and able to save his mother's life. This quest narrative formula is a common feature between *The Talisman* and the *Dark Tower* series. Roland's quest is all-encompassing: it is an obsession and his driving, defining motivation. Jack's quest can be read as a miniature version of Roland's own: Roland's quest is to save the Dark Tower, with the destruction of all worlds hanging in the balance, while Jack's quest is to save his mother, who is his whole world. Both Roland and Jack are called to their duty as young men, each faces thrilling victories and crushing defeats, and each suffers almost unbearable losses along the way. Both Roland and Jack are transformed by their quests: the men they become and the way they see the world around them are a direct result of their quests and the experiences they have along those journeys. In this respect, Jack gets off easier than Roland does: Jack returns to his mother, saves her life, and grows into a man who has forgotten the wonderful and horrible things he has experienced (though these memories return to him in *Black House*). Roland, however, is not so lucky, as just when his journey's end is in sight, he finds himself again and again sent back to the beginning, a purgatorial repetition of a quest that may remain eternally unresolved.

Black House

While *The Talisman* may bear some similarities to King's *Dark Tower* universe, *Black House* is an overtly *Dark Tower*-connected novel, with its actions impacting and being impacted by the Crimson King's acquisition of Breakers to further his goal of the Tower's fall. As Wiater, Golden, and Wagner note, while it is a direct sequel to *The Talisman*, "structurally, *Black House* is more reminiscent of *Insomnia* than *The Talisman* because of its slow movement from the 'real' to the fantastic, and in the fact that its characters ... are merely pawns in a much larger cosmic chess game" (69). *Black House* picks up Jack Sawyer's story as an adult: following an illustrious career as one of the youngest and best detectives with the LAPD, he retires early to move to French Landing, Wisconsin, in part because it is reminiscent of the yet-unremembered Territories. Like *The Talisman*, *Black House* carries echoes of Twain, with French Landing located on the banks of the Mississippi River, where in Twain "on the river, at home with nature and free to indulge an appreciation for the primitive.... Huck and Jim discover a sanctuary from the evils of nineteenth-century civilization" (Magistrale, *Landscape* 102). French Landing is initially just such a respite for Jack as well, where he makes friends, forgets the horrors of his time as a policeman, and represses the memories that are fighting their way to the surface. But then a cannibalistic monster referred to as The Fisherman begins to prey upon French Landing's children and the novel becomes "Part murder-mystery and part mythic end-of-the world struggle" (Smith), as Jack is called back to action and back to his boyhood memories, both of which are essential in solving the case and stopping the murders.

The murderer ends up being a local geriatric with a dark and violent history named Charles Burnside, though the key to stopping him runs deeper: Burnside is undeniably a human monster, but he is also being possessed by a supernatural being referred to as Mr. Munshun, which is itself an emissary of the Crimson King,[4] using Burnside to bring him children in the hopes of finding psychically-talented ones that he can press into service as Breakers to help bring about the fall of the Dark Tower. French Landing is a thin place between the worlds, a borderland,[5] and as King and Straub write, a "strange flavor of the dreamlike and slightly unnatural is characteristic of borderlands. It can be detected in every seam between one specific territory and another" (*Black House* 30). As a result, the work of the Crimson King extends its influence into French Landing, through Burnside's violence and select residents' awareness of this permeability. In addition to Jack's returning awareness of these other worlds, Judy Marshall senses the Crimson King and his dark intent, information conveyed by Sophie, her "twinner" on the other side. Judy and Sophie's relationship proves indispensable in retrieving Judy's son Tyler when he is taken. However, this awareness also gets Judy institutionalized in the local hospital's psychiatric ward, which brings into stark contrast the versatility and suspension of disbelief of which children are capable, as opposed to the rigid perceptions of reality adhered to by most of their adult counterparts. The mysterious word "opopanax" is invoked repeatedly throughout *Black House* and, as the same word Callahan uses in *Wolves of the Calla* when he sends the feather around to call people to meeting (King 20), hints at a gathering and collective confrontation, though the characters initially remain unaware of this coming together or its enormous consequences, which extend well beyond the Fisherman and the immediate horrors effecting French Landing.

When Jack begins to remember and flips from French Landing back to the Territories of his youth, he finds them darkly changed: not only does he discover Tyler Marshall's baseball cap and know that the killer has brought Tyler into this world, there is also "a kind of vibration.... A black and nasty vibration like a headache, [and] a smell like ancient smoke" (King and Straub, *Black House* 204). The Territories are no longer the idyllic, fresh-aired reprieve of Jack's childhood. In fact, he has found himself further afield, in a part of Roland the gunslinger's world that has moved on. The vibration comes from The Big Combination (or as Roland knows it, *An-tak*), a factory where non-psychically gifted children are worked to death, the Crimson King's "terrible power source in End-World" (Vincent, *The Road to the Dark Tower* 216). The journey of Roland's *ka-tet* comes close to overlapping here with Jack's own, as this same awful machine "is responsible for the red glow Susannah sees in the distance from the ramparts of Castle Discordia" (*ibid.*) in *Song of Susannah*. The reach of the Big Combination and its terrible power extends well beyond End-World, as it is also used to "fuel evil—despots, pedophiles, tyrants and torturers—in a great numberless string of universes" (*ibid.*). While Jack is unaware of these details, this unsettling

11. The Talisman *and* Black House

vibration is his first indication that while he is in another world, it is not the Territories he knew and came to love on his boyhood quest.

In his journeys to this other world, Jack gets drawn into the tales of End-World and the gunslingers, even hearing specific mention of Roland and his *ka-tet*. At one point when he flips over, Jack finds himself in an abandoned medical tent, the setting of Roland's vampiric horror in the *Dark Tower* story "The Little Sisters of Eluria." Sophie quickly leads Jack away from the tent, telling him, "The Little Sisters don't come out when the sun shines ... [and] we'll be gone our separate ways from here long before dark" (King and Straub, *Black House* 432). When Jack is reunited with his old friend Speedy Parker/Parkus, he finds that Parkus may have been a gunslinger, one of those tasked with protecting the Mid-World that was, "before the world moved on" (King and Straub, *Black House* 436), though Parkus himself denies this (King and Straub, *Black House* 436, 443). Jack, Parkus, and Sophie palaver in a now-deserted speaking ring, where Parkus explains as much as he can about the Crimson King, the Dark Tower, and the gunslingers who seek to keep it from falling, regretting that it is "hard telling what you need to know and what you don't.... I leave out the wrong piece of information, maybe all the stars go dark. Not just here, but in a thousand thousand universes" (King and Straub, *Black House* 441). This palaver also draws upon the shared lexicon of the Western genre tradition, which is foundational to the *Dark Tower* series as a whole. Westerns also hold special personal significance for Jack, in his fond memories of his mother's acting in these genre films, though when Jack imagines himself and his friends as the cavalry, Parkus corrects him, noting that this power is well beyond Jack's own and "the cavalry is Roland of Gilead and his new gunslingers" (King and Straub, *Black House* 444). Another key element of this interconnection that is central to Jack, Parkus, and Sophie's palaver is the definition and use of the Crimson King's Breakers. Parkus tells Jack that of the six original Beams holding up the Tower, three have been destroyed, two hold some power, and "only one still holds true" (King and Straub, *Black House* 443). Tyler Marshall could well be the Breaker who tips the scales and brings about the fall of the Dark Tower, as Parkus tells Jack that Tyler is "potentially, one of the two most powerful Breakers in the history of all the worlds" (King and Straub, *Black House* 446), second only to Ted Brautigan (*Hearts in Atlantis*, *The Dark Tower*).

If French Landing occupies a borderland between the worlds, Black House itself is the direct portal that connects them. Just as a person may be able to sense something special in these borderlands places, Black House repels those who may seek to find it: stories about it fail to travel far, eyes refuse to see the overgrown drive that leads to it, and even those who have been there soon forget the way. Those who persevere and make their way toward the house are beset by all manner of monstrous defenses. When the Thunder Five are sent by Jack on a reconnaissance mission to find the house, they encounter psychological and physical horrors that work to keep them from Black House's door, including ghosts from their own pasts, searing pain, and a monstrous dog, whose bite not only kills but literally liquefies one of the bikers (King and Straub, *Black House* 393–403). When the omniscient narrative perspective allows the reader to look directly at Black House, what is seen is unsettling. As King and Straub write,

> Black House—like Shirley Jackson's Hill House, like the turn-of-the-century monstrosity in Seattle known as Rose Red—is *not* sane. It is not entirely of this world. It's hard to look at from the outside—the eyes play continual tricks—but if one *can* hold it steady for a few seconds, one sees a three-story dwelling of perfectly ordinary size.... Inside, however, it is different. Inside, Black House is *large*. Black House is, in fact, almost infinite [*Black House* 537–8, emphasis original].

Black House is a haunted house story on an epic, universe-spanning scale. Bruce Fretts argues that "once Jack and his posse enter the titular structure, *Black House* becomes an old-fashioned haunted house story" and McAleer notes the interconnections with King's larger body of work and King's television miniseries *Rose Red* (2002), as "the constantly changing floor plans of Rose Red recall the slippage and constant transformation seen in Black House" (160). However, for all the familiar haunted house elements engaged and negotiated by *Black House*, its position as a portal to End-World raises those stakes substantially.

Once Jack and his *ka-tet* have navigated the supernatural and human horrors of Black House—which include their own worst memories, a depthless chasm, otherworldly monsters, and a wall of preserved human faces (King and Straub, *Black House* 584–5)—they find themselves in End-World. Here, elements of the other worlds of the larger *Dark Tower* universe are synthesized, as Tyler encounters the carnivorous trees that nearly snared *The Talisman*'s twelve-year-old Jack Sawyer (King and Straub, *Black House* 550) and Burnside tells Tyler they will be taking a monorail to get to their audience with the Crimson King, the last monorail in End-World, though "once there were two others. Patricia ... and Blaine. They're gone. Went crazy. Committed suicide" (King and Straub, *Black House* 560), a narrative thread included in the *Dark Tower* novels *The Waste Lands* and *Wizard and Glass*. The Talisman's lingering power that Jack has carried with him into adulthood, as well as their combined powers as a cohesive group, allow the men to stand against Mr. Munshun, defeat him, and rescue Tyler. Armand "Beezer" St. Pierre, the leader of the Thunder Five, had his daughter taken by The

Fisherman and his righteous anger as a bereaved father gives him the power to help destroy Mr. Munshun, while police chief Dale Gilbertson's outrage against these atrocities and his desire to protect his town and its people allow him to do the same. Jack's recollection of his childhood quest and his reclamation of the power he discovered within himself upon that journey consolidate their collective abilities as they destroy Mr. Munshun. In the end, however, the ultimate power is Tyler Marshall's: Jack and his *ka-tet* can rescue Tyler and flee End-World, but it is only Tyler who can destroy the Big Combination and set free the tortured children condemned to power it. Turning his prodigious psychic power against the machine, Tyler brings it down, an action that echoes through multiple levels of the Tower as "in worlds strung side by side in multiple dimensions throughout infinity ... evils shrivel and disperse" (King and Straub, *Black House* 601) and "up, up in his high faraway confinement, the Crimson King feels a deep pain in his gut and drops into a chair, grimacing. Something, he knows, something fundamental, has changed in his dreary fiefdom" (*ibid.*). Neither Tyler nor Jack can save the Dark Tower—that is well beyond even their remarkable abilities— but they have forestalled the final confrontation, deprived the Crimson King of an ultimate Breaker, and freed the children of the Big Combination, who follow them home and out into the light of a Wisconsin summer day.

The conclusion of *Black House* pulls Jack out of the real world of French Landing, permanently exiling him to the Territories. As the town celebrates the end of The Fisherman's reign of horror and the safe return of Tyler Marshall, Jack is shot by Wanda Kinderling, the furious wife of the murderer Jack first came to French Landing to find and stop. Wounded beyond any hope of survival, Speedy Parker/Parkus flips Jack back to the Territories, where his survival is far from assured, but at least possible. Jack's final transition is fittingly narrated in fairy tale fashion, marking the start of Jack's new chapter with the opening "Once upon a time (as all the best old stories used to begin when we all lived in the forest and nobody lived anywhere else)" (King and Straub, *Black House* 621). This channels the fairy tale cadence of some of Roland's favorite stories and the "Once upon a bye, long before your grandfather's grandfather was born" of his own telling in *The Wind Through the Keyhole* (King 109). In addition to this larger, established narrative tradition, the cadence of this line also brings Jack back to himself and his own personal mythology, in his childhood recollection of "when everyone had lived in California and no one had lived anyplace else" (King and Straub, *The Talisman* 201). This is a new start for Jack, one that is equally true to both his longing for the Territories and the man he has grown to become in the real world. While Parkus speculates in *Black House*'s closing pages that Jack may yet have another role to play in the fate of the Dark Tower (King and Straub 624), Jack does not reappear in the series' final books.

As with *The Talisman*—and so much of King's larger body of work—*Black House* is intricately connected to a wide range of other literary influences beyond King's own. The Mississippi River setting and central position of an adolescent male protagonist on a transformative journey continues to evoke Twain. Charles Dickens's *Bleak House* is invoked in King and Straub's title and serves a key narrative role, as Jack reads Dickens's novel to his blind friend Henry Leyden. As Fretts notes, "*Black House* also qualifies as Dickensian in other respects: its size (625 pages), scope (spanning two worlds—small-town Wisconsin and a parallel realm called the Territories), and sprawling cast of characters." The opening pages of *Bleak House*, as Jack reads them to Henry, are evocative of their own situation as well, and as Jack reads of the London fog, "what he is reading unhappily reminds him of French Landing ... all of it choked by unseen fog ... [which] glides hungry and searching down the valleys" (King and Straub, *Black House* 188). However, the most significant literary influence in *Black House* is arguably that of Edgar Allan Poe and particularly his poem "The Raven," from whose lines are drawn the title of the novel's third section, "Night's Plutonian Shore." Tansy Freneau, the bereaved mother of Irma, one of The Fisherman's victims, recalls this poem from her high school English class. This recollection—and Tansy's dead-voiced recitation—of Poe's poem prefigures the appearance of a crow named Gorg "a'tappin" (*ibid.*) on her door. Like Poe's raven, Gorg has come to torment Tansy in her grief, but its larger role is as an agent of the Crimson King, and it also tempts Tyler Marshall to the hedges from which Burnside is able to grab him. In coming to Tansy, Gorg works to incite her to rally her fellow citizens to angry mob violence as they descend on the police station with the intention of taking and lynching the man the police have in custody as the suspected Fisherman. This crow also brings to mind the many permutations and dark powers of Randall Flagg in *The Stand* (as well as his multiple forms and identities throughout King's *Dark Tower*-related works and within the series itself), who has the power to call upon several animals and inhabit crows, allowing him to watch his adversaries and spy upon them undetected. In similar fashion, *Black House*'s Gorg wreaks havoc and tracks Jack's *ka-tet*, observing them as they approach Black House. Recognizing the crow's threat, in a move reminiscent of the gunslingers themselves, Jack turns, "firing almost before he sees with his eyes" (King and Straub, *Black House* 573), the description here echoing the oath of the gunslingers, as Jack shoots so quickly that his friends can't count the shots.

King and Straub's collaborative writing style evolved significantly between *The Talisman* and *Black House* and one of the distinguishing narrative characteristics that marks this evolution is the collective third-person narration in *Black House*, ushering the reader alongside as part of the "royal we." For example, in an early tour of French Landing, King and Straub write that "moving toward the sun, we glide away from the river and over the shining tracks, the backyards and roofs of Nailhouse Row, then a line of Harley-Davidson motorcycles tilted on their kickstands" (*Black House* 6). This omniscient perspective provides foreshadowing, such as in brief mention of Black House's "No Trespassing" sign emerging from the creeping Dickensian fog, though Jack remains "completely unaware of the black house he one day will have to enter" (King and Straub, *Black House* 188). King uses a similar approach in the later *Dark Tower* books, particularly in foreshadowing significant losses, as when he describes Roland, Eddie, Susannah, and Jake in *The Dark Tower* with the direct address that "I'd have you see them this way ... because now they are ka-tet for the last time" (383). As King uses this direct address in *The Dark Tower* to warn his readers of the impending loss, as well as to mourn and apologize ("Say sorry" [*ibid.*]), the use of this omniscient "royal we" in *Black House* has emotionally resonant and comforting capabilities as well, as Jack's friends find his wounded body gone and are reassured in the hope that he may survive in the Territories. As King and Straub—and their readers—bid this group farewell, they say "we think that here we must leave them for good.... Let us leave them hoping" (*Black House* 617).

While *Black House* draws readers more deeply into King's *Dark Tower* universe, it is interconnected with Straub's fictional worlds as well, particularly "when Milton Wanderley, brother of Don Wanderley from Straub's novel *Ghost Story*, is mentioned in passing" (Wiater, Golden, and Wagner 70), as one of the victims whose faces hang on the wall of Black House. *Black House* is an amalgamation of King and Straub's approaches to horror, encompassing narrative, description, and theme, as "serial killers in Wisconsin are squarely in Straub territory, [and] it's clear that the book is set in the Stephen King universe" (*ibid.*). With *The Talisman* and *Black House*, King and Straub merge their two universes, providing countless connections and paths to follow, and reminding readers once more—as all familiar with the Dark Tower well know—that there are other worlds than these.

Conclusion

King's *The Dark Tower*, the final novel of the series, was published in 2004, but like the gunslinger's ongoing journey, the *Dark Tower* universe remains a constant presence in King's work. Following the publication of his seven-book series, King published an additional *Dark Tower* novel, *The Wind Through the Keyhole*, in 2012, whose action takes place between the end of the fourth book (*Wizard and Glass*) and the start of the fifth (*Wolves of the Calla*). The influence of the *Dark Tower* series continues to resonate throughout King's larger body of fiction following the series' conclusion in 2004 as well: the narrator in the short story "N." (included in the 2008 collection *Just After Sunset*) has a madness-inducing encounter with a presence in a circle of stones that bears a strong resemblance to a speaking demon or the Lovecraftian horrors that lurk in the *todash* space between worlds. *Lisey's Story* (2006) includes mention of the Territories, connecting that novel to *The Talisman, Black House, The Eyes of the Dragon*, and King's larger *Dark Tower* universe.[1] In *11/22/63* (2011), Jake Epping goes through a magic door to travel to a different time; in this journey, he also sees a Takuro Spirit, the make and model Roland and his *ka-tet* encounter in post–Captain Trips Topeka at the start of *Wizard and Glass*. In an interview discussing the novel, however, King says "he made a special effort not to have *11/22/63* turn into a Dark Tower book because it is so firmly rooted in real history," with Vincent arguing that the appearance of Nozz-A-La cola and Takuro Spirits "should probably be treated as indicators of a parallel or altered time line rather than as a strong connection to the series" (*The Dark Tower Companion* 93). Roland's old adversary Flagg/Marten Broadcloak/Walter o' Dim/The Man in Black may be back in a new form with a new name (Richard Farris this time) in *Gwendy's Button Box*, the 2017 Castle Rock novel King wrote with Richard Chizmar, where Farris tempts Gwendy with an unfathomable power that has disastrous consequences.[2] The Dark Tower is at the nexus of so much of

King's vast universe that it seems likely these connections will continue to appear in and engage with King's work throughout the entirety of his career. In addition to the Dark Tower's continuing presence and influence in King's writing, the Dark Tower narrative has continued beyond the page in a wide variety of forms, including an online game called *Discordia*, an extensive series of comics, and a feature film starring Idis Elba and Matthew McConaughey. Even now, new possibilities for the *Dark Tower* universe are on the horizon.

Discordia was launched as a free-to-play game on King's website in 2009, inviting players to enter into and interact with the *Dark Tower* universe. The game was developed by Brian Stark, Judy Hahn, Marsha DeFillippo, and Robin Furth, who is one of King's former assistants, a *Dark Tower* expert, and author of *The Dark Tower: A Complete Concordance*. As Jack Gardner explains, the team capitalized on one of the existing major conflicts within the series, that between the Tet and Sombra Corporations. The game's playable character, however, was an entirely new creation: an agent called Op19, who is "working for the Tet Corporation's Investigation and Surveillance Unit" (Vincent, *The Dark Tower Companion* 112) and must search the Dixie Pig Restaurant, travel the tunnels to the Fedic Dogan, then return to Keystone Earth. Jack Gardner describes *Discordia* as "basically a hidden-object game mixed with some gunslinging action sequences" as the player must find a series of magical objects. Originally planned as a continuing episodic game, after this initial chapter, there was a long wait until the second chapter came out in 2013. While the first chapter of *Discordia* adhered closely to the narrative and key elements of King's *Dark Tower* series, the second chapter tells a story all its own. The game is situated in real time, so four years have passed for the characters within the game, just as they have for its players. At the center of this second chapter is another new character, Arina Yokova. Breaking down the walls between fiction and reality, just as King did in *Song of Susannah* and *The Dark Tower*, Yokova is familiar with the *Dark Tower* novels, believes the Dark Tower turning Roland back to the Mohaine Desert is essentially a technological glitch, and dedicates herself to "free[ing] Roland from this loop by any means necessary" (Vincent, *The Dark Tower Companion* 114), well-armed with her extensive knowledge of Roland's life and adventures from the novels. As Furth explains, *Discordia*'s addition of new characters and its meta-textual engagement are part of the *Dark Tower*'s "expanded universe" (qtd. in Vincent, *The Dark Tower Companion* 117), separate but connected, without the aim of adhering to the narrative or facts of King's series. There have been no additional chapters of the game released as yet, though that does not mean that King's team could not return to the project at a later date. Gardner argues that if new *Discordia* game play is developed, it would be an ideal fit for virtual reality (VR) format, which was an approach used in *IT: Escape from Pennywise*, a VR experience released in tandem with Andy Muschietti's 2017 film adaptation of *IT, Chapter 1*.

The most expansive adaptation of and engagement with King's *Dark Tower* series outside of the novels themselves has been a series of *Dark Tower* comics published by Marvel, which were well-received by fans. As Graeme McMillan reports on the initial *Dark Tower* series of comics, the first issue "was the second-best-selling comic of February 2008, with the rest of the seven-part series remaining at the top of the charts." Running from 2007 to 2017, these adaptations have now been collected and released in three major volumes: *The Dark Tower, The Dark Tower: The Gunslinger,* and *The Dark Tower: The Drawing of the Three*. Each collection includes five to six collected narrative runs, of five to seven issues each. The first of these Marvel adaptations, *The Dark Tower*, took a particularly unique approach to adapting King's series. Rather than retelling the familiar story and adapting the established narrative in a new medium, the authors and artists instead chose to fill in some of the blanks in Roland's past, telling stories that had not been included in King's series, though many had been briefly mentioned in passing. Marvel's *The Dark Tower* includes *The Gunslinger Born, The Long Road Home, Treachery, Fall of Gilead,* and *Battle of Jericho Hill*. While some of this narrative focuses on Roland and his *ka-tet*'s mission in Mejis, including the death of Susan Delgado, as recounted in *Wizard and Glass*, other issues and narrative arcs bring in new or expanded information. This approach to adaptation raises the question of the role these comics—and other adaptations, like *Discordia* and the feature film—play in understanding King's series and the *Dark Tower* universe, namely whether or not their narratives should be considered as *Dark Tower* canon (Vincent 145), which has resulted in significant debate among fans. This is an interesting question, particularly because while King has authorized these adaptations—even serving as creative director and executive director of the Marvel Comics versions—they are not of his own creation. Furth, who is credited with plotting and consultation on the full run of the Marvel Comics adaptations of the *Dark Tower* stories, argues that in the multiplicity of worlds that surround the Dark Tower, "I always view the *Dark Tower* comics as existing in one of these parallel worlds. If the *Dark Tower* novels exist in Tower Keystone, or the central world of the *Dark Tower* universe, the *Dark Tower* comics exist in a spinoff world, one which is very similar to, but not exactly the same as" those of King's novels (*The Gunslinger: The Man in Black* i). In the world imagined by the authors and artists of *The Dark Tower* comics series, readers witness the rise of Aileen, the first and only female gunslinger of Gilead (*The Dark Tower: Treachery*) and learn the details of the Battle of Jericho Hill (*The Dark Tower: Battle of Jericho Hill*), where Roland loses nearly all of his original *ka-tet* and which he recalls in only brief moments of largely unexamined recollection in King's *Dark Tower* series, the most detailed of which is featured in one of Roland's dreams in *Wolves of the Calla* (King 169–172). Throughout the Marvel Comics series, readers similarly get other blanks filled in, including increased narrative development of the murder of Roland's father and the fall of Gilead (*The Dark Tower: The Fall of Gilead*).

Following the initial *Dark Tower* run of comics that delved into Roland's backstory and untold tales, the other Marvel Comics—*The Gunslinger* and *The Drawing of the Three*—take a more traditional approach to adaptation, sticking closely to the narrative of King's series, though still bringing a new perspective and voice to the telling of those stories. *The Gunslinger* series includes *The Journey Begins*, *The Little Sisters of Eluria*, *The Battle of Tull*, *The Way Station*, *The Man in Black*, and a series of individual stories collected as *Last Shots*. Furth and team deviate some from King's series—including Roland and Jake briefly separating as Roland leaves Jake behind and begins his trek through the mountain alone (*The Gunslinger: The Man in Black*)—but by and large, the story remains a fairly traditional adaptation of King's first *Dark Tower* book, *The Gunslinger*, and the *Dark Tower* story "Little Sisters of Eluria." The same is true of Marvel's *The Drawing of the Three*, in which Roland brings Eddie, Susannah, and Jake into his world, though the comics present each character taking a first-person narrative position in turns, providing a more intimate perspective on their thoughts, feelings, and recollections of their former lives as they join Roland. Marvel's *The Drawing of the Three* also shifts the narrative break in King's series as Roland, Eddie, and Susannah draw Jake into their world by the series' end (*The Drawing of the Three: The Sailor*), while in King's series this is a more protracted process, highlighting the threatening madness of Jake and Roland's doubled memories, and with Roland and Jake not reunited until midway through *The Waste Lands*, the series' third book. In addition, Marvel's *The Drawing of the Three* adds an extra layer of interconnection, as the emissaries of the Crimson King sense the future power of Roland's *ka-tet* and attempt to kill both Eddie and Susannah as children (*The Drawing of the Three: The Prisoner*; *The Drawing of the Three: The Lady of Shadows*), expanding the mythos of the Dark Tower and further emphasizing the paths of Eddie and Susannah's lives that brought them into Roland's quest.[3]

The Marvel comics also feature some of the legends of Arthur Eld, including Roland's telling of "The Fall of Lord Perth" in *The Gunslinger: Last Shots* and a treasure trove of information provided in essays by Furth, ranging from the creation of Maerlyn's Rainbow and the smelting of Excalibur to make the guns of the Eld to the *charyou tree* tradition of which Susan Delgado becomes a tragic part (Vincent 149–53). These Marvel adaptations also take the opportunity to more fully explore some of the series' peripheral but significant characters, like Sheemie Ruiz, who Roland meets in Mejis and encounters again outside Algul Siento in the final novel of King's series. Sheemie plays a significant role throughout *The Dark Tower* arc of comics, following Roland and his *ka-tet* home to Gilead and being captured along the way by a dogan robot, through whom he gains extraordinary powers (*The Dark Tower: The Long Road Home*). Sheemie tells more of his own heroic story in detail in *Sheemie's Tale* (collected in *The Gunslinger: Last Shots*), including his fight against monsters in the vein of Lovecraftian Great Old Ones, who wish to harness Sheemie's formidable power and use him to destroy the universe (26–39).

While some of the Marvel Comics' narrative stays close to King's original and other parts deviate significantly, McMillan notes that these variations underscore the multiple realities engaged by King's series, arguing that "in the complicated, parallel-world reality of the larger *Dark Tower* mythology … [the Marvel Comics are a] separate but equal take on a series of recurring events—and one that might end up going in an entirely different direction at any point, depending on the whims of the creators involved." In 2018, the *Dark Tower* graphic novels' intellectual property was acquired from Marvel by Gallery 13, the graphic novel imprint of Simon and Schuster, King's long-time publisher (Johnston), which may well result in these adaptations taking a different path forward, should additional comics be released.

Dozens of King's stories and novels have been adapted for film and television, with their quality running the gamut from excellent (*The Shawshank Redemption*, *The Green Mile*) to awful (*The Lawnmower Man*, countless *Children of the Corn* sequels). Given the sheer scope of King's *Dark Tower* series, it is one of King's few works that was long considered "unfilmmable" (Harp and Warner), a challenge which was echoed in the *Dark Tower* film project's decade-long stay in development as it passed through various hands, treatments, and approaches. *The Dark Tower* finally made it to the big screen in 2017, directed by Nikolaj Arcel and starring Idris Elba as Roland, Matthew McConaughey as the Man in Black, and Tom Taylor as Jake Chambers. Much like the Marvel Comics adaptations, *The Dark Tower* film is perhaps most productively considered as presenting another possible world, events as they are playing out on another level of the Dark Tower and "exist[ing] on its own terms as a sort of companion piece" (Seddon) rather than a traditional adaptation. Producer Ron Howard describes the film as "another go-around in the universe. It allows us to use the language and the characters, but it liberated us from a literal adaptation" (qtd. in *The Dark Tower: The Art* 15). In this film, Jake is plagued by visions of Roland and his world, much as he is at the start of King's novel *The Waste Lands*, though these visions are explained by Jake's telepathic ability (described as "the shine," in reference to King's *The Shining* and later, its sequel *Doctor Sleep*) rather than because he has been to Mid-World, loved and been betrayed by Roland, and died twice, once in his own world and once in the gunslinger's. Roland's quest has shifted from protecting the Dark Tower to seeking vengeance on the Man in Black, though he rediscovers his true purpose by the film's end. The film draws in disparate elements from throughout King's *Dark Tower* series, including the significance of the number nineteen, the hybrid *taheen*, and a momentary passing reference to billy-bumblers' ability to speak, while leaving others out entirely, like Roland's vast history, Eddie, and Susannah. Along with the film's reference to Jake's "shine," the film is a compendium of King universe Easter eggs, as screenwriter Akiva Goldman notes that "I thought the more the movie can suggest a connectedness with the larger Stephen King universe, the better" (qtd. in *The Dark Tower: The Art* 199). These visual cues serve to underscore the interconnection of the *Dark Tower* with King's larger body of work—including a Saint Bernard, a model Plymouth Fury, a portal numbered 1408, a deteriorating amusement park marquee reading "Pennywise," and a poster of Rita Hayworth, among others—and while nothing substantial ever comes of these connections, they work to firmly establish the viewer within King's world.

Despite this parallel universe possibility, however, reviews were negative and the film is generally considered a failure. One of the kindest reviews praised the film's "visual spectacle of action and fantasy" (Reyes), though the majority described *The Dark Tower* with assessments ranging from "underwhelm[ing]" (DeFore) and "astoundingly awful" (Ryan), to "a complete disaster" (Callahan). Most reviewers praised the performances of the lead actors, particularly Elba and McConaughey, finding fault instead with the film's organization and narrative, which had some interesting moments, though like the King references, these largely failed to come together in a cohesive way. Matt Goldberg analyzes these shortcomings from a genre perspective, arguing that "there's no half-assing a fantasy epic. Either you want to draw people into a big, strange new world or you want to keep them grounded in ours.... Despite strong performances from leads Idris Elba and Matthew McConaughey, *The Dark Tower* is too meager to feel grandiose, and too haphazard to feel grounded." Howard has some thoughts on genre and the film's failure as well, reflecting in hindsight that the PG-13 rating and "boy's adventure" approach to the narrative was a misstep, arguing that "it should've been horror" (qtd. in Reyes). While these genre considerations are significant, as the hybridity of King's series has demonstrated, allying an adaptation with the traditions of a single genre is not necessarily the key to success in making and marketing an effective film adaptation of King's *Dark Tower*, which may make it a challenge for the standard Hollywood feature film formula.

However, King's *Dark Tower* series continues to enchant readers and fans, and there seems to be a new adaptation approach on the horizon, with *The Dark Tower* optioned and cast by Amazon Studios as a long-form series. The series will reportedly take on Roland's story chronologically, beginning with an adaptation of *Wizard and Glass*, with a sweeping scope and the time necessary for extensive world creation and character development. This adaptation seems to be drawing on tried-and-true fantasy and horror approaches by following in the structural footsteps of the enormously popular HBO series *Game of Thrones* (2011–2019) and bringing in former *Walking Dead* (2010–present) showrunner Glen Mazzara. As Mazzara notes of this new adaptation's approach, King's *Dark Tower* stories "need a long format to capture the complexity of Roland's coming of age—how he became The Gunslinger, how Walter became The Man in Black and how their rivalry cost Roland everything and everyone he ever loved" (qtd. in Seddon). While not much is known about this new adaptation at the time of this writing, it definitely promises to provide another perspective on and approach to Roland's quest, adding yet another layer of engagement and negotiation to King's *Dark Tower* universe.

The *Dark Tower* series is central to King's canon and in many ways, serves as a litmus test of his growth and maturation as a writer over the course of his long and prolific career thus far, from the early ruminations on the man who would become Flagg in King's college poem "The Dark Man" and his early stories of Roland in *The Gunslinger*'s installment publication in *The Magazine of Fantasy and Science Fiction* to its dramatic conclusion in the final pages of *The Dark Tower* and beyond. King's complex genre engagements throughout the series also put King's work into conversation with both the classic and contemporary literary traditions, highlighting his engagement with—and often dramatic negotiation of—those who have preceded him, as he reflects upon, refers to, and remakes the narratives which have come before. Though it has been more than a decade since *The Dark Tower*'s publication and the end—and resumption—of Roland's quest, the series' impact on and interconnection with King's larger body of work remains central to and in many cases, an integral context for understanding the universes King creates and the tales he tells, whether set in familiar Derry and Castle Rock or the more fantastical and far-flung realms beyond, like the Boo'ya Moon of *Lisey's Story*. Both King himself and the stories he writes have been drawn again and again back to the world of Roland Deschain and the Dark Tower, with interconnections and overlappings abounding throughout the entirety of his work. When it comes to King, all roads lead to the Dark Tower.

Chapter Notes

Introduction

1. The limited-edition publication of *The Gunslinger* went unremarked by most readers until the book was included in the list of King's novels that appeared in the prefacing materials of *Pet Sematary* in 1983. When that happened, "fans bombarded King and his publishers with letters asking how to obtain a copy of this elusive book" (Vincent, *The Stephen King Illustrated Companion* 140), highlighting an interesting dynamic of acquisitiveness and even a sense of entitlement to King's work by his fans. King describes this experience in the diary section that closes *Song of Susannah*, noting the letters and outrage of fans who found *The Gunslinger* listed on the *Pet Sematary* ad card and clamored for a book that was unavailable. As King writes, "They just assume that if there's a book anywhere in the world they want, then they have a perfect right to that book.... I love being able to make my living writing stories, but anyone who sez there's no dark side to it is full of shit" (*Song of Susannah* 393).

Chapter 1

1. Shakespeare likely drew inspiration from a Scottish ballad, "Child Rowland and Burd Ellen," in which a hero named "Rowland, a son of King Arthur, rescues his sister, Lady Ellen, from the King of Elfland's Dark Tower after his older brothers try and fail to return" (Vincent, *The Road to the Dark Tower* 281), another connection between the figure of Roland and the Arthurian tradition.

2. Chrétien was also the first writer to introduce Lancelot and his love affair with Guinevere (Ashley 59), highlighting the lines of creation, interconnection, and inspiration that radiate throughout the Arthurian narrative tradition.

3. This aridity, thirst, and potential death are emphasized again later in the poem, when Eliot laments this lack with his yearning "If there were water / And no rock / If there were rock / And also water / And water / A spring / A pool among the rock .... But there is no water" (lines 346–359). In the world Eliot describes here, even the usually regenerative coming of spring offers no hope, with this hopelessness established in the poem's opening lines "April is the cruelest month, breeding / Lilacs out of the dead land, mixing / Memory and desire" (lines 1–3).

4. Wolfe is also a significant reference when Eddie and Jake are sharing one another's lives through their dreams. Eddie finds that he is carrying a copy of Wolfe's *You Can't Go Home Again* (1940), though it is a very unique copy, stamped on the front with a key, a rose, and a door, and its opening lines are those of *The Gunslinger* rather than Wolfe's own (King, *The Waste Lands* 77). This notion of home is complex and contested, in Eddie's initial homesickness for New York and his growing sense of belonging in Mid-World, Jake's yearning for Mid-World as his true home, and Roland's loss of home through the passage of time and the world's cataclysmic moving on. This notion of home

is similarly complicated in the series' reflections on the *Wizard of Oz* narrative in *Wizard and Glass*, when Susannah tells Flagg, "New York isn't home for us anymore.... No more than Gilead is home for Roland. Take us back to the Path of the Beam. That's where we want to go, because that's our way home. Only way home we got" (King 669). In this way, home for the gunslingers becomes the journey and their companions, rather than any single fixed place.

5. Creekmore offers a detailed analysis of the tarot reading in Eliot's "The Waste Land," including explanation of individual cards, their influence on one another, and Eliot's use of and deviation from established tarot practice in her article "The Tarot Fortune in The Waste Land."

6. In addition to this tarot reading, the role of divination is significant throughout the *Dark Tower* series, with a wide range of seers. In *The Gunslinger*, for example, "Roland receives information about the future from three seers, all having parallels to those in 'The Waste Land': the sibyl wishing for death becomes a demon in a wall; Madame Sosostris becomes the man in black; and the blind gender-shifting Tiresias becomes a succubus" (Auger 197).

Chapter 2

1. I have explored the role of Baum's story and its adaptations in establishing, considering, and negotiating national identity at length in *The Wizard of Oz as American Myth: A Critical Study of Six Versions of the Story, 1900–2007* (McFarland, 2012).

2. This is another example of the ways in which narratives between Mid-World and the world of Roland's companions often intersect and then diverge, in this case within the horror tradition. While the Skin-Man bears some similarities to the traditional werewolf (as a human transforming into a beast which can be stopped by silver bullets), there are also notable differences, such as the fact that the moon has no impact on this particular Skin-Man's transformations and that the Skin-Man can transform into a wide variety of animals—including a bear, an alligator, and a snake—rather than having one fixed, bestial form.

3. The Covenant Man is a sadistic tax-collector and malicious trickster, and is yet another permutation of one of King's central antagonists, Randall Flagg, who appears under different names and in different guises in a number of novels, including *The Eyes of the Dragon* and *The Stand*, as well as throughout the larger *Dark Tower* series. In *The Wind Through the Keyhole*, he signs his note to Tim Stoutheart as RF/MB (King 238), abbreviations for Randall Flagg (or, by extension, any of his other RF monikers), Marten Broadcloak, and perhaps even The Man in Black; additionally, Maerlyn refers to the Covenant Man as "he of the broad cloak" (King 250).

Chapter 3

1. While the full alphabet is not detailed in the *Dark Tower* series, specific letters or phrases are included, such as a pattern resembling "the Great Letter Zn" carved around the rim of one of the Sisters of Oriza's deadly plates, a symbol which simultaneously means "both *zi* (eternity) and *now*" (King, *Wolves of the Calla* 330). There are also more symbolic forms of writing, such as the series of intricate designs which mark and identify the Unfound Door, which are rewritten and transformed to "Found" when Roland reaches the door of the Dark Tower (King, *The Dark Tower* 820).

2. King's description of Shardik here also briefly echoes that of the rabid Saint Bernard Cujo in his 1981 novel of the same name. Much like the impact of rabies on Cujo's brain, Shardik is suffering a similar neurological breakdown, in this case due to "a rapidly multiplying colony of parasites foraging within his fabulous brain" (King, *The Waste Lands* 32).

3. Rowling's *Harry Potter* series is invoked in *Wolves of the Calla* as well, when Roland and his friends discover a crate of flying grenades called sneetches which are armed with spinning blades and explosives, and marked as the "Harry Potter Model ... Serial # 465-11-AA-HPJKR" (683), in a nod to the name and magical

flying abilities of the wizarding world's golden snitch.

4. A frequent theme in science fiction narratives is also the entertainment value such technological advancement may provide, like leisure travel to exotic other worlds, and the doors seem to have served this function—though of a darker sort—at one time as well, with posters advertising trips to witness John F. Kennedy's assassination (King, *The Dark Tower* 78) and 9/11 (King, *The Dark Tower* 87).

Chapter 4

1. The inclusion of Garlan in Roland's boyhood geography explicitly connects the *Dark Tower* series with the world of King's *The Eyes of the Dragon*, as discussed in Chapter 7.

2. While these boys who leave by the west gate generally pass out of the narrative and into obscurity, some of the failed gunslingers prove dangerous in their own right as well, going west to be armed by Farson and trained for revolution and treachery (King, *The Wind Through the Keyhole* 36). Eldred Jonas in *Wizard and Glass* is just such a failed gunslinger and exile from Gilead, made formidable through his rejection and rage. Though these men may gain power and fame, they are still viewed as failures and traitors, and as Roland tells Jonas, "the soul of a man such as you can never leave the west" (King, *Wizard and Glass* 499), further marking the west as a personal reflection on one's shortcomings and an inescapable purgatory.

3. This proves not to be true arthritis, but rather an echo or doubling between worlds as Roland is feeling the injuries King will sustain when struck and nearly killed by a van, at which time the pain leaves Roland and passes to King (King, *The Dark Tower* 452).

Chapter 5

1. "The Mist" is another King work that can be read as having connections to the *Dark Tower* series, with the tear between worlds bearing striking similarities to the *todash* space of the *Dark Tower* universe, which separates worlds from one another and is occupied by horrors and monsters akin to those that lurk within the mist itself.

2. The violence of this physical transformation is similarly described in *The Wind Through the Keyhole* in the more benevolent transformation of Maerlyn of the Eld from a mythical tiger into his more human form, accompanied by "a grinding sound as the very bones inside its body rearranged themselves" (King 249), as well as in the more terrifying transformation and rampage of the discovered Skin-Man (King 291).

3. "The Masque of the Red Death" is an especially significant Gothic inspiration in King's *The Shining* as well, and has been explored by Leonard Mustazza in detail in "Poe's 'The Masque of the Red Death' and King's *The Shining*: Echo, Influence, and Deviation," in Tony Magistrale's 1991 edited collection *Discovering Stephen King's 'The Shining.'*

4. King combines this moment of cosmic terror with more traditional Gothic horror, evoking Poe as well when, with the house coming apart around him, "Jake could hear the whole house collapsing, like the one in that story of Edgar Allan Poe" (King, *The Waste Lands* 294). The horror of "The Fall of the House of Usher" is also internalized in Susannah's imagined dogan where she attempts to control her shared body's labor and Mordred's coming birth, knowing the walls and floors around her will soon begin to crack and fail and sardonically thinking "Ladies and gentlemen, welcome to the House of Usher" (King, *Song of Susannah* 71).

5. This characteristic raises the possibility of a thinny being central to the oddness of the Castle Rock, Maine, in the Hulu original series, *Castle Rock* (2018–2019), which is inspired by and engages with many of King's works, while moving well beyond a direct adaptation of any of them. In the series' first season, the mysterious Kid (played by Bill Skarsgård) repeatedly asks Henry Deaver (Andre Holland), "do you hear it now?" and claims to have come from an alternate reality in which The Kid himself is the true Henry Deaver, though the veracity of these claims is suspect and uncertain.

Chapter 6

1. In the revised and expanded edition of *The Gunslinger*, released in 2003 as the *Dark Tower* series neared its conclusion, Jake senses Callahan's presence, telling Roland as they move on from the Way Station, "I feel like something's watching us," to which Roland agrees, "Something or someone" (King 126).

2. Vampires also appear in King's larger body of short fiction, including "One for the Road" (a continuation of the story of Jerusalem's Lot, published in the 1978 collection *Night Shift*), "The Night Flier" (in the 1993 collection *Nightmares & Dreamscapes*) and "Popsy" (also in *Nightmares and Dreamscapes*). *Wizard and Glass*'s Rhea of the Cöos has some vampiric qualities, feeding on Cordelia Delgado's blood to revive herself (King 575) and defining vampires more metaphorically, beyond those who are sustained by blood, Mia's possession of Susannah is described in terms of vampirism (King, *Song of Susannah* 375) and Roland faces a vampire that feeds on emotion late in the *Dark Tower* series (King, *Dark Tower* 701). The Plymouth Fury Christine has a vampiric relationship with Arnie Cunningham, drawing his energy, life force, and identity to fuel her rage in *Christine* (1983) and the True Knot of *Doctor Sleep* can be read as vampires as well, feeding on the "steam" released by torturing and killing children with paranormal abilities. King's *Dark Tower*-related novel *Insomnia* features metaphorical vampirism, as Ralph and Lois "feed" on the auras and life force of others to gain the psychic energy they need to stand against evil and attempt to derail the disastrous events threatening Derry. Finally, the figure of the vampire is deployed as one among a horrific ensemble cast in King and Straub's *Black House*, when the bikers open the door to the eponymous house and Doc sees Daisy Temperly, a girl he accidentally killed with a dosage miscalculation, who smiles at him and "exposes a mouthful of bulging vampire teeth" (581).

3. This date echoes throughout the last three books of the *Dark Tower* series in the recurrence, repetition, and increasing significance of the numbers 19, 99, and 1999.

Chapter 7

1. *The Colorado Kid* may have some *Dark Tower* connections as well, though these are ephemeral and undeveloped. For example, while there were no Starbucks franchises in Denver in 1980 and one appears in *The Colorado Kid*, King notes that "The Constant Readers of the Dark Tower series may realize that that is not necessarily a continuity error, but a clue" (qtd. in Vincent, *The Dark Tower Companion* 103). The Colorado Kid's impossibly quick transport from Colorado to Maine may also hint at a portal or travel through an alternate world akin to *The Talisman*'s Territories (*ibid.*).

2. Captain Trips first appears in King's "Night Surf" in the *Night Shift* collection, a short story about a handful of young adults in the immediate aftermath of the superflu.

3. While he has been known by a wide range of names, Flagg is one of the most commonly used, and I have used it consistently throughout this chapter to avoid confusion.

4. Flagg's pervasive presence is difficult to pin down, uncertain and shifting throughout the series. For example, early on, in *The Drawing of the Three*, Marten and Walter are described as two separate individuals (King 9–10), though they are later revealed to be one and the same (King, *Wolves of the Calla* 412).

5. Several of these names are drawn from H.P. Lovecraft's mythos of cosmic horror, including Nyarlathotep and R'yelah, and while Glen may have been speaking metaphorically, this has led some critics, like *Nerdist*'s Kyle Anderson, to include Flagg among the pantheon of "Stephen King's Lovecraftian Gods."

6. "The Dark Man" has not to date been included in any of King's short fiction collections. It was originally published in 2004 in Thomas Piccirilli's poetry anthology *The Devil's Wine* and has also been released as a Cemetery Dance special

edition (2013), with illustrations by Glenn Chadbourne.

Chapter 8

1. Another often unacknowledged group whose perspective is periodically privileged throughout *Insomnia* is that of abused women. After Helen Deepneau leaves her husband, she and her daughter join other women at a shelter in the countryside. In this way, these women remain unseen and protected, hidden for their own safety. This theme of the unseen also echoes through the novel in the ways in which domestic abuse is spoken about and just as significantly, in the silence which surrounds it, as these women and their children have few people to depend on and protect them aside from one another. While Ralph and Lois worry about being disbelieved and thought crazy or senile if they tell anyone about what they have been seeing around Derry, Helen Deepneau and her fellow domestic violence survivors are all too familiar with keeping secrets, not being listened to, and being disbelieved. This is a theme that King explores further in *Rose Madder*, which similarly blends the real-life horror of domestic abuse with mythological fantasy, in this case negotiating the legend of Theseus, the Minotaur, and his maze.

2. Atropos's presence can also be felt throughout King's larger body of work, whether overtly noted or more subtly engaged. An example of this is when Ralph and Lois are in Atropos's underground lair, which is filled with his macabre trophies, one of which is the sneaker of *Pet Sematary*'s young Gage Creed (King, *Insomnia* 535).

3. Their names also echo Edgar's line in Shakespeare's *King Lear* from which Browning drew inspiration for "Childe Roland to the Dark Tower Came" (and from which King, in turn, drew inspiration for the *Dark Tower* series), with Edgar's "'Fie, foh, and fum'" (III.iv.196). This also connects these figures to the fairy tale tradition and the "fee, fie, fo, fum" of the giant in "Jack and the Beanstalk," making this a particularly dynamic intertextual engagement, with multiple layers of allusion and meaning (Vincent, *The Road to the Dark Tower* 176).

4. Though Roland asks if these figures are representations of King's personal id, ego, and superego, Fimalo explains that they have simply taken on a form that would be familiar to Roland and Susannah, though this form is not directly related to King himself as either author or character within the series (King, *The Dark Tower* 604).

5. This sharing of a body is echoed in Roland's "coming forward" to take control of Eddie Dean's body at multiple points throughout *The Drawing of the Three*, though in this case, Roland is decidedly an outsider, a presence which ranges from uncomfortable at its best to invasive at its worst, a distinct difference from the separate but coexisting parts of Detta/Odetta and Susannah/Mia's personality throughout the series.

6. This connection is further developed in *Insomnia*, where the Crimson King, like It, is associated with *"deadlights"* (King, *Insomnia* 607, emphasis original).

7. The Civic Center was designed by *IT*'s Losers' Club Ben Hanscom, commissioned to replace the older building that was destroyed in the flood of 1985 (King, *Insomnia* 414), once again underscoring the interconnection between *Insomnia*, the *Dark Tower* series, and the far-reaching scope of Derry's dark history within King's larger canon.

8. Patrick is referred to as "Son of Sonia" in *The Dark Tower* (709), establishing him as the same Patrick Danville from *Insomnia*, though paintings Roland and Susannah see in the final leg of their journey with Patrick Danville's signature may be those Patrick will go on to paint after his time with the gunslingers or those created by an alternate timeline/universe Patrick Danville (King, *The Dark Tower* 705).

Chapter 9

1. *Rose Madder* is another of King's novels that has possible connections to the *Dark Tower* series through characters' travel to other worlds, with possible overlaps with Roland's own, though these

never come to fruition (Vincent, *The Dark Tower Companion* 98).

2. As Furth notes, the *can-toi* appear in *Desperation* as well, though in a different incarnation, as there "the can-toi are the animal servants of the demon Tak .... [and] Unlike our can-toi, the can-toi of *Desperation* have neither human bodies nor the ability to reason or speak" (52).

3. The story itself echoes the acclaimed 1961 *The Twilight Zone* episode "It's a Good Life," which was adapted from a 1953 short story by Jerome Bixby, and features a supernaturally gifted child.

4. Stark was also the pseudonym of Donald Westlake, adding an additional layer to the negotiation of name, identity, and pseudonym engaged by *The Dark Half*.

5. The second season of *Castle Rock* expands this engagement to build on the established Castle Rock setting while also expanding to include Jerusalem's Lot and the backstory of Annie Wilkes (played by Lizzy Caplan), as well as digging into the larger area's dark history, in which The Kid seems to play an integral part.

Chapter 10

1. The recurring figure of Flagg is another thread that ties *Hearts in Atlantis* as a whole to the *Dark Tower* series and King's larger multiverse, with Flagg mentioned in *Hearts in Atlantis* as "the elusive Raymond Fiegler" (King 453), leader of Militant Students for Peace, and who is adept at "[t]he trick of being *dim*" (King 516, emphasis original).

2. This is also an approach used to restrict the power of particularly strong Breakers, as when Charles Burnside forces Tyler Marshall to wear a similar hat as he ushers him to End-World in *Black House* (King and Straub 548). Once this is removed, the immense destructive potential of Tyler's psychic power becomes clear as he destroys the Crimson King's Big Combination and sets free the children who have been sentenced to work and suffer there. This same tool is used much less effectively by Flagg in *The Dark Tower* as he tries to shield his thoughts and prevent the mind control of young Mordred.

3. Similarly, in the *Dark Tower* series' "world of twins and mirror images" (King, *The Dark Tower* 76), Ted briefly thinks he has been reunited with Bobby in Jake's striking resemblance to the other boy and the two young men's connection as potential "twinners" (King, *The Dark Tower* 215).

4. In this story, published in King's 2002 short story collection of the same name, Dinky features as a first-person narrator with a suspiciously cushy job, much like that which first tempted Ted into service as a Breaker. Dinky's training and stated purpose—that "the targets were bad guys, dictators and spies and serial killers" (King, "Everything's Eventual" 291)—is similar to that experienced by the children in King's novel *The Institute* (2019), though these children are kidnapped and abused rather than recruited, managed, and manipulated like Dinky. While Dinky, like his fellow Breakers at Algul Siento, craves the high that comes with using his power, he also proves himself capable of resistance and revolution near the conclusion of "Everything's Eventual," a capacity for strength and resolve that is once more essential in Algul Siento.

5. "Ur" was later published in King's 2015 collection *The Bazaar of Bad Dreams*. The page numbers of that print version are cited here.

6. Like "Ur," "Mile 81" was originally published as an ebook exclusive and later collected in *The Bazaar of Bad Dreams*, whose page numbers are cited here.

7. Children's heightened awareness and the subversive potential of their belief is also integral in *IT* and the Loser's Club's defeat of Pennywise as children. For example, Eddie uses his inhaler as a weapon, thinking, "*acid. it's acid if I want it to be*" (King, *IT* 1042, emphasis original), with this belief and Eddie's claiming of its power allowing the kids to rally against the monster. Eddie's seizing of agency is also a refusal of his mother's control and deception of him, following his discovery that his inhaler contains nothing but camphor-flavored water, a placebo designed to keep him complacent and obedient in his belief of his own frailty. In this case, Eddie's belief actually reshapes the world around him, restructuring his relationship with his mother,

Chapter 11

1. While King is most often invoked as a singular household name, he has also periodically collaborated with other authors, including working with Stuart O'Nan to write the non-fiction book *Faithful: Two Diehard Boston Red Sox Fans Chronicle the Historic 2004 Season* (2005); contributing to Scott Snyder and Rafael Albuquerque's *American Vampire, Volume 1* (2010); writing with Joe Hill on the short stories "Throttle" (2009) and "In the Tall Grass" (2012), as well as the graphic novel adaptation of "Throttle" included in *Road Rage* (2012); and co-authoring *Sleeping Beauties* (2017) with Owen King.

2. Another Victorian echo is in the writing itself, which King and Straub passed back and forth as each continued their respective sections, a kind of two-man serial reading and writing experience. As King recalls, this process was akin to "*the old days, when I got the* Saturday Evening Post *with its serial stories. When Peter said he was going to send something, I would get excited because I was going to get to read some more of the story*" (qtd. in Winter 142, emphasis original). King also embraced this serial writing practice in 1996 with his installment publication of *The Green Mile,* and in his online publication of his unfinished novel *The Plant* (privately distributed 1982–85; online 2000), which was released in a series of individual chapters.

3. The possibility of multiple realities resonates darkly here as well, as Strengell notes that Jack succeeds in *The Talisman* only for his mother to be killed by a drunk driver in the version of reality recounted in *The Tommyknockers* (1987) (Strengell 11), though in *Black House* Jack tells Fisherman suspect George Potter that his own understanding of himself, and his and his friends' ability to stand against the monster. mother died of cancer which returned later in her life (King and Straub 343). Jack could be withholding the truth or, as with *Desperation* and *The Regulators*, this discrepancy could indicate how Jack and his mother's lives may have played out on different levels of the Tower.

4. In *Black House*, the Crimson King is also referred to as Abbalah, an alternate name used only in *Black House* and King's unfinished online novel *The Plant* (Vincent, *The Road to the Dark Tower* 216).

5. These borderlands abound in King's fiction and while some of them demarcate the porous boundaries between Roland's world and that of the real, there are plenty of other worlds as well, from the roads that run through "places that ain't on any map of Maine" in "Mrs. Todd's Shortcut" (221), to the Lovecraftian-influenced horrors of "The Mist" and "Crouch End," and the land of Boo'ya Moon at the heart of *Lisey's Story* (2006).

Conclusion

1. This mention in *Lisey's Story* also invokes Twain as well, once more blurring the lines of inspiration and invention as Lisey Landon reflects that her husband "Scott had left Boo'ya Moon behind. Like Huck, he'd lit out for the Territories" (King 432).

2. This possibility is expanded and further complicated with Farris's return in the sequel *Gwendy's Magic Feather* (2019), in which Chizmar continues Gwendy's story on his own, rather than in collaboration with King.

3. *The Drawing of the Three: The Prisoner* also connects Eddie's story explicitly to themes from "Low Men in Yellow Coats," including lost pet posters as the low men try to find Eddie (1) and investing the car Henry Dean steals with malevolent life, with a snarling face (32) and a seatbelt that is reluctant to let Eddie go (34–5).

Works Cited

Adams, Richard. *Shardik*. Avon, 1974.
Anderson, Kyle. "A Guide to Stephen King's Lovecraftian Gods." *Nerdist*, 17 Oct. 2017, https://nerdist.com/article/stephen-king-lovecraft-gods-cthulhu-it-dark-tower/.
Ashley, Mike. "Arthur." *The Encyclopedia of Fantasy*, edited by John Clute and John Grant. St. Martin's Press, 1997, pp. 57–63.
Asimov, Isaac. *I, Robot*. Bantam Books, 2004 (1950).
Auerbach, Nina. *Our Vampires, Ourselves*. University of Chicago Press, 1995.
Auger, Emily E. "Tarot and T.S. Eliot in Stephen King's Dark Tower Novels." *Mythlore*, no. 2, 2018, pp. 185–213. *EBSCOhost*, search.ebscohost.com/login.aspx?direct=true&db=edsgao&AN=edsgcl.539213024&site=eds-live&scope=site.
Badley, Linda. "Stephen King Viewing the Body." *Stephen King* (Modern Critical Views), edited by Harold Bloom. Chelsea House Publishers, 1998, pp. 163–190.
Baum, L. Frank. *The Wonderful Wizard of Oz*. Illustrated by W.W. Denslow. Barnes & Noble Classics, 2005 (1900).
Beahm, George. *The Stephen King Companion: Four Decades of Fear From the Master of Horror*. Thomas Dunne Books, 2015.
Beale, Lewis. "Why Akira Kurosawa's 'Seven Samurai' keeps inspiring new retellings like 'The Magnificent Seven.'" *The Los Angeles Times*, 23 Sept. 2016, https://www.latimes.com/entertainment/movies/la-ca-mn-seven-samurai-magnificent-seven-20160913-snap-story.html.
Bender, Todd K. "Robert Browning." *Critical Survey of Poetry, English Language Series, Volume 1, A-Cae*, Revised edition, edited by Frank N. Magill. Salem Press, 1992, pp. 405–417.
Bettelheim, Bruno. *The Uses of Enchantment: The Meaning and Importance of Fairy Tales*. Alfred A. Knopf, 1977.
Biderman, Shai. "'Do Not Forsake Me, Oh, My Darling': Loneliness and Solitude in Westerns." *The Philosophy of the Western*, edited by Jennifer L. McMahon and B. Steve Csaki. University Press of Kentucky, 2010, pp. 13–29.
Braun, Michele. "Roland the Gunslinger's Generic Transformation." *Stephen King's Modern Macabre: Essays on the Later Works*, edited by Patrick McAleer and Michael A. Perry. McFarland, 2014, pp. 66–80.
Browning, Robert. "Childe Roland to the Dark Tower Came." *My Last Duchess and Other Poems*. Dover, 1993 (1855), pp. 59–65.
Buday, Maroš. "Exploring The Dark Tower: Stephen King's Postmodern Epic." *Zeszyty Naukowe Uniwersytetu Rzeszowskiego*, 12 Dec. 2015, https://repozytorium.ur.edu.pl/bitstream/handle/item/1639/12%20buday-exploring.pdf?sequence=1&isAllowed=y.
Callahan, Dan. "'The Dark Tower' Review: Big Screen Adaptation of Stephen King's Gunslinger Epic Misfires." *The Wrap*, 2 Aug. 2017, https://www.thewrap.com/dark-tower-review-big-screen-adaptation-stephen-kings-gunslinger-epic-misfires/.

Works Cited

Campbell, Joseph. *The Hero with a Thousand Faces.* Princeton UP, 1968 (1949). Bollingen Series XVII.
Casebeer, Edwin F. "Stephen King's Canon: The Art of Balance." *A Dark Night's Dreaming: Contemporary American Horror Fiction,* edited by Matthew J. Bruccoli. University of South Carolina Press, 1996, pp. 42–54.
Castle Rock. Created by Sam Shaw and Dustin Thomason. Perf. André Holland, Melanie Lynskey, Bill Skarsgård, Sissy Spacek. *Hulu.com,* Hulu Originals, 2018.
Cawelti, John G. *The Six-Gun Mystique Sequel.* Bowling Green State University Popular Press, 1999.
Chizmar, Richard. *Gwendy's Magic Feather.* Cemetery Dance, 2019.
Clark, Alex. "Shardik by Richard Adams review—beware the bear." *The Guardian,* 26 Nov. 2014, https://www.theguardian.com/books/2014/nov/26/shardik-richard-adams-watership-down-beware-bear.
Clayton, Wickham. "Alien on the Inside: Adaptation of Stephen King's Alien Possession Tales." *Science Fiction Film and Television,* vol. 10, no. 2, 2017, pp. 177–196.
Clover, Carol. *Men, Women, and Chainsaws: Gender in the Modern Horror Film.* Princeton University Press, 1993.
Clute, John. "Fantasy." *The Encyclopedia of Fantasy,* edited by John Clute and John Grant. St. Martins, 1997, pp. 337–339.
Collings, Michael. "Michael Collings on *Insomnia* (1994)." In George Beahm's *The Stephen King Companion: Four Decades of Fear from the Master of Horror.* Thomas Dunne Books, 2015, pp. 324–325.
_____. "Michael Collings on The Eyes of the Dragon." In George Beahm's *The Stephen King Companion: Four Decades of Fear from the Master of Horror.* Thomas Dunne Books, 2015, p. 239.
_____. "Michael Collings on *The Stand* (1978)." In George Beahm's *The Stephen King Companion: Four Decades of Fear from the Master of Horror.* Thomas Dunne Books, 2015, pp. 139–140.
Conlon, John J. "T.S. Eliot." *Critical Survey of Poetry, English Language Series, Volume 3, Ebe-Holl,* Revised edition, edited by Frank N. Magill. Salem Press, 1992, pp. 1065–1079.
Cotrell, Arthur, and Rachel Storm. *The Encyclopedia of World Mythology.* Hermes House, 2006.
Cowan, Douglas E. *America's Dark Theologian: The Religious Imagination of Stephen King.* New York University Press, 2018.
Creekmore, Betsey B. "The Tarot Fortune in The Waste Land." *ELH,* vol. 49, no. 4, 1982, pp. 908–928. *JSTOR,* www.jstor.org/stable/2872904.
Cruz, Gilbert. "Stephen King on His 10 Longest Novels." *Time,* 6 Nov. 2009, http://entertainment.time.com/2009/11/09/mutations-king-on-his-10-longest-novels/.
Cruz, Ronald Allan Lopez. "Mutations and Metamorphoses: Body Horror is Biological Horror." *Journal of Popular Film and Television,* vol. 40, no. 2, 2012, pp. 160–168.
Cuddon, J. A. *A Dictionary of Literary Terms and Literary Theory,* 3rd ed. Blackwell Reference, 1991.
Curran, Ronald T. "Complex, Archetype, and Primal Fear: King's Use of Fairy Tales in *The Shining*." *The Dark Descent: Essays Defining Stephen King's Horrorscape,* edited by Tony Magistrale. Greenwood Press, 1992, 33–46.
The Dark Tower, The Drawing of the Three: Bitter Medicine. By Robin Furth, Peter David, Jonathan Marks, and Lee Loughridge. Marvel, 2016.
The Dark Tower, The Drawing of the Three: House of Cards. By Robin Furth, Peter David, Piotr Kowalski, and Nick Filardi. Marvel, 2015.
The Dark Tower, The Drawing of the Three: The Lady of Shadows. By Robin Furth, Peter David, Jonathan Marks, Lee Loughridge, and Jonathan Marks. Marvel, 2016.
The Dark Tower, The Drawing of the Three: The Prisoner. By Robin Furth, Peter David, Piotr Kowalski, and Nick Filardi. Marvel, 2015.
The Dark Tower, The Drawing of the Three: The Sailor. By Robin Furth, Peter David, Juanan Ramírez, Cory Hamscher, Jesus Aburtov, and Federico Blee. Marvel, 2017.

Works Cited

The Dark Tower, The Gunslinger: Last Shots. By Robin Furth, Peter David, and Richard Isanove. Marvel, 2013.
The Dark Tower, The Gunslinger: The Battle of Tull. By Robin Furth, Peter David, Richard Isanove. Gallery 13, 2019 (2011).
The Dark Tower, The Gunslinger: The Journey Begins. By Robin Furth, Peter David, Sean Phillips, and Richard Isanove. Marvel, 2011.
The Dark Tower, The Gunslinger: The Little Sisters of Eluria. By Robin Furth, Peter David, Luke Ross, and Richard Isanove. Marvel, 2013.
The Dark Tower, The Gunslinger: The Man in Black. By Robin Furth, Peter David, Alex Maleev, and Richard Isanove. Marvel, 2013.
The Dark Tower, The Gunslinger: The Way Station. By Robin Furth, Peter David, Laurence Campbell, and Richard Isanove. Marvel, 2011.
The Dark Tower Omnibus: The Gunslinger Born, The Long Road Home, Treachery, Fall of Gilead, Battle of Jericho Hill. By Robin Furth, Peter David, Jae Lee, and Richard Isanove. Marvel, 2011.
The Dark Tower: The Art of the Film. Text by Daniel Wallace. Melcher Media and Scribner's, 2017.
Day, Kirsten. *Cowboy Classics: The Roots of the American Western in the Epic Tradition.* Edinburgh University Press, 2016.
DeFore, John. "'The Dark Tower': A Film Review." *The Hollywood Reporter,* 2 Aug. 2007, https://www.hollywoodreporter.com/review/dark-tower-1026375.
"Desperation." *Publisher's Weekly,* n.d., https://www.publishersweekly.com/978-0-670-86836-0.
Discordia. Created by Brian Stark, Judy Hahn, Marsha DeFillippo, and Robin Furth. *StephenKing.com,* 2009, https://stephenking.com/darktower/discordia/.
Downey, Dara, and Darryl Jones. "King of the Castle: Shirley Jackson and Stephen King." *Shirley Jackson: Essays on the Literary Legacy,* edited by Bernice M. Murphy. McFarland, 2005, pp. 214–236.
Ebert, Roger. "The Good, The Bad, and The Ugly." *Roger Ebert.com,* 3 Aug. 2003, https://www.rogerebert.com/reviews/great-movie-the-good-the-bad-and-the-ugly-1968.
Egan, James. "Apocalypticism in the Fiction of Stephen King." *Extrapolation* vol. 25, no. 3, Fall 1984, pp. 214–227. *EBSCOhost,* doi:10.3828/extr.1984.25.3.214.
———. "*The Dark Tower*: Stephen King's Gothic Western." *The Gothic World of Stephen King: Landscape of Nightmares,* edited by Gary Hoppenstand and Ray B. Browne. Bowling Green State University Popular Press, 1987, pp. 95–106.
Eliot, T.S. "The Waste Land." *The Waste Land and Other Poems.* Signet Classic, 1998 (1922), pp. 32–59.
Evans, Beryl. *Charlie the Choo-Choo.* Illustrated by Ned Dameron, Simon & Schuster, 2016.
Flieger, Verlyn. *There Would Always Be a Fairy Tale: More Essays on Tolkien.* Kent State UP, 2017.
Franich, Darren. "*Magnificent Seven: Seven Samurai* is much more than the original." *Entertainment Weekly,* 22 Sept. 2016, https://ew.com/article/2016/09/22/magnificent-seven-original-seven-samurai/.
Franklin, Ruth. *Shirley Jackson: A Rather Haunted Life.* Liveright, 2016.
Fretts, Bruce. "Back in 'Black.'" *Entertainment Weekly,* no. 616, Sept. 2001, p. 76. *EBSCOhost,* search.ebscohost.com/login.aspx?direct=true&db=ulh&AN=5227685&site=ehost-live.
Freud, Sigmund. *The Uncanny.* Trans. David McLintok. Penguin, 2003 (1899).
"From a Buick 8 (Review)." *Publisher's Weekly,* vol. 249, no. 22, June 2002, p. 58. *EBSCOhost,* proxy.culver.edu:2048/login?url=https%3a%2f%2fsearch.ebscohost.com%2flogin.aspx%3fdirect%3dtrue%26db%3daph%26AN%3d6779562%26site%3deds-live%26scope%3dsite.
Fugere, Mike. "*Castle Rock* Embraces Stephen King's The Dark Tower (and It's Super Weird)." *Comic Book Resources (CBR),* 5 Sept. 2018, https://www.cbr.com/castle-rock-embraces-dark-tower-continuity/.

Works Cited

Furth, Robin. *Stephen King's The Dark Tower: A Concordance, Volume 2*. Scribner's, 2005.

Gardner, Jack. "The Dark Tower Game That Time Forgot." *Extra Life*, 4 May 2017, https://community.extra-life.org/articles.html/features/the-dark-tower-game-that-time-forgot-r971/.

Gilman, Greer. "The languages of the fantastic." *The Cambridge Companion to Fantasy Literature*, edited by Edward James and Farah Mendlesohn. Cambridge UP, 2012, pp. 134–146.

Goldberg, Matt. "'The Dark Tower' Review: You Can't Do an Epic on the Cheap." *Collider*, 2 Aug. 2017, http://collider.com/the-dark-tower-review/?utm_source=twitter&utm_campaign=collidersocial&utm_medium=social#poster.

The Good, The Bad, and The Ugly. Directed by Sergio Leone, performances by Clint Eastwood, Eli Wallach, and Lee Van Cleef. United Artists, 1967.

Grundhauser, Eric. "Why Is the World Always on the Back of a Turtle?" *Atlas Obscura*, 20 Oct. 2017, https://www.atlasobscura.com/articles/world-turtle-cosmic-discworld.

Handy, Bruce. "Books: Stephen King: Monster Writer." *Time*, no. 11, 1996, p. 60. EBSCOhost, search.ebscohost.com/login.aspx?direct=true&db=edsgea&AN=edsgcl.246570439&site=eds-live&scope=site.

Harp, Justin, and Sam Warner. "The Dark Tower's first reviews are in—is it a Stephen King classic or supernatural sludge?" *Digital Spy*, 8 Mar. 2017, https://www.digitalspy.com/movies/a834646/dark-tower-first-reviews-round-up/.

Hendrix, Grady. "The Great Stephen King Reread: Desperation." *Tor*, 26 June 2015, https://www.tor.com/2015/06/26/the-great-stephen-king-reread-desperation/.

Herron, Don. "Horror Springs in the Fiction of Stephen King." *Fear Itself: The Horror Fiction of Stephen King*, edited by Tim Underwood and Chuck Miller. New American Library, 1984 (1982), pp. 75–100.

Iglesias, Gabino. "Blood, Parasites, and Mutilation: Celebrating 10 Masters of Body Horror." *Lit Reactor*, 12 Oct. 2017, https://litreactor.com/columns/blood-parasites-and-mutilation-celebrating-10-masters-of-body-horror.

Indick, Ben P. "King and the Literary Tradition of Horror and the Supernatural." *Stephen King*, edited by Harold Bloom. Chelsea House, 1998, pp. 15–26. Modern Critical Views Series.

_____. "Stephen King as an Epic Writer." *Discovering Modern Horror Fiction*, edited by Darrell Schweitzer. Starmont House, 1985, pp. 56–67. Starmont Studies in Literary Criticism No. 4.

Jackson, Matthew. "All of the Stephen King Easter Eggs in *Castle Rock*." *SyFy Wire*, 13 Sept. 2018, https://www.syfy.com/syfywire/all-of-the-stephen-king-easter-eggs-in-castle-rock-so-far.

Jackson, Shirley. *The Haunting of Hill House*. Penguin Classics, 2006 (1959).

_____. "The Lottery." *The Lottery and Other Stories*. Farrar, Straus and Giroux, 1991, pp. 291–302.

Johnston, Rich. "Exclusive: Gallery 13 Grab Stephen King's The Dark Graphic Novel Rights from Marvel." *Bleeding Cool*, 19 June 2018, https://www.bleedingcool.com/2018/06/19/gallery-13-stephen-king-dark-tower-graphic-novel-rights-marvel/.

Jones, Diana Wynne. "Magic." *The Encyclopedia of Fantasy*, edited by John Clute and John Grant. St. Martins, 1997, pp. 615–618.

Joshi, S.T. "Introduction." H.P. Lovecraft, *The Annotated Supernatural Horror in Literature*, edited by S.T. Joshi. Hippocampus, 2012, pp. 9–24.

Juranovszky, Andrea. "Trauma Reenactment in the Gothic Loop: A Study on Structures and Circularity in Gothic Fiction." *Inquiries Journal/Student Pulse*, vol. 6, issue 5. Retrieved from http://www.inquiriesjournal.com/a?id=898.

Kaveney, Roz, and David Langford. "Plot Devices." *The Encyclopedia of Fantasy*, edited by John Clute and John Grant. St. Martins, 1997, pp. 767–769.

King, Stephen. "Afterword." *The Dark Tower III: The Waste Lands*. Signet, 2003 (1991), pp. 589–90.

_____. "Afterword." *The Dark Tower IV: Wizard and Glass*. Signet, 2003 (1997), pp. 695–9.

———. *Bag of Bones*. Scribner's, 1998.
———. *Cell*. Pocket Star Books, 2006.
———. *The Colorado Kid*. Hard Case Crime, 2005.
———. "Crouch End." *Nightmares and Dreamscapes*. Viking, 1993, pp. 559–591.
———. *Cujo*. Signet, 1981.
———. *Danse Macabre*. Gallery Books, 2010 (1981).
———. *The Dark Half*. Signet, 1989.
———. *The Dark Man*. Illustrated by Glenn Chadbourne. Cemetery Dance, 2013.
———. *The Dark Tower I: The Gunslinger*, revised and expanded ed. Signet, 2003 (1982).
———. *The Dark Tower II: The Drawing of the Three*. Signet, 1987.
———. *The Dark Tower III: The Waste Lands*. Signet, 1991.
———. *The Dark Tower IV: Wizard and Glass*. Signet, 1997.
———. *The Dark Tower V: Wolves of the Calla*. Donald M. Grant, Publisher & Scribner's, 2003.
———. *The Dark Tower VI: Song of Susannah*. Donald M. Grant, Publisher & Scribner's, 2004.
———. *The Dark Tower VII: The Dark Tower*. Donald M. Grant, Publisher & Scribner's, 2004.
———. *Desperation*. Signet, 1996.
———. *Doctor Sleep*. Scribner's, 2013.
———. *End of Watch*. Scribner's, 2016.
———. "Everything's Eventual." *Everything's Eventual: 14 Dark Tales*. Pocket Books, 2002, pp. 211–263.
———. *The Eyes of the Dragon*. Signet, 1987.
———. "Fair Extension." *Full Dark, No Stars*. Pocket Books, 2010, pp. 357–403.
———. "The Final Argument." *The Dark Tower V: Wolves of the Calla*. Donald M. Grant, Publisher & Scribner's, 2003, pp. xi-xvi.
———. *Finders Keepers*. Scribner's, 2015.
———. *From a Buick 8*. Scribner's, 2002.
———. *Hearts in Atlantis*. Scribner's, 1999.
———. *Insomnia*. Signet, 1994.
———. *The Institute*. Scribner's, 2019.
———. *IT*. Scribner's, 1986.
———. *Joyland*. Hard Case Crime, 2014.
———. *Lisey's Story*. Scribner's, 2006.
———. "The Little Sisters of Eluria." *Everything's Eventual: 14 Dark Tales*. Pocket Books, 2002, pp. 145–209.
———. "Mile 81. *The Bazaar of Bad Dreams: Stories*. Scribner's, 2015, pp. 7–50.
———. "The Mist." *Skeleton Crew*. Signet, 1985, pp. 24–154.
———. *Mr. Mercedes*. Scribner's, 2014.
———. "Mrs. Todd's Shortcut." *Skeleton Crew*. Signet, 1985, pp. 206–231.
———. "N." *Just After Sunset*. Scribner's, 2008, pp. 185–238.
———. "Night Flier." *Nightmares & Dreamscapes*. Viking, 1993, pp. 109–146.
———. "Night Surf." *Night Shift*. Signet, 1978, pp. 52–60.
———. "On Being Nineteen (and a Few Other Things)." *The Dark Tower I: The Gunslinger*, revised and expanded ed. Signet, 2003 (1982), pp. ix-xix.
———. *Pet Sematary*. Doubleday, 1983.
———. "Popsy." *Nightmares & Dreamscapes*. Viking, 1993, pp. 147–160.
———. *The Regulators*. Dutton, 1996.
———. *Rose Madder*. Signet, 1995.
———. *'Salem's Lot*. Pocket Books, 1975.
———. *The Shining*. Doubleday, 1977.
———. *The Stand, The Complete & Uncut Edition*. Signet, 1990.
———. "Stephen King on the Kindle and iPad." *Entertainment Weekly*, 26 Mar. 2010, https://ew.com/article/2010/03/26/stephen-king-kindle-and-ipad/.
———. "Ur." *The Bazaar of Bad Dreams: Stories*. Scribner's, 2015, pp. 209–266.

———. "Why I Was Bachman." *The Bachman Books: Four Early Novels by Stephen King.* Plume, 1985, v-x.
———. *The Wind Through the Keyhole: A Dark Tower Novel.* Scribner's, 2012. King, Stephen (as Richard Bachman). *Blaze.* Pocket Books, 2007.
King, Stephen, and Joe Hill. "Throttle." *He is Legend: An Anthology Celebrating Richard Matheson,* edited by Christopher Conlon. Tor, 2009, pp. 17–55.
King, Stephen, and Owen King. *Sleeping Beauties.* Scribner's, 2017.
King, Stephen, and Peter Straub. *Black House.* Random House, 2001.
———. *The Talisman.* Ballantine Books, 1984.
King, Stephen, and Richard Chizmar. *Gwendy's Button Box.* Cemetery Dance, 2017.
King, Stephen, and Stewart O'Nan. *Faithful: Two Diehard Boston Red Sox Fans Chronicle the Historic 2004 Season.* Scribner's, 2004.
King, Stephen, Joe Hill, and Richard Matheson. *Road Rage.* IDW Publishing, 2012.
King, Stephen, Scott Snyder, and Rafael Albuquerque. *American Vampire, Volume 1.* Vertigo, 2011.
Korstophine, Kevin. "Introduction." *The Palgrave Handbook to Horror Literature,* edited by Kevin Korstophine and Laura R. Kremmel. New York: Palgrave, 2018, pp. 1–17.
Kozackzka, Adam S. "Genre Exchange on the Supernatural Frontier in Stephen King's *The Gunslinger*: The Gunfighter Archetype Meets the Ravenous Other." *Undead in the West II: They Just Keep Coming,* edited by Cynthia J. Miller and A. Bowdoin Van Riper. Scarecrow Press, 2013, pp. 87–105.
"La Chanson de Roland." *Encyclopædia Britannica,* 2019, https://www.britannica.com/topic/La-Chanson-de-Roland.
Lacy, Norris J. "Fisher King." *The Arthurian Encyclopedia,* edited by Norris J. Lacy. Peter Bedrick Books, 1986, p. 183.
Lovecraft, H.P. "The Call of Cthulhu." *The Call of Cthulhu and Other Weird Stories.* Penguin Classics, pp. 139–169.
———. "Supernatural Horror in Literature." *The Annotated Supernatural Horror in Literature,* edited by S.T. Joshi. Hippocampus, 2012, pp. 25–96.
Lupack, Alan. *The Oxford Guide to Arthurian Literature and Legend.* Oxford University Press, 2005.
Lüthi, Max. *Once Upon a Time: On the Nature of Fairy Tales.* Indiana University Press, 1976.
MacDonald, George. "The Gray Wolf." *Terrifying Transformations: An Anthology of Victorian Werewolf Fiction, 1838–1896,* edited by Alexis Easley and Shannon Scott. Valancourt, 2013, pp. 112–120.
Magistrale, Tony. *Landscape of Fear: Stephen King's American Gothic.* Bowling Green State University Popular Press, 1988.
———. *Stephen King: America's Storyteller.* Praeger, 2009.
———. *Stephen King: The Second Decade,* Danse Macabre *to* The Dark Half (Twayne's United States Authors Series). Twayne, 1992.
The Magnificent Seven. Directed by John Sturges, performances by Steve McQueen, Eli Wallach, Yul Brynner, Charles Bronson, Robert Vaughn, and Horst Buchholz. United Artists, 1960.
Malory, Sir Thomas. *Le Morte Darthur,* The Winchester Manuscript, edited by Helen Cooper. Oxford World's Classics, 1998.
Maslin, Janet. "Books of the Times: Invasion of the Ring Tone Snatchers." *New York Times,* 23 Jan. 2006, https://www.nytimes.com/2006/01/23/books/invasion-of-the-ring-tone-snatchers.html.
May, Charles E. *Edgar Allan Poe: A Study of the Short Fiction.* Twayne, 1991.
McAleer, Patrick. *Inside the* Dark Tower *Series: Art, Evil and Intertextuality in the Stephen King Novels.* McFarland, 2009.
McLeod, Saul. "Id, Ego and Superego." *Simply Psychology,* 2016, https://www.simplypsychology.org/psyche.html.
McMillan, Graeme. "'Dark Tower' Is Even More Complicated Than You Think."

Hollywood Reporter, 3 Aug. 2017, https://www.hollywoodreporter.com/heat-vision/dark-tower-comics-books-roland-story-more-complicated-you-think-1026681.

McMurray, Rachel. "'Because Some Stories *Do* Live Forever': Stephen King's The Dark Tower Series as a Modern Romance." 2012. University of Kansas. Master's Thesis. https://kuscholarworks.ku.edu/handle/1808/10677?show=full.

McNicol, Nancy. "From a Buick 8 (Review)." *Library Journal*, vol. 127, no. 12, July 2002, p. 118. *EBSCOhost*, proxy.culver.edu:2048/login?url=https%3a%2f%2fsearch.ebscohost.com%2flogin.aspx%3fdirect%3dtrue%26db%3daph%26AN%3d6984152%26site%3deds-live%26scope%3dsite.

"Mile 81." *Publisher's Weekly*, 26 Mar. 2012, https://www.publishersweekly.com/978-1-4423-4913-1.

Miller, Cynthia J., and A. Bowdoin Van Riper. "Blending Genres, Bending Time: Steampunk on the Western Frontier." *Westerns: The Essential* Journal of Popular Film and Television *Collection*, edited by Gary R. Edgerton and Michael T. Marden. Routledge, 2012, pp. 233–248.

Miller, Georgiana O. "A Rose, a Stone, an Unfound Door: Metaphor and Intertextuality in The Dark Tower Series." *Stephen King's Modern Macabre: Essays on the Later Works*, edited by Patrick McAleer and Michael A. Perry, McFarland, 2014, pp. 107–120.

Miller, Jennifer L. "In the Shadow of the Dark Tower: Stephen King's Fantasy Epic as 9/11 Literature." *The Modern Stephen King Canon: Beyond Horror*, edited by Philip L. Simpson and Patrick McAleer, Lexington, 2019, pp. 203–218.

Mitchell, Lee Clark. *Westerns: Making the Man in Fiction and Film*. University of Chicago Press, 1996.

Murphy, Bernice M. *Key Concepts in Contemporary Popular Fiction*. Edinburgh University Press, 2017. Key Concepts in Literature Series.

Mustazza, Leonard. "Poe's 'The Masque of the Red Death' and King's *The Shining*." *Discovering Stephen King's 'The Shining,'* edited by Tony Magistrale. Starmont House, 1991, pp. 62–73.

Owen, D.D.R. "Introduction" *The Song of Roland*, edited and translated by D.D.R. Owen, The Boydell Press, 1990, pp. 1–39.

Paquette, Jenifer. *Respecting* The Stand: *A Critical Analysis of Stephen King's Apocalyptic Novel*. McFarland, 2012.

Parrinder, Patrick. "Science Fiction: Metaphor, Myth or Prophecy?" *Science Fiction, Critical Frontiers*, edited by Karen Sayer and John Moore, Palgrave Macmillan, 2000, pp. 23–34.

Perry, Michael. "Storytelling and a Story Told: Stephen King's Narrators in *From a Buick 8, The Colorado Kid,* and *Blaze*." *The Modern Stephen King Canon: Beyond Horror*, edited by Philip L. Simpson and Patrick McAleer. Lexington Books, 2019, pp. 21–32.

Phipps, Keith. "Stephen King's *The Stand*." *AV Club*, 14 Feb. 2011, https://www.avclub.com/stephen-king-s-the-stand-1798224288.

Poe, Edgar Allan. "The Fall of the House of Usher." *The Unabridged Edgar Allan Poe*. Running Press, 1983, pp. 532–548.

_____. "The Masque of the Red Death." *The Unabridged Edgar Allan Poe*. Running Press, 1983, pp. 739–744.

_____. "The Tell-Tale Heart." *The Unabridged Edgar Allan Poe*. Running Press, 1983, pp. 799–803.

Polito, Robert. "Apocalypse Now." *The New York Times*, 20 Oct. 1996, https://www.nytimes.com/1996/10/20/books/apocalypse-now.html.

Punter, David, and Glennis Byron. *The Gothic*. Blackwell Publishing, 2004. (Blackwell Guides to Literature).

Quigley, Kevin. "A Novel Critique." *Charnel House*, n.d., charnelhouse.tripod.com/regulators.html.

Quinn, Judy. "King of the Season." *Publisher's Weekly*, vol. 243, no. 32, 1996, pp. 292+, http://arldocdel.iii.com/1426241.pdf.

"The Regulators." *Publisher's Weekly*, n.d., https://www.publishersweekly.com/978-0-525-94190-3.

Reino, Joseph. *Stephen King: The Second Decade,* Carrie *to* Pet Sematary (Twayne United States Authors Series). Twayne, 1988.
Reyes, Mike. "Ron Howard Says He 'Made a Mistake' With The Dark Tower." *Cinema Blend,* 3 June 2019, https://www.cinemablend.com/news/2474323/ron-howard-says-he-made-a-mistake-with-the-dark-tower.
"Robot Science Fiction." *Best Science Fiction Books,* 2015, http://bestsciencefictionbooks.com/robot-science-fiction.php.
Rose Red. Directed by Craig R. Baxley, written by Stephen King, performances by Julian Sands, Emily Deschanel, Nancy Travis, Melanie Lynskey, Kimberly J. Brown. ABC, 2002.
Rushdie, Salman. *The Wizard of Oz.* British Film Institute, 1992.
Ryan, Mike. "'The Dark Tower' Review: What The Hell Happened?" *UPROXX,* 2 Aug. 2017, https://uproxx.com/movies/the-dark-tower-review/.
Sanders, Jason. "The Good, the Bad, and the Ugly." *University of California, Berkeley Art Museum & Pacific Film Archive,* 2019, https://bampfa.org/event/good-bad-and-ugly-1.
Scheub, Harold. "Bumba Vomits Up the Universe (Bushongo/DR Congo)." *A Dictionary of African Mythology.* Oxford University Press, 2000. Accessed through *Oxford Reference,* http://www.oxfordreference.com/view/10.1093/oi/authority.20110803095535192.
Sears, John. *Stephen King's Gothic.* University of Wales Press, 2011. Gothic Literary Studies Series.
Seddon, Dan. "Why is Amazon TV resurrecting a flop movie franchise from Stephen King?" *Digital Spy,* 4 Feb. 2019, https://www.digitalspy.com/tv/ustv/a27004614/amazon-dark-tower-reboot/.
Senior, W.A. "Quest fantasies." *The Cambridge Companion to Fantasy Literature,* edited by Edward James and Farah Mendlesohn. Cambridge UP, 2012, pp. 190–199.
Seven Samarai. Directed by Akira Kurosawa, performances by Toshirô Mifune, Takashi Shimura, Keiko Tsushima. Toho Company, 1954.
Shakespeare, William. *King Lear,* edited by Barbara A. Mowat and Paul Werstine. Washington Square Press, 1993 (1606). (Folger Shakespeare Library).
Smythe, James. "Rereading Stephen King, Chapter 22: The Eyes of the Dragon." *The Guardian,* 20 June 2013, https://www.theguardian.com/books/booksblog/2013/jun/20/rereading-stephen-king-eyes-of-the-dragon.
_____. "Rereading Stephen King, Week 6—The Stand." *The Guardian,* 3 Aug. 2012, https://www.theguardian.com/books/2012/aug/03/rereading-stephen-king-the-stand.
Stoker, Bram. *Dracula.* Signet Classic, 1992 (1987).
Strengell, Heidi. *Dissecting Stephen King: From the Gothic to Literary Naturalism.* Popular Press, 2005.
Tanjeem, Namera. "The Best High Fantasy Books: A Beginner's Guide to the Genre." *Book Riot,* 6 Dec. 2018, https://bookriot.com/2018/12/06/best-high-fantasy-books/.
Teverson, Andrew. *Fairy Tale.* Routledge, 2013. The New Critical Idiom Series.
Thompson, Raymond H. "Mordred (Modred, Medraut)." *The Arthurian Encyclopedia,* edited by Norris J. Lacy. Peter Bedrick Books, 1986, p. 394.
Tolkien, J.R.R. "On Fairy-Stories" *Tree and Leaf.* HarperCollins, 1988 (1964), pp. 3–81.
Tritel, Barbara. "What the Wicked Magician Did." *The New York Times,* 22 Feb. 1987, https://www.nytimes.com/1987/02/22/books/what-the-wicked-magician-did.html.
Turold. *The Song of Roland.* Translated by Dorothy L. Sayers. Penguin Classics, 1957.
Twain, Mark. *The Works of Mark Twain, Volume 8: Adventures of Huckleberry Finn,* edited by Walter Blair and Victor Fischer. University of California Press, 1988 (1884).
Vincent, Bev. *The Dark Tower Companion: A Guide to Stephen King's Epic Fantasy.* New American Library, 2013.
_____. *The Road to the Dark Tower: Exploring Stephen King's Magnum Opus.* New American Library, 2004.
_____. *The Stephen King Illustrated Companion: Manuscripts, Correspondence, Drawings, and Memorabilia from the Master of Modern Horror.* Metro Books, 2009.
Webster, Fiona. "Desperation/The Regulators." *Fantastic Fiction,* n.d., https://www.fantasticfiction.com/k/stephen-king/desperation-regulators.htm.

Wheat, Patricia H. "The Mask of Indifference in 'The Masque of the Red Death.'" *Studies in Short Fiction,* vol. 19, no. 1, Winter 1982, p. 51–56. *EBSCOhost,* proxy.culver.edu:2048/login?url=https%3a%2f%2fsearch.ebscohost.com%2flogin.aspx%3fdirect%3dtrue%26db%3daph%26AN%3d9267845%26site%3deds-live%26scope%3dsite.

White, T. Gilchrist. "'Childe Roland to the Dark Tower Came': The Heroic Aspects of the Gunslinger." *Stephen King's Modern Macabre: Essays on the Later Works,* edited by Patrick McAleer and Michael A. Perry. McFarland, 2014, pp. 81–92.

Wiater, Stanley, Christopher Golden, and Hank Wagner. *The Complete Stephen King Universe: A Guide to the Worlds of Stephen King.* St. Martin's, 2006.

Winter, Douglas. *Stephen King: The Art of Darkness,* rev. and expanded. Plume, 1986 (1984).

Wisker, Gina. *Horror Fiction: An Introduction.* Continuum, 2005.

Wister, Owen. *The Virginian: A Horseman of the Plains.* Macmillan, 1902.

Wolfe, Thomas. *Look Homeward, Angel.* Charles Scribner's Sons, 1929.

Wood, Rocky. *Stephen King: A Literary Companion.* McFarland, 2011.

Wright, Will. *Six Guns and Society: A Structural Study of the Western.* University of California Press, 1975.

Yarbro, Chelsea Quinn. "Cinderella's Revenge—Twists on Fairy Tale and Mythic Themes in the Work of Stephen King." *Fear Itself: The Horror Fiction of Stephen King,* edited by Tim Underwood and Chuck Miller. New American Library, 1984 (1982), pp. 63–73.

Zipes, Jack. *Fairy Tale as Myth/Myth as Fairy Tale.* University Press of Kentucky, 1994.

_____. *The Irresistible Fairy Tale: The Cultural and Social History of a Genre.* Princeton University Press, 2012.

Index

Allgood, Cuthbert 14, 19, 20, 22, 23, 72
Arthurian legend 5, 6, 11, 13–18, 183n; see also Excalibur
Asimov, Isaac 46, 60, 61

Bachman, Richard 2, 9, 42, 136, 140–146
Beam-Breakers 10, 32–33, 36, 47, 54, 65, 148, 152–153, 163, 167–168, 169, 188n
Bill Hodges trilogy 4, 110; see also Mr. Mercedes
Black House 2, 10, 103, 107, 121, 152, 162–173, 174, 186n, 188n, 189n; see also Straub Peter; Talsiman
Blaine the monorail 25, 32, 34, 42, 48, 49, 59–60, 94, 157, 170
Brautigan, Ted 5, 10, 65, 103, 150–153, 154, 156, 160, 169, 188n
Broadcloak, Marten 9, 35, 52, 84, 113, 117, 174; see also Flagg

Calla Bryn Sturgis 8, 9, 31, 33, 39, 48, 49, 60–61, 63, 64–65, 66, 69, 71, 74, 77–78, 94, 99, 100 102, 103, 106, 164
Callahan, Donald 2, 5, 8–9, 15, 53–54, 55, 94, 97–109, 114, 124, 130, 131, 133, 149, 150, 165 168, 186n
Carrie 29, 100
Castle Rock (series) 2, 147–148, 185n, 188n
Castle Rock, Maine 2, 97, 146–148, 174, 181, 185n, 188n
Cell 43
Chambers, Jake 3, 5, 14, 15, 19, 20, 24–25, 27, 30–32, 34, 36, 37, 40–42, 47, 48, 49, 50, 53–54 55, 56, 57, 61, 65–66, 69, 72, 73, 75, 78, 85, 91, 92–93, 94, 95–96, 103, 104, 108–109 119, 120, 130, 131, 142, 134, 147, 152, 165, 173, 183n, 185n, 186n, 188n

Charlie the Choo-Choo 66, 41–43, 131; print book 33, 141; as Roland's son 14, 71, 72; train 42
"Childe Roland to the Dark Tower Came" (Robert Browning) 5, 6, 7, 8, 11, 18, 21–23, 24–26 28, 187n
Christine 147, 179, 186n
The Colorado Kid 4, 110, 186n
Cort 12, 20, 82
cosmic horror 79, 80–81, 92–96, 104, 113, 161, 185n, 186n
Covenant Man 39, 60, 116, 117, 184n
Crimson King 5, 10, 12, 14, 15, 17, 36, 37, 47, 50, 52, 53, 54, 55, 56, 69, 85, 87, 92–93, 99, 102, 103, 105, 106, 111, 118, 119, 123, 124–125, 127, 128, 129, 131, 132–135, 149, 150, 152, 153, 163, 165, 167–168, 170, 171, 172, 177, 187n, 188n, 189n
Cujo 50, 179, 184n

Dandelo 22, 61, 134, 142, 186n
Danse Macabre 8, 80–81, 84, 97
Danville, Patrick 9, 48, 61, 71, 111, 124–125, 130, 132–135, 149, 150, 154–155, 187n
The Dark Half 80, 104, 143, 188n
"The Dark Man" 9, 113–114, 180, 186–187n
The Dark Tower (film) 2, 174, 176, 178–180
The Dark Tower (novel) 1, 5, 15–16, 22–23, 36, 47, 50, 60, 61, 65, 68, 71, 72, 73, 75, 83, 87, 91 95–96, 101–102, 103–104, 109, 111, 112, 113, 117–119, 121, 124, 126–128, 130–131, 133 134, 135, 142, 143, 149, 153, 169, 173, 174, 175, 180, 181, 184n, 185n, 186n, 187n, 188n
Dean, Eddie 5, 14, 15, 16, 19, 20, 24, 27, 30–32, 34, 36, 37, 40, 42, 44, 48, 49, 50, 53, 55, 56 57, 59, 61, 63, 65–66, 68,

69, 70, 72, 73, 77, 89, 93, 94, 95–96, 119, 120, 173, 183n, 187n
Dean, Susannah 5, 15, 17, 19, 20, 27, 30–33, 34, 36, 37, 40, 48, 49, 55, 56, 57, 58, 59, 61, 68 69, 70, 72–73, 77, 78, 83, 85–87, 89, 92, 93, 94, 95–96, 119, 120, 126–128, 133, 134, 168 173, 184n, 185n, 186n, 187n; see also Holmes, Odetta; Walker, Detta
Delgado, Susan 19, 23, 26, 52, 53, 72, 73, 88, 102, 106, 153
Derry, Maine 7, 9, 37, 38, 123–135, 146–147, 181, 186n, 187n
Deschain, Roland 4–5, 7, 12–13, 14, 15–16, 19–20, 22–23, 24–28, 31–32, 35–36, 38–40, 48, 49, 54–55, 56–57, 63, 65–66, 67–73, 76, 77, 85, 90–91, 93, 94–95, 96, 101–102, 106–107, 11, 112 117, 119, 121, 124, 126–128, 132–133, 134, 143, 152, 164, 165, 166–167, 168, 169, 171 173, 175, 180, 181, 186n, 187n
Desperation 2, 9, 100, 136–148, 188n, 189n
Dickens, Charles 150, 166, 172, 173
Discordia 175–176
Dr. Jekyll and Mr. Hyde (Robert Louis Stevenson) 80, 104, 127
Doctor Sleep 43, 142, 179, 186n
Dracula (Bram Stoker) 80, 82, 97–98, 104, 105, 115
The Drawing of the Three 1, 5, 19, 21, 32, 47, 50, 54, 55, 61, 69, 72–73, 82–83, 85, 91, 96, 121, 128, 157, 158, 186n, 187n

Eastwood, Clint 8, 75, 76
Eld, Arthur 12, 14–15, 18, 178; see also Way of the Eld
epic 2, 5, 7, 8, 11–13, 18, 21, 22, 28, 29, 44, 45, 46, 48, 56, 62, 63, 64, 65, 74, 76, 78, 107, 110–111, 163, 170, 179
"Everything's Eventual" 153, 188n
Excalibur 14, 178
The Eyes of the Dragon 2, 4, 9, 10, 52, 84, 110, 112–113, 116–117, 118, 119, 120–122, 124, 157 164, 174, 184n, 185n

"Fair Extension" 50–51
fairy tale 2, 7, 29–43, 44, 45, 49, 62, 110, 112, 117, 121, 127, 171, 187n; "Hansel and Gretel" 29, 31, 32–33, 43; "Jack and the Beanstalk" 32, 127, 187n; "Little Red Riding Hood" 29, 32, 33; Peter Pan 32, 45; "The Pied Piper of Hamlin" 33
"The Fall of the House of Usher" 84–85, 185n; see also Poe, Edgar Allan

Fannin, Richard 9, 84, 113, 117, 120; see also Flagg
fantasy 2, 4, 5, 6, 7, 9, 23, 29, 44–57, 58, 60, 62, 74, 79, 110, 121, 178, 179, 180, 187n
Fisher King 23–24, 26
Flagg 2, 9, 23, 35, 43, 52, 83–84, 112–119, 120, 121, 174, 180, 184n, 186n, 188n; see also Broadcloak, Marten; Covenant Man; Fannin, Richard; Man in Black; Paddick, Walter; Walkin' Dude; Walter o' Dim
Frankenstein (Mary Shelley) 46, 80, 82, 104
From a Buick 8 2, 10, 103, 149, 156–159, 160, 161

Gilead 12, 14, 19, 20, 39, 53, 114, 117, 121, 169, 184n, 185n
The Good, the Bad, and the Ugly (film) 2, 7, 8, 63, 75–77, 78
Gothic tradition 25–26, 74–75, 80, 82, 89, 90–91, 113, 127, 185n
The Green Mile 136, 138–139, 189n
The Gunslinger 1, 3, 4–5, 12, 19, 27, 41, 45, 47, 48, 54, 55, 56, 61, 63, 64, 65, 66, 68, 70, 72, 74 75, 76, 82, 91, 94–95, 96, 103, 107, 111, 113, 117, 132, 133, 147, 150, 152, 177, 183n, 184n, 186n

Harry Potter series (J.K. Rowling) 60, 184–185n
Hearts in Atlantis 2, 5, 10, 36, 103, 133, 138, 138, 149, 150–153, 154, 156, 160–161, 169, 188n; 189n
Holmes, Odetta 55, 61, 72, 83, 85, 128, 187n; see also Dean, Susannah; Walker, Detta
Horn of Eld 16, 20
horror 2, 4, 5, 7, 8, 25–26, 29, 41, 44, 48, 74–75, 79–96, 98, 104, 109, 110, 115, 123, 127, 137 139, 144, 145, 161, 162–163, 173, 180, 184n, 185n, 186n

Insomnia 2, 9, 103, 111, 123–135, 154–155, 159, 167, 186n, 187n
IT 7, 16, 33, 37–38, 43, 61, 79, 123, 124, 128, 129, 132, 142, 147, 187n, 188–189n; see also Derry, Maine; Pennywise

Jackson, Shirley 2, 8, 80, 84, 87–90, 91, 92, 170; *The Haunting of Hill House* 2, 89–90, 170; "The Lottery" 87–89
Jericho Hill 16, 19–20, 72, 73, 102, 107, 117, 177

Index

Jerusalem's Lot, Maine 8, 98, 102, 103–104, 106, 108, 124, 186n, 188n
Johns, Alain 20, 72

King as character 9, 15, 22, 73, 91, 96, 107–108, 109, 127, 136, 142, 143, 146, 187n

legend 2, 6, 7, 11, 13–28, 29, 31, 44, 45, 178, 187n
Lisey's Story 174, 181, 189n
"Little Sisters of Eluria" 76, 106–107, 121, 138, 169, 177
Lovecraft, H.P. 4, 8, 80, 81, 92, 94, 95, 96, 104, 186n
Lud 24, 25, 32, 41, 47, 48, 57–58, 59, 60, 67, 83, 89–90, 94, 120, 130

magic 7, 44, 45, 51–54, 57, 61, 74, 76, 121, 142
The Magnificent Seven 8, 63, 75, 76, 77–78
Man in Black 9, 12, 22, 27, 55, 61, 63, 64, 70, 72, 75, 83, 94–95, 101, 107, 113, 117, 174, 184n; see also Flagg
Marvel Comics 2, 176–178, 189n
"The Masque of the Red Death" 85–87, 185n
Mejis 19, 23, 35, 47, 48, 50 52, 63, 65, 72, 73, 88, 93–94, 106–107, 117, 153, 176, 178
Mia 17, 57, 58, 83, 85–87, 92–93, 94, 138, 186n, 187n
"Mile 81" 2, 10, 103, 147, 149, 156, 159–161, 188n
Misery 79, 147, 188n
"The Mist" 80, 92, 100, 185n, 189n
Mr. Mercedes 79, 80, 110; see also Bill Hodges trilogy
Mordred 12, 14, 15, 16–18, 54, 73, 83–84, 85–87, 91, 118–119, 121, 185n, 188n; see also Arthurian legend
Le Morte Darthur (Sir Thomas Malory) 1, 7, 13–18, 24, 29
"Mrs. Todd's Shortcut" 189n
myth 13, 14, 30, 31, 32, 33, 36, 37, 44, 74, 113, 121, 125–126, 142, 163, 167, 178, 185n, 187n

"N." 80, 92, 174

Oy 5, 15, 17, 35, 56, 57, 72, 73, 94, 95, 108–109, 142

Padick, Walter 83–84, 113, 117; see also Flagg

Pennywise 37, 79, 128, 132, 179, 188–189n; see also IT
Pet Sematary 79, 80, 160, 183n, 187n
Poe, Edgar Allan 4, 8, 26, 80, 84–87, 91, 92, 154, 172, 185n; see also "The Fall of the House of Usher"; "The Masque of the Red Death"; "The Raven"; "The Tell-Tale Heart"

"The Raven" 172; see also Poe, Edgar Allan
The Regulators (as Richard Bachman) 2, 9, 136–148, 189n
religion 99–104, 138–139, 145
Revival 80, 104, 139
Rhea of the Cöos 23, 32, 35, 52–53, 72, 88, 186n
robots 7, 45, 46, 57, 60–61, 74, 78, 120, 178
Rose Madder 79, 137, 140, 147, 187–188n
roses 25, 47, 65, 85, 128, 129, 130–131, 134, 135, 152, 154, 165, 183n

'Salem's Lot 2, 5, 8–9, 80, 97–109, 110, 111, 124, 138, 149
science fiction 2, 5, 7, 44–45, 46, 57–62, 67, 74, 90, 110, 137, 141, 185n
The Seven Samurai 8, 76, 77–78
Shakespeare, William 21, 45, 183n, 187n
Shardik (Guardian) 36, 47, 58–59, 60, 184n
Shardik (Richard Adams) 58–59
The Shining 29, 43, 80, 147, 160, 179, 185n
Song of Roland 7, 11, 18–21, 23, 28
Song of Susannah 1, 5, 11, 15, 20, 41, 42, 53–54, 55, 57, 58, 77, 85–87, 91, 92–93, 94, 96, 104 105, 108, 121, 130, 133, 138, 143, 164–165, 168, 175, 183n, 185n, 186n
The Stand 1, 2, 9, 16, 34–35, 84, 94, 110–122, 124, 138, 142, 172, 184n
Straub, Peter 2, 4, 10, 103, 162–173, 188n, 189n; see also Black House; The Talisman

The Talisman 2, 4, 10, 103, 107, 121, 123, 124, 162–173, 174, 189n; see also Black House; Straub, Peter
tarot 26–27, 61, 184n
"The Tell-Tale Heart" 84, 85; see also Poe, Edgar Allan
territories 2, 4, 10, 107, 121, 162–173, 174, 186n, 189n
thinnies 61, 83, 93–94, 138, 148, 156, 185n

Index

Tolkien, J.R.R. 1–2, 7, 11, 44, 45–47, 48, 49–50, 52, 62, 76, 115, 166; *Lord of the Rings* 1–2, 7, 11, 45
The Tommyknockers 111, 189*n*
Tull 12, 19, 47, 55, 63, 64, 65, 69, 76, 111
Turtle 7, 12, 33, 36–38, 43, 104, 109, 129–130
Twain, Mark 165–166, 167, 172, 189*n*

"Ur" 2, 10, 103, 149, 153–155, 156, 159, 161, 188*n*

vampires 8, 15, 55, 83, 97–109, 130, 133, 142, 158, 169, 186*n*, 189*n*

Walker, Detta 55, 61, 73, 83, 85, 93, 128, 187*n*; *see also* Dean, Susannah; Holmes, Odetta
Walkin' Dude 9, 113, 119; *see also* Flagg
Walter o'Dim 9, 113, 117, 133, 174, 180, 186*n*
"The Waste Land" (T.S. Eliot) 6, 7, 11, 23–28, 29, 184*n*
The Waste Lands 1, 5, 19, 24–26, 32, 36–37, 41–42, 47, 49, 50, 55, 57–60, 61, 65–66, 67, 69, 72 73, 75, 83, 85, 89–90, 91, 93, 94, 95, 120, 130, 131, 152, 157, 165, 170, 177, 179, 183*n*, 184*n*, 185*n*
Way of the Ed 14, 19; *see also* Eld, Arthur
Western 2, 5, 7–8, 44, 63–78, 79, 137, 139, 141, 145, 169
The Wind Through the Keyhole 1, 5, 7, 10, 12, 29, 33, 37, 38–40, 47, 70, 76, 83, 116, 117, 138 158, 171, 174, 184*n*, 185*n*
Wizard and Glass 1, 5, 10, 19, 23, 32, 33, 34–36, 38, 42, 47, 49, 52–53, 63, 65, 70, 72, 74, 83 88, 89, 91, 93–94, 102, 106–107, 112–113, 117, 119, 121, 130, 133, 152, 153, 170, 174 176, 180, 184*n*, 185*n*
The Wizard of Oz (L. Frank Baum) 7, 31, 33–36, 45, 86, 166, 184*n*
Wizard's Glass 52–53, 54, 95, 164; Black Thirteen 53–54, 103, 104
Wolfe, Thomas 25, 183*n*
Wolves of the Calla 1, 5, 10, 14, 16, 19, 20, 31, 32, 33, 38, 42, 44, 47, 48, 49, 50, 53, 55, 60, 61 64–65, 66, 68, 69, 71, 77–78, 83, 85, 91, 94, 99, 103, 105, 106, 108, 109, 130, 131, 133 168, 174, 177, 184–185*n*, 186*n*